HOPE Beyond HELL

THE RIGHTEOUS PURPOSE OF GOD'S JUDGMENT.

BY

GERRY BEAUCHEMIN

MALISTA PRESS
OLMITO, TEXAS

THE PROBLEM

*P*icture yourself as a missionary to the Muslim nation of Senegal, West Africa. The date? September 26, 2002. About a year prior, you befriended your neighbor, Abdou Ndieye, a Muslim merchant. Only a few weeks ago, he graciously accepted your invitation to study the Bible with you. You are thrilled. Abdou is the first Muslim with whom you have begun sharing the Good News.

Today you prepare to explore another portion of God's Word with him, but something terrible has happened. You cannot believe what you are hearing and seeing on the news. The Joola, a Senegalese ferry, has capsized killing almost 2,000 people. You remember Abdou's wife, Astou, and his 14 year old daughter, Fatou, are on that ship. You are in shock and cannot believe what you are seeing—a ship's underside sticking up out of the sea with helicopters hovering overhead. You hurry next door. As you knock on the door, you hear deep groans and wailing. You slowly enter. Abdou is prostrate on the floor. He pleads before Yalla (Wolof for Allah), "Why? Why? How could you let this happen?" He goes into spasms of weeping, beating his hands against the floor.

Feeling utterly helpless, you pray, "God help me comfort my friend."

Abdou lifts his eyes, hardly able to recognize you for the tears. "My wife and daughter have died a terrible death! Tell me I will see them again. Tell me they are safe in God's arms! Has your Jesus taken them to His heaven?" You are lost for words. The silence is deafening.

"Answer me, Christian, will I see them again? Are they in a better place? Tell me!"

You remain speechless. What can you say? Where is the "Good News" when you need it most?[1]

THE *CRAZY* UNCLE

I applaud Gerry Beauchemin for his excellent book, *Hope Beyond Hell*, and for the courage to write it....This book is a "must-read" for those Christians who have lost their way because they couldn't reconcile a Bible that declares that "God is Love" while simultaneously teaching that the fate of the sinner is eternal damnation.

The doctrine of "endless punishment" has for centuries been the "crazy uncle" that the Church, with justifiable embarrassment, has kept locked in the back bedroom. Unfortunately, from time to time, he escapes his confinement, usually when there are guests in the parlor, and usually just at the time when we are telling them about a loving God who gave His Son to die for their sins. It's no wonder that the guests run away never to return. But instead of shunting the "crazy uncle" back to his asylum, and trying to cover our embarrassment (by ever more loudly shouting "God is Love!"), we need to get our "crazy uncle" healed.

A good place to start this healing process is Gerry Beauchemin's book. Layer by layer, concept by concept, Gerry's message will loose the bonds of insanity that has plagued the Church for centuries.

From the guilt-ridden psyche of Augustine to the tormented fantasies of Dante, the Church has been victimized by the terrors of pagan nonsense. It has been "corrupted from the simplicity that is in Christ" (2Cor. 11:3 KJV). Books like *Hope Beyond Hell* are pointing us back to TRUE "Good News."

Grady Brown, MTh., DLitt.
Author of *That All May Be Fulfilled* and *That's What I Have, That's Who I Am!*
Director and Founder of Dayspring Bible Ministries
623 Jack Drive, Lindale, Texas 75771

CONTENTS

PRELIMINARY NOTE

*T*his book as been written especially for Christians who have mis-understood God's judgments. That misunderstanding has led to a false concept of God that has kept millions of people from coming to Christ. God is the most awesome and marvelous Being in the universe. He loves all people with an everlasting love and has demon-strated that love in Jesus Christ.

It would be best to read this book with an open Bible while studying all quotes in light of the context. Not to do so will increase the risk of misunderstanding. In order to provide the weight of Scriptural evidence that this study demands, I have abbreviated many passages. This approach is similar to what Rick Warren, author of The Purpose Driven Life, does in his writings. He wrote:

> Verse divisions and number were not included in the Bible until 1560 A.D., I have not always quoted the entire verse, but rather focused on the phrase that was appropriate. My model for this is Jesus and how he and the apostles quoted the Old Testament. They often just quoted a phrase to make a point.

The author has added all use of *italics* and **bolding** for emphasis. All quotations are from the New King James Version (©1979) unless otherwise noted. Note the following book abbreviations:

Ge.	Genesis	1Ch.	1 Chronicles
Ex.	Exodus	2Ch.	2 Chronicles
Le.	Leviticus	Ezr.	Ezra
Nu.	Numbers	Ne.	Nehemiah
De.	Deuteronomy	Es.	Esther
Jos.	Joshua	Job	Job
Jud.	Judges	Ps.	Psalms
Ru.	Ruth	Pr.	Proverbs
1S.	1 Samuel	Ec.	Ecclesiastes
2S.	2 Samuel	So.	Song of Solomon
1K.	1 Kings	Is.	Isaiah
2K.	2 Kings	Jer.	Jeremiah

La.	Lamentations	1Co.	1 Corinthians
Ez.	Ezekiel	2Co.	2 Corinthians
Da.	Daniel	Ga.	Galatians
Hos.	Hosea	Ep.	Ephesians
Joe.	Joel	Ph.	Philippians
Amo.	Amos	Col.	Colossians
Oba.	Obadiah	1Th.	1 Thessalonians
Jon.	Jonah	2Th.	2 Thessalonians
Mic.	Micah	1Ti.	1 Timothy
Nah.	Nahum	2Ti.	2 Timothy
Hab.	Habbakuk	Tit.	Titus
Zep.	Zephaniah	Phil.	Philemon
Hag.	Haggai	He.	Hebrews
Zec.	Zechariah	Ja.	James
Mal.	Malachi	1Pe.	1 Peter
Mt.	Matthew	2Pe.	2 Peter
Mk.	Mark	1Jn.	1 John
Lu.	Luke	2Jn.	2 John
Jn.	John	3Jn.	3 John
Ac.	Acts	Ju.	Jude
Ro.	Romans	Re.	Revelation

KJV	King James Version (1611)
NKJV	New King James Version (1982)
NAS	New American Standard (1960)
RSV	Revised Standard Version (1947)
YLT	Young's Literal Translation (1898)
JB	Jerusalem Bible (1966)
CLT	Concordant Literal Translation (1926)
ROTH	Rotherham Literal Translation (1902)
WEY	Weymouth Translation (1912)
NIV	New International Version (1973)
IGNT	Interlinear Greek New Testament
DOUAY	DOUAY Bible Translation (1989)

ACKNOWLEDGMENTS

I appreciate you, Denise, (my dear wife) for your openness, patience, and partnership with me in our quest to know God. You have been a faithful wife who has stood by, prayed for, and encouraged me in my search for truth. God knew I needed someone who was willing to face the hard questions with me. I pray God will give us both the courage and zeal to fearlessly proclaim His glorious and unfailing purpose for all people.

I am deeply thankful to you, Renée, (my daughter) for the hard work you have done on the technical side to make this book possible. It was such a joy to work with you. I can't imagine having done it without you. Your insights, comments, and suggestions were priceless.

I thank my dear friends, Steve and Dave. Steve for introducing me to this hope; and Dave for spurring me on in it.

Special thanks to Derek and Pat McLean for your work of love in cover design and editing.

Thanks to all who have read the manuscript for your encouragement and comments!

I thank all our brothers and sisters in Christ who have partnered with Denise and I over the last 20 years in bringing the Good News of Jesus Christ to a lost and hurting world.

DEDICATION

I DEDICATE THIS BOOK TO:

- Our heavenly Father, that the world may know what You are really like.
- The Church, Christ's Body: that we would know and proclaim God's unfailing purpose for all.
- All afflicted by the idea of everlasting punishment.
- My girls: Denise, Renée, Anna, and Nicole.

FOREWORD

*L*OVE NEVER FAILS! (1Co. 13:8) Words of victory, power, encouragement, and hope. Oh, do we dare believe? Can it really be possible?
For most of my life, I have embraced teachings built on well-defined
arguments for why LOVE SOMETIMES FAILS. Not that it wanted to
fail or lacked the power to succeed; it just didn't work out sometimes.
As a matter of fact, it didn't work out most of the time. The simple
but profound truth in this study has radically altered the way I now
see the One who is Love.

Friends have warned me that truth can be found in the strangest
places. The truth in this book found me on the road back from a
medical outreach in the Aztec villages of Mexico. For the past few
years, I had watched Gerry labor in what he calls his "helps" ministry
for the Kingdom—a dental ministry where he would labor for days
well into the night; demonstrating
practically the Father's love. As we went
on different outreaches, I came to notice
a pattern—one that to this day continues:
Gerry would be the first one up and
running, working late into the night, with
a gentle, caring spirit throughout. On the day scheduled for return,
when everyone else would be packed and waiting, he was finishing up
one last patient. After watching him for several clinics, I had to know
what made him tick. What was his secret? As the trips down would
sometimes take 8 to 10 hours we had plenty of time to talk. The study
you hold in your hands reflects his view of God, and the life I saw
lived is the fruit of that. It is a simple truth that can be summed up in
three mighty words—LOVE NEVER FAILS!

> *Love never fails.*
> (1Co. 13:8)

I confess that when I first heard him expound on this, it hit me
like a ton of bricks. So simple and yet so radically different from that
which I had heard all my life. A truth that will, as all truth does, set
you free. When this truth caught up with me, I was marveling at
God's never-ending love for Israel as shared by the Apostle Paul in
Romans, in spite of their persistence in unbelief. With two little
words, Gerry turned my world upside down, or should I say right side
up, "Why Israel?" And with that began a deeper study into this One

who is Love, who is working out His victory and will not stop until He becomes "all in all."

Come hear again the Good News shared by the angel with some shepherds one night outside of Bethlehem—Good News of great joy to all people! Rekindle the fire as you hear again of the One who is making all things new. Rejoice again as you ponder our Father who will not rest until all His children are safely home. Marvel at His wisdom in working out His master plan for the ages to see His will accomplished—that none should perish. Worship afresh the living God, who is the Savior of all men. Watch the Word unfold before you, as the mystery (hidden for ages) brings a peace that passes all understanding. Stand in amazement as you experience the One, who is Love, doing what He does best—transforming His creation into His likeness. Our God truly is an awesome God and this study is another affirmation to His never-ending, never-failing LOVE.

My prayer for you as you journey through this was expressed so well by the Apostle Paul—"that the God of our Lord Jesus Christ, the Father of glory, may give you a spirit of wisdom and of revelation in the knowledge of Him, having the eyes of your hearts enlightened, that you may know what is the hope to which He has called you....that according to the riches of His glory He may grant you to be strengthened with might through His Spirit in the inner man, and that Christ may dwell in your hearts through faith; that you, being rooted and grounded in love, may have power to comprehend with all the saints what is the breadth and length and height and depth, and to know the love of Christ which surpasses knowledge, that you may be filled with all the fullness of God. Now to Him who is able to do immeasurably more than all we ask or imagine, according to His power that is at work within us, to Him be glory in the church and in Christ Jesus throughout all generations, for ever and ever. Amen!" (Ep. 1:17-18; 3:16-19 RSV; 3:20-21 NIV)

David Nuckols
Director of Bread of Life Frontier Missions,
Brownsville Texas

INTRODUCTION

Are you at peace regarding the eternal destiny of your children, parents, brothers, sisters, grandfather, grandmother, aunts, uncles, cousins, and friends? Are you experiencing abundant joy in your "personal" salvation while unsure if some of your loved ones might suffer throughout all eternity? How is that possible? You see, we Christians have a problem, a very serious problem. The problem is in our belief that hell is "eternal" and that most of humanity will go there. Deep inside we know something is not right, but we suppress our questions and doubts because we "think" the Bible teaches it. What inner conflict rages within! It is futile to find satisfying answers to the problems it raises. For example:

+ How can an all-powerful, all-knowing, and all-loving God create billions of people knowing most will be tormented in hell forever?
+ Why must our free will to damn ourselves be "absolute," greater than God's "free will" to save us—His property?
+ How can Adam's power to condemn us be greater than Christ's power to save us?

Please do not accept pat answers to these critical questions. Jesus commands us to judge for ourselves what is right (Lu 12:57). What is right about a punishment that never ends?

How has this teaching affected the spread of the "Good News"— the Gospel? Think about it, an "eternal" hell...

+ Maligns God's character before the world.
+ Contradicts His unending and unfailing love for all people.
+ Makes our worship stem from fear instead of true affection.
+ Denies His unlimited power to accomplish His will.
+ Makes man's will greater than God's will.
+ Infinitely minimizes Christ's triumph over Satan.
+ Denies Christ fully accomplished His mission on earth.
+ Violates the divine witness revealed in every conscience.
+ Negates the most glorious promises in the Bible.
+ Ignores the testimony of the early Church.
+ Robs us of peace and joy.
+ Affects what we become; like father—like son.

♦ Hinders world evangelism. (Remember Abdou?)

"Test all things" (1Th. 5:21). Have you tested this teaching?

For most of my life the fear of hell stalked me, ever waiting for an opportune moment to raise its ugly head. Just the idea was like a sword slicing through me. It has been the greatest stumbling block to my faith. In fact, I almost gave up on Christianity because of it.

Hell is a horrifying thought. Millions have been terrorized by it. Some have even killed their children to spare them such a fate. If we would truly grasp the horror of it, we would go insane. Our every waking moment would have to be spent snatching whoever we can out of the fire or nothing but constant guilt would torment us. Can you imagine the horror of suffering "forever?" What is a billion years? It is but a second in eternity. Who could possibly imagine such horror? What if you or one of your loved ones should go there? Does this thought affect how you feel about God?

This theme has gripped my heart as it afflicts millions of people and dishonors God before the world. After years of wrestling with this topic, studying the Bible, and reading the works of others, I have found that hell is a judgment given from the disciplinal hand of a loving Father. Though severe, it serves a good and remedial purpose.

One of our greatest presidents agreed. In *Abraham Lincoln the Christian*, William Johnson, stated:

> Abraham Lincoln did not nor could not believe in the end-less punishment of anyone of the human race. He under-stood punishment for sin to be a Bible doctrine; that the punishment was parental in its object, aim, and design, and intended for the good of the offender; hence it must cease when justice is satisfied. All that was lost by the transgression of Adam was made good by the atonement.[1]

That is the message of this book. It is indeed good news for those tormented over the destiny of lost loved ones! Millions in our land can relate. Though the subject is hell, the book is really about God. What is He like? Have you heard the cliché: "God is good—all the time?" Well you will find solid support for it here. God is good even in His judgments. They are not infinite and horrendously cruel, but just, righteous, and remedial.

If you find I am manipulating the Scriptures in this book, then please leave it. But if not, be ready to fall in love with an amazing and wonderful God!

Tradition

You invalidate the word of God
for the sake of your tradition.
(Mt. 15:6 NAS; Mt. 15:3,9)

If religious leaders of Christ's time could invalidate the word of God for the sake of tradition, is it not possible today? Is the Church somehow immune? Only in 1995 did the Southern Baptist Convention finally submit an official apology regarding their stand on slavery.[2] Yes, slavery used to be accepted in Christendom. Many debates took place for and against slavery with each side quoting the Bible. However, when one considers that the letter kills and the Spirit gives life, and our beliefs must harmonize with the spirit and tenor of the Bible as a whole, the argument against slavery takes on new force. The same applies with the case against an "eternal" hell.

Traditions endure for generations, are highly revered, and are extremely difficult to change. There are no harder forms of error to confront and correct. When Paul and Steven declared to their fellow Israelites that God's mercy extended to the Gentiles, they were stoned. Do we hold to any traditions for which Christ might rebuke us? If we refuse to acknowledge any inconsistencies in our beliefs, how will we ever know?

This book examines the Augustinian tradition of everlasting punishment, so called because it stems principally from the theology of Augustine, who is said to be the father of the western Church.[3] This tradition assumes that the vast majority of the human race will never be saved. This is based on passages such as, "Narrow is the gate and difficult is the way which leads to life, and there are few who find it" (Mt. 7:14). But is this what Christ meant by these words? This book presents strong evidence why this could not be what Christ and the Apostles taught.

Most Christians have not fully thought through the serious implications of this tradition. In essence, it teaches that an all-powerful and loving God has created a world knowing full well the majority of His creation would spend eternity in suffering. How can this be?

Although this is what tradition assumes, most Christians, in their heart of hearts, do not embrace it. In *Hell Under Fire*, Daniel Block, professor of systematic theology at Westminster Theological Seminary, wrote, "The traditional doctrine of hell now bears the marks of *odium theologium*—Its defenders are seemingly few."[4] Though its defenders may be few, the doctrine itself continues to terrorize millions.

> *The tradition that an all-knowing, all-loving, and all-powerful God, would create a world where the majority of His human creatures are destined to spend eternity suffering is incomprehensible.*

The tradition that an all-knowing, all-loving, and all-powerful God would create a world where the majority of His human creatures are destined to spend eternity in suffering is incomprehensible. What greater horror has the world ever known?

Implications

These people draw near with their mouths and honor Me with their lips, but have removed their hearts far from Me, and their fear toward Me is taught by the commandment of men.
(Is. 29:13)

What is this passage saying? It is warning us about a fear toward God taught by the commandment of men. Could Augustine's teaching on hell be just such a commandment? Certainly, it removes our hearts far from God! Can we honestly say our affection toward God has not been influenced by this horrid doctrine? Has the thought that God might punish you or your loved ones forever in hell ever hindered your love toward Him?

This tradition seriously affects our understanding of God, including our whole outlook on life and how we relate to people. Do we not reflect, at least to a degree, the character of the God we worship? If we think seriously about the implications of this teaching, it will lead to certain undeniable conclusions as mentioned on page 15.

Confronting Our Tradition

A tradition begins when someone's interpretation (in this case Augustine's) is accepted by others and passed down through the generations. How many Hindus, Buddhists, Muslims, and Christians hold to beliefs solely because they have been passed down to them? Should we not critically evaluate for ourselves our tradi-

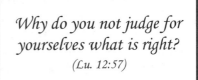

Why do you not judge for yourselves what is right?
(Lu. 12:57)

tions? "Test all things; hold fast what is good" (Th. 5:21). "Why do you not judge for yourselves what is right" (Lu. 12:57)? Christ strongly warns us about our traditions (Mt. 15:3, 6, 9). Perhaps you have struggled with hell as I have. Maybe you have longed that somehow, in this case, tradition is wrong. If so, read on. But before starting, let us consider one important point.

The Scriptures

The Bible has been translated from ancient tongues and cultures by men who carry their own ideas into their translations. They cannot help reading the ancient manuscripts through the lens of their personal theology. They are only human. Since most have held the doctrine of eternal torment, they unwittingly filtered all they translated from that mindset. That is why we must constantly be on our guard, like the Bereans (Ac. 17:11), comparing Scripture with Scripture based on the original Greek and Hebrew words. It is naïve and irresponsible not to do so.

Unless God gives us ears to hear, the Bible will remain a mystery (Pr. 20:12; Lu. 8:8). For unless He opens our minds and hearts, we toil in vain. "For our sufficiency is from God and not of the letter...for the letter kills, but the Spirit gives life" (2Co. 3:5, 6). The Ku Klux Klan are known to have based their evil actions on the "letter" of Scripture, but did they know its Spirit?[5] "Be diligent to present yourself approved to God, a worker who does not need to be ashamed, rightly dividing the word of truth" (2Ti. 2:15).

To help you rightly divide the word of truth, I submit the following basic principles of interpretation for your consideration:

- Pray for understanding.
- Trust Scripture to interpret Scripture rather than commentaries.
- Remember that the ancient eastern custom was to use language in the most vivid possible way.[6] (Appendix III, #16)

"Are you not therefore mistaken, because you do not know the Scriptures nor the power of God" (Mk. 12:24)? I encourage you to meditate on the Scriptures presented in this study, for they focus strongly on God's power. Follow the example of the Bereans, who were "more noble" than the rest, for they did not just take someone's word for it, but searched it out for themselves (Ac. 17:11). To do this you will need a concordance listing words according to Greek usage, not English. I highly recommend the *The Word Study Concordance*, by George Wigram and Ralph Winter. You do not need to know Greek to use it. Winter explained:

> The Word Study Concordance traces not English but Greek words. You can find listed every passage where a given Greek word occurs regardless of how many different ways it may be translated into English. Even the best lexicons are basically some scholar's reflections on the data drawn from a concordance. Once you have read these Bible passages yourself, you have acquired something no dictionary can easily give you—a certain instinctive feel for the word. You have become conditioned by the actual use of the word (which is the most normal and reliable way to learn any word in any language), not to equate it to some other word. Students often try to short-circuit this process and go directly to a lexicon.[7]

We are blessed to have access to excellent Bible study tools enabling us to better understand God's Word. With a humble spirit and prayerful attitude, let us look intently into God's written revelation seeking to understand His character and purpose in His judgments. Let us now critically examine the foundation pillars that have made belief in everlasting punishment possible.

CHAPTER ONE

PÌLLΛRS

Examining the scriptures...to see if these things were so.
(Ac. 17:11 NAS)

"*T*est all things: hold fast what is good" (1Th. 5:21). The doctrine of everlasting punishment, in my view, is supported by four pillars. These pillars represent a misunderstanding of three key Greek words, and one concept. They are *Aion, Gehenna, Apollumi,* and "Free" Will. Once these are understood as the biblical writers understood them, our comprehension of God's judgments take on a glorious new meaning.

Aion

The first pillar we will examine is the Greek word, *aion*. It is mostly translated "eternal," "everlasting," and for "ever" in the King James Version. However, some translations read "age-abiding," "age-during," or "eon," as noted below. "Robert Young, author of the highly respected *Young's Analytical Concordance*, in his literal translation of the Bible, always translates it 'age' and never once as 'everlasting,' or 'eternal.'"[1]

Old Testament (Greek Septuagint)

In *History of Opinions on the Scriptural Doctrine of Retribution*, Edward Beecher, D.D., pointed out:

> The Septuagint is the Greek translation of the Old Testament and was the Bible of the early church. The word *aion* occurs in it about four hundred times in every variety of combination. The adjective *aionios* derived from it, is used over one hundred times....*Aion* denoted an age, great or small, so the adjective *aionios* expressed the idea pertaining to or belonging to the *aion*, whether great or small. But in every case this adjective derives its character and duration from the *aion* to which it refers.[2]

In the Septuagint the Greek word, *aion,* is used to translate the Hebrew word *olam.* Thus, if we want to get a sense of the New Testament meaning of *aion,* we need to understand the meaning of *olam* in the Old Testament. Numerous passages referring to *olam* show clearly it cannot mean "never-ending." Note these few:

- Jonah was in the fish forever [*olam*] *until* he left three days later (Jon. 1:17; 2:6).
- Sodom's fiery judgment is eternal [*olam*] *until* God returns them to their former state (Ez. 16:53-55; Ju. 7).
- A Moabite is forbidden to enter the Lord's congregation forever [*olam*] *until* the 10ᵗʰ generation (De. 23:3).
- Hills are everlasting [*olam*] *until* made low...earth is burned up (Ge. 49:26; De. 33:15; Is. 40:4; 2Pe. 3:10).
- Mountains are everlasting [*olam*] *until* they are scattered (Hab. 3:6).
- A slave serves his master forever [*olam*] *until* death ends his servitude (Ex. 21:6).
- The Mosaic covenant is everlasting [*olam*] *until* it vanishes away (Le. 24:8; He. 8:7-13).

> *Numerous passages referring to olam show clearly it cannot mean "never-ending."*

- The Aaronic priesthood is everlasting [*olam*] *until* the likeness of Melchizedek arises (Ex. 40:15; Nu. 25:13; He. 7:14-22).
- These "stones" are to be a memorial forever *until* (Jos. 4:7)? Where are they now?
- The leprosy of Naaman shall cling forever [*olam*] *until* his death, of course (2K. 5:27).
- God dwells in Solomon's temple forever [*olam*] *until* it is destroyed (2Ch. 7:16; 1K 8:13; 9:3).
- Animal sacrifices were to be offered forever [*olam*] *until* ended by the work of Christ (2Ch. 2:4; He. 7:11-10:18).
- Circumcision was an everlasting [*olam*] covenant *until* the new covenant (Ge. 17:9-13; 1Co. 7:19; Ga. 5:6).
- Israel's judgment lasts forever [*olam*] *until* the Spirit is poured out and God restores it (Is. 32:13-15).
- I will make you an eternal [*olam*] excellence *until* many generations (Is. 60:15).

Even passages that do not use *olam* but signify unchanging are not so when God is involved. Nothing can deter Him from achieving His purposes. For example:

- Israel's affliction is incurable *until* the Lord restores health and heals her wounds (Jer. 30:12, 17).
- Samaria's wounds are incurable *until* the Lord brings them back and restores them (Mic. 1:9; Ez. 16:53 DOUAY).
- Egypt and Elam will rise no more *until* the Lord brings back their captives (Jer. 25:27; 49:39; Ez. 29:14).
- Moab is destroyed *until* the Lord brings back the captives of Moab (Jer. 48:4, 42, 47).

New Testament

Turning from the Greek Old Testament, consider the New Testament use of *aion*. Does "eternity" make any sense in the following passages?

- *What will be the sign...of the end of [**eternity**]* (Mt. 24:3)?
- *I am with you...to the end of the [**eternity**]* (Mt. 28:20).
- *The sons of this [**eternity**] are more shrewd* (Lu. 16:8).
- *The sons of this [**eternity**] marry* (Lu. 20:34).
- *Worthy to attain that [**eternity**]* (Lu. 20:35).
- *Since the [**eternity**] began* (Jn. 9:32; Ac. 3:21).
- *Conformed to this [**eternity**]* (Ro. 12:2).
- *Mystery kept secret since the [**eternity**] began but now made manifest* (Ro. 16:25-26).
- *Where is the disputer of this [**eternity**]* (1Co. 1:20)?
- *Wisdom of this [**eternity**], nor of the rulers of this [**eternity**]...ordained before the [**eternities**]...which none of the rulers of this [**eternity**]...* (1Co. 2:6-8).
- *Wise in this [**eternity**]* (1Co. 3:18).
- *Upon whom the ends of the [**eternities**] have come* (1Co. 10:11).
- *God of this [**eternity**] has blinded* (2Co. 4:4).
- *Deliver us from this present evil [**eternity**]* (Ga. 1:4).
- *Not only in this [**eternity**] but also in that which is to come* (Ep. 1:21).
- *Walked according to the [**eternity**] of this world* (Ep. 2:2).
- *In the [**eternities**] to come* (Ep. 2:7).

- *From the beginnings of the [**eternities**]* (Ep. 3:9).
- *Hidden from [**eternities**]...but now...revealed* (Col. 1:26).
- *Loved this present [**eternity**]* (2Ti. 4:10).
- *Receive him [**for eternity**]* (Phil. 1:15). Forever or until Onesimus, Philemon's former slave, dies?
- *Powers of the [**eternity**] to come* (He. 6:5).
- *At the end of the [**eternities**]* (He. 9:26).
- *We understand the [**eternities**] have been prepared by a saying of God* (He. 11:3).

How can we say...

- "before eternity" or "eternity began"? Eternity has no beginning (Jn. 9:32; Ac. 3:21; 1Co. 2:7; Ep. 3:9).
- "present eternity," "eternity to come," and "end of eternity"? Eternity transcends time. Only God is eternal (Mt. 24:3; 28:20; 1Co. 10:11; 2Ti. 4:10; He. 6:5; 9:26).
- "this eternity," "that eternity," or "eternities"? There is only one eternity (Lu. 16:8; 20:34-35; Ro. 12:2; 1Co. 1:20; 2:6-8; 3:18; 10:11; 2Co. 4:4; Ga. 1:4; Ep. 1:21; 2:2, 7; 3:9; Col. 1:26; 2Ti. 4:10; He. 11:3).
- "eternal secret" if the secret is revealed (Ro. 16:25-26; Col. 1:26)? It is no longer a "secret" at that point.
- Onesimus will be Philemon's slave for eternity? Is he still his slave (Phil. 1:15)?

Scores of passages demonstrate that *aion* is of limited duration. In his book *God's Methods with Man*, G. Campbell Morgan (scholar, associate of D.L. Moody, and a highly respected expositor of Scripture), said:

> Let me say to Bible students that we must be very careful how we use the word "eternity." We have fallen into great error in our constant use of that word. There is no word in the whole Book of God corresponding with our "eternal," which, as commonly used among us, means absolutely without end. The strongest Scripture word used with reference to the existence of God, is—"unto the ages of the ages," which does not literally mean eternally.[3]

In his *Word Studies in the New Testament*, Marvin Vincent, D.D., Baldwin Professor of Sacred Literature at Union Theological Seminary, New York, explained:

> *Aion*, transliterated *aeon*, is a period of longer or shorter duration, having a beginning and an end, and complete in itself. Aristotle (*peri ouravou*, i. 9, 15) said, "The period which includes the whole time of one's life is called the aeon of each one." Hence, it often means the life of a man, as in Homer, where one's life (*aion*) is said to leave him or to consume away (Il v.685; Od v.160). It is not, however, limited to human life. It signifies any period in the course of the millennium, the mythological period before the beginnings of history. The word has not "a stationary and mechanical value" (De Quincey). It does not mean a period of a fixed length for all cases. There are as many aeons as entities, the respective durations of which are fixed by the normal conditions of the several entities. There is one *aeon* of a human life, another of the life of a nation, another of a crow's life, another of an oak's life. The length of the *aeon* depends on the subject to which it is attached....The adjective *aionious* in like manner carries the idea of time. Neither the noun nor the adjective, in themselves, carry the sense of endless or everlasting. They may acquire that sense by their connotation....*Aionios* means "enduring through" or "pertaining to a period of time." Both the noun and the adjective are applied to limited periods....Out of the 150 instances in LXX, [Greek Old Testament] four-fifths imply limited duration. For a few instances, see Gen. xlviii. 4; Num. x. 8; xv. 15; Prov. xxii. 28; Jonah ii.6; Hab. iii. 6; Isa lxi. 17.[4]

> *"Aion, transliterated aeon, is a period of longer or shorter duration, having a beginning and an end, and complete in itself."*[4]

> *"The length of the aeon depends on the subject to which it is attached."*[4]

So what if the Greek word *aion* has been erroneously translated "eternal" instead of "age"? What does that have to do with everlasting punishment? It has everything to do with it, since one of the key texts used in defense of the Augustinian view of hell is Mt. 25:46: "And these will go away into everlasting [*aionian*] punishment." If this passage as translated here is accurate, then I would have to admit the Bible teaches that hell is forever. But what if it is not? What if *aion* does not mean "everlasting"? What would that do to the "biblical support" of an infinite hell? It would negate the use of any verses resting on the word *aion* used in its defense.

Consider how the following translations word this phrase:

+ Young's Literal Translation: "punishment age-during."
+ Rotherham Translation: "age-abiding correction."
+ Weymouth Translation: "punishment of the ages."
+ Concordant Literal Translation: "chastening *eonian*."

These reputable and literal translations use the word "age" and not "eternal." These two concepts are diametrically opposed to one another. They are not the same by any means. An age has a beginning and an end; eternity does not.

Augustine raised the argument that since *aionios* in Mt. 25:46 referred to both life and punishment, it had to carry the same duration in both cases.[5] However, he failed to consider that the duration of *aionios* is determined by the subject to which it refers. For example, when *aionios* referred to the duration of Jonah's entrapment in the fish, it was limited to three days. To a slave, *aionios* referred to his life span. To the Aaronic priesthood, it referred to the generation preceding the Melchizedek priesthood. To Solomon's temple, it referred to 400 years. To God it encompasses and transcends time altogether.

Thus, the word cannot have a set value. It is a relative term and its duration depends upon that with which it is associated. It is similar to what "tall" is to height. The size of a tall building can be 300 feet, a tall man six feet, and a tall dog three feet. Black Beauty was a great horse, Abraham Lincoln a great man, and Yahweh the GREAT God. Though God is called "great," the word "great" is neither eternal nor divine. The horse is still a horse. An adjective relates to the noun it modifies. In relation to God, "great" becomes GREAT only because of who and what God is. This silences the contention that *aion* must always mean forever because it modifies God. God is described as the God of Israel or the God of Abraham. This does not mean He is not the God of

Gentiles or the God of you and me. Though He is called the God of the "ages," He nonetheless remains the God who transcends the ages.

In addition, Augustine's reasoning does not hold up in light of Ro. 16:25, 26 and Hab. 3:6. Here, in both cases, the same word is used twice—with God and with something temporal. "In accord with the revelation of a secret hushed in times *eonian*, yet manifested now...according to the injunction of the *eonian* God" (Ro. 16:25, 26 CLT). An *eonian* secret revealed at some point cannot be eternal even though it is revealed by the *eonian* God. *Eonian* does not make God eternal, but God makes *eonian* eternal. "And the everlasting mountains were scattered....His ways are everlasting" (Hab. 3:6). Mountains are not eternal, though they will last a very long time. God's ways however, are eternal, because He is eternal.

Matthew 25:46 contains an additional clue confirming the temporary nature of God's judgment. The Greek word, translated "punishment," is *kolasis*. William Barclay, world-renowned Greek scholar, translator, and author of the popular Bible commentary, *The Daily Study Bible* and *New Testament Words,* notes:

> The Greek word for punishment here [Mt. 25:46] is *kolasis*, which was not originally an ethical word at all. It originally meant the pruning of trees to make them grow better. I think it is true to say that in all Greek secular literature *kolasis* is never used of anything but remedial punishment.[6]

Thomas Talbott, philosophy professor at Willamette University in Oregon and author of *The Inescapable Love of God*, explained:

> According to Aristotle, there is a difference between revenge and punishment; the latter (*kolasis*) is inflicted in the interest of the sufferer, the former (*timōria*) in the interest of him who inflicts it, that he may obtain satisfaction. Plato also appealed to the established meaning of *kolasis* as support for his theory that virtue could be taught: "For if you will consider punishment (*kolasis*)...and what control it has over wrong-doers, the facts will inform you that men agree in regarding virtue as procured." Even where a punishment may seem harsh and unforgiving, more like retribution than parental chastisement, this in no way excludes a corrective purpose. Check out the punish-

ment that Paul prescribes in I Corinthians 5:5. One might never have guessed that, in prescribing such a punishment—that is, delivering a man to Satan for the destruction of the flesh—Paul had in mind a corrective purpose, had Paul not explicitly stated the corrective purpose himself ("that his spirit may be saved in the day of the Lord Jesus"). So as this text illustrates, even harsh punishment of a seemingly retributive kind can in fact serve a redemptive purpose.[7-9]

"And these will go away into everlasting [*aionian*] punishment [*kolasis*], but the righteous into eternal [*aionian*] life" (Mt. 25:46). Isn't it ironic that the passage most often used to support everlasting punishment is in fact one strongly opposing it when accurately understood?

Alternative Views

Aionian (eternal), when associated with God, may simply refer to that which comes forth from Him and relates to His purposes; a quality of essence rather than of duration. Is this not what our Lord intends in John 17:3: "And this is eternal life, that they may know You"? If this is so, perhaps the Matthew passage could be paraphrased this way: "And these will go away into the chastisement of God, but the righteous into the life of God."

Professor Talbott confirms this:

> *Aionian (eternal), when associated with God, may simply refer to that which comes forth from Him and relates to His purposes; a quality of essence rather than of duration.*

When the letter of Jude describes the fire that consumed Sodom and Gomorrah as "eternal fire," the point is not that the fire literally burns forever without consuming the cities; it is not that the fire continues to burn even today. The point is that the fire is a form of divine judgment upon those cities...that has its causal source in the eternal God himself. And similar for Jesus' reference to "eternal fire" in Matthew 25:41 and to "eternal punishment" in Matthew 25:46. The fire to which he alludes is not eternal in the sense that it burns forever without consuming anything—without consuming, for example, that which is false within a person (see 1 Co. 3:15)—and neither is the punishment eternal in the sense that it continues forever without accomplishing its corrective purpose. Both the fire and the punishment are eternal in the sense that they have their causal source in the eternal God himself.[10]

Similarly Barclay wrote:

The simplest way to put it is that *aionios* cannot be used properly of anyone but God; it is the word uniquely, as Plato saw it, of God. Eternal punishment is then literally that kind of remedial punishment which it befits God to give and which only God can give.[11]

Talbott continues:

The Gospel writers thought in terms of two ages, the present age and the age to come, and they associated the age to come with God himself; it was an age in which God's presence would be fully manifested, his purposes fully realized, and his redemptive work eventually completed. They therefore came to employ the term, "αἰώνιος," [*aionios*] as an eschatological [doctrine of end times] term, one that functioned as a handy reference to the realities of the age to come. In this way, they managed to combine the more literal sense of "that which pertains to an age" with the more religious sense of "that which manifests the presence of God in a special way." Eternal life, then, is not merely life that comes from God; it is also the mode of living associated with the age to come. And similarly for eternal punishment: It is not merely punishment that comes from God; it is also the form of punishment associated with the age to come. Now in none of this is there any implication that the life that comes from God and the punishment that comes from God are of an equal duration."[12]

Likewise, Beecher demonstrates that in the days of the early church the idea was "punishment of the world to come." The early Church establishes that fact through the ancient creeds. In fact, in none of its creeds did the early Church teach everlasting punishment.[13]

Arguing that eternal punishment must be of unending duration because it is contrasted with eternal life (Mt. 25:46) misses the point. It fails to recognize that eternal life is a quality of relationship with God (Jn. 17:3), and is an end in itself; while eternal punishment is God's corrective discipline and a means to an end. In any case, whether *aion* means "age-abiding," "of God," or "of the world to come," none of these expressions state, imply, or require that the punishment be never-ending.

So then, if *aion* does not strictly mean eternal, what word does? There are a number of Greek words that imply eternal. They are usually translated "indestructible," "imperishable," "unfading," "immortality," and "incorruptible." See Ro. 1:23; 2:7; 1Co. 9:25; 15:42, 51-54; He. 7:15-16; 1Pe. 1:3-4; 5:4; 1Ti. 1:17; 6:16; 2Ti. 1:10. Our hope of immortality does not reside in the word *aionios*, but in God's very nature (unfailing love and unlimited power) and promises. (See Appendix I).

This short discussion on the word *aion* is just an introduction. I highly recommend you read *The History of Opinions on the Scriptural Doctrine of Retribution* by Dr. Edward Beecher. I found his research and findings incontestable. You may read it on our website: HopeBeyondHell.net (Church History). So long as we have a flawed understanding of this four letter Greek word, we will remain blinded to the truth in relation to God's judgments.

Gehenna

The second pillar in support of the doctrine of everlasting punishment is *Gehenna*. It is one of three words translated "hell" in the New Testament. It is the most common, used 12 times. *Hades* is used 11 times, and *Tartarus* only once. William Barclay stated:

> *Gehenna*...means the Valley of Hinnom, a valley to the south-west of Jerusalem. It was notorious as the place where Ahaz had introduced the fire worship of the heathen God Molech, to whom little children were burned....2 Chronicles 28:2-4. Josiah had stamped out that worship and ordered that the valley should be forever after an accursed place...it became the place where the refuse of Jerusalem was cast out and destroyed. It was a kind of public incinerator. Always the fire smoldered in it, and a pall of thick smoke lay over it, and bred a loathsome kind of worm

which was hard to kill (Mark 9:44-48). So *Gehenna*, the Valley of Hinnom, became identified in people's minds with all that was accursed and filthy, the place where useless and evil things were destroyed.[14]

Hades is the Greek word for the Hebrew, *Sheol*, which the *New Strong's Concise Dictionary* defines as "unseen," the place (state) of departed souls.[15] Throughout the Old Testament, it refers to the state following death for both righteous and unrighteous. The NIV translates it "grave" or "death." *Tartarus* is a holding area prior to judgment for angels who have sinned (2Pe. 2:4).

Gehenna is not mentioned in the Old Testament or by John, Paul, Peter, Jude, or James in all their writings (except once indirectly regarding the tongue—Ja. 3:6). Nor is it mentioned in the book of Acts or Hebrews. The New Testament records Jesus as using the term on what seems like only four occasions. How can such a horrible fate—to which most people are destined—not be warned against everywhere? How can we explain this?

The First Time "*Gehenna*" Is Used by Christ

[Please read Mt. 5:21-22.]

At the very outset of the New Testament, Christ established the limited nature of the *Gehenna* judgment. This is extremely significant. For in the context of His first mention of it, He confirmed the Mosaic code of justice: "An eye for an eye, and a tooth for a tooth" (Mt. 5:38 derived from Ex. 21:24; Mt. 5:17-19). This code established that each crime merits a just and fit punishment, one obviously measurable: "You shall give life for life, eye for eye, tooth for tooth, hand for hand, foot for foot, burn for burn, wound for wound, stripe for stripe" (Ex. 21:23-25). If Christ understood *Gehenna* to be everlasting, He could not have associated it with the Mosaic code. What is measurable about everlasting? And furthermore, He specifically confirmed this by saying that the same measure we use on others will be used on us! (Mt. 7:2). This indicates *Gehenna* is not eternal. For example, no derogatory remark (*raca* or "fool") afflicts everlasting pain, and therefore cannot merit everlasting punishment in return.

[Please read Mt. 5:23-26.]

"Prison" here is a metaphor for *Gehenna*. (This harmonizes with the "prison" of 1Pe. 3:19, and the Father's sentence of Mt. 18:34-35). It is directly linked to *Gehenna* in the preceding verse (Mt. 5:22) by the word "therefore," and it is immediately followed by another *Gehenna* judgment in the very next passage (Mt. 5:27-32). Thus, Mt. 5:23-26 is "sandwiched" between two *Gehenna* judgments. The final clincher is that the Lord identifies the *Gehenna* judgment as a most serious judgment we are all to fear. He says, "**Assuredly** I say unto you." That is serious. What other judgment could he possibly be referring to in this context but the *Gehenna* judgment?

"**Truly** [Assuredly] I say to you, you will not come out of there [Gehenna] **until** you have paid up the last cent." vs. 26 (NAS) The word "until" unmistakably confirms *Gehenna* is of a limited duration. Once the penalty is exacted, release follows, but not before. Note He addressed these words to a mixed audience of believers and unbelievers (Mt. 5:1; 7:28; 8:1). (See also Mt. 18:34-35).

[**Please read Mt. 5:27-30.**]

Here, He describes the consequences of sinning lustfully. We can all imagine the scene—not pleasant. Nevertheless, these are concepts we can identify with in this physical world. With *Gehenna*, however, we know little. We have to trust Christ implicitly. So what does He say? It is "more profitable" to lose an eye or a hand, than to experience *Gehenna*. That's it. That is all He chose to say. If *Gehenna* were unending (a concept horrible beyond description), how could He describe it merely as "less profitable"? Is this all He could say to contrast momentary and unending pain? Such a phrase can only describe another finite penalty, though to a degree more severe.

> *Whatever the lake of fire entails, we can be confident it consists of judgment that conforms to the character of our Father.*

For the complete exposition of Christ's use of *Gehenna*, including: "Fire Not Quenched," "Refining Fire," "Undying Worm," and "Lake of Fire," see Appendix IV.

Whatever the lake of fire entails, we can be confident it consists of a judgment conforming to the character of our Father. Are not His purifying fires inflicted in the presence of the Lamb who was slain for us (Re. 14:10)? He certainly will not rest day and night as He looks on our sufferings with His unchanging heart of compassion (Mt. 9:36; He. 13:8).

Additional passages do not use the word *Gehenna*, but seem to refer to the same judgment (Mt. 3:10, 12; 7:19; 13:40-42, 49-53; 25:41; Lu. 3:9, 17; 17:29; Jn. 15:6; Ju. 1:7). The strongest language among them is "gnashing of teeth." In *Christ Triumphant*, Thomas Allin, D.D., historian, author, and clergyman of the English Episcopal Church North London (late 19th and early 20th centuries), observed:

> The whole Bible is Oriental. Every line breathes the spirit of the East, with its hyperboles and metaphors, and what to us seem utter exaggerations. If such language be taken literally, its whole meaning is lost. When the sacred writers want to describe the dusky redness of a lunar eclipse, they say the moon is "turned into blood." He who perverts Scripture is not the man who reduces this sacred poetry to its true meaning. Nay, that man perverts the Bible who hardens into dogmas the glowing metaphors of Eastern poetry—such conduct LANGE calls "a moral scandal." So with our Lord's words. Am I to hate my father and mother or pluck out my right eye literally? Or take a case by Farrar. Egypt is said to have been an iron furnace to the Jews (De. 4:20; Jer. 11:4), and yet they said, "it was well with us there," and sighed for its enjoyments (Nu. 11:18). Therefore I maintain that no doctrine of endless pain can be based on Eastern imagery, on metaphors mistranslated very often, and always misinterpreted.[16]

Likewise, Barclay wrote, "It was the eastern custom to use language in the most vivid possible way. Eastern language is always as vivid as the human mind can make it."[17] Though men will weep and even gnash their teeth, they will not do so forever. "Weeping may endure for a night, but joy comes in the morning" (Ps. 30:5). "[I] will rest in *hope*. For *You will not leave my soul in Sheol*." (Ps. 16:9-10).

Apollumi (Greek for "destruction")

Most Christians think death and destruction, whether of unbelievers or unfaithful believers, refer to an eternal hell of suffering or to a state of annihilation. Thus, they are understood to be a permanent state. I think if we closely compare Scripture with Scripture, line upon line, we will see this falls short of what God is really all about.

Even in death and destruction, He will not be defeated. His promises to restore all (Ac. 3:21; 2Co. 5:19; Ep. 1:10; Col. 1:19-21) will come to pass in their appointed times (Ep. 1:9-11; 1Ti. 2:6). In his *An Expository Dictionary of Biblical Words* regarding *apollumi*, W. E. Vine stated, "The idea is not extinction but ruin, loss, not of being, but of well being...."[18]

Andrew Jukes, graduate of Harrow and Trinity College, Cambridge and pastor of St. John's Church, was a well-respected Christian author in 19th century England. Also the author of *The Law of the Offerings*, *Four Views of Christ*, *Types in Genesis*, *The Names of God*, and the *Restitution of all Things*, he wrote:

> Death for man is simply an end to, or separation from, some given form of life which he has lived in... We must... by Christ die to this dark spirit-world, to return to live in God's light-world... [It] is a ceasing from some particular form of life which has been lived in by man, yet it is never non-existence absolutely; rather the means to bring the fallen creature into a new life, a chaos being ever the necessary condition for a new creation.[19]

Here are a few passages for you to think about:

- *In the day that you [Adam] eat of it you shall surely die* (Ge. 2:17).
- *You [Israel] shall surely perish [apollomi—Septuagint[20]]* (De. 30:18).
- *I will...destroy [apolia—presumed derivative of apollumi—Strong[21]] that nation* (Jer. 12:17).
- *I kill and I make alive; I wound and I heal* (De. 32:39).
- *He destroys [apollumi—Septuagint[22]] the blameless and the wicked* (Job 9:22).
- *The righteous perishes [apollumi—Septuagint[23]], and no man takes it to heart* (Is. 57:1).
- *The wineskins are marred [apollumi]* (Mk. 2:22 KJV).
- *He is not the God of the dead but of the living, for all live to Him* (Lu. 20:38).
- *But if it [grain of wheat] dies, it produces much grain* (Jn. 12:24).
- *He who has died has been freed from sin* (Ro. 6:7; 7:9; 8:6; 2Co. 4:11; Ep. 2:1; 1Ti. 5:6).

- *Neither death nor life...shall be able to separate us from the love of God* (Ro. 8:38-39).
- *What you sow is not made alive unless it dies* (1Co. 15:36).
- *Death is swallowed up in victory* (1Co. 15:54).

Please take a moment to reflect on what we have just read. Adam dies on the same day he sins, yet lives 900 more years. Israel and Jerusalem perish. The blameless are destroyed. The righteous perish. Wineskins are marred. The dead are alive to God. Death produces grain and frees from sin. Death cannot separate from God's love. What is sown is not made alive unless it dies.

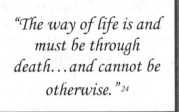

"The way of life is and must be through death...and cannot be otherwise." [24]

Utter or permanent annihilation cannot be the true meaning of death and destruction in any of these cases. Destruction is the prerequisite for subsequent change. Is this not what the cross is all about in the life of the believer? He kills and makes alive. He destroys to make new.

The Cross

Andrew Jukes wrote:

> The meaning of Christ's cross is not understood, but rather perverted and therefore death is shrunk from. It is not welcomed as God's appointed means to deliver us from him that has the power of death....Christians misunderstand destruction and judgment are the only way for fallen creatures to be delivered from their bondage, and brought back to God's life in His kingdom. This is a point of all importance. It lies at the very root of the cross of Christ and of His members. It is the clue to all His judgments, who "kills and makes alive," who "brings down to the grave and brings up" (1Sa. 2:6; Dt. 32:39). The way of life is and must be through death...and cannot be otherwise. [24]

As followers of Jesus Christ, we have been called to carry our cross, to die (Mk. 8:34; Jn. 12:24-25). Unless we do, we will not have His life abiding in us (Jn. 15:4-5). We are to partake of the divine nature (2Pe. 1:3-12). What does this mean except that we are to die?

Our salvation is not brought to perfection until we have died to sin and live to righteousness (Ro. 6). Death is not optional. Only in dying to our self-will do we truly live and bear fruit to God (Jn. 12:24). Scripture frequently alludes to this purpose in salvation (Ro. 6:3; 8:13; 12:1, 2; 2Co. 4:11, 16; 5:15; Ga. 2:20; Ph. 3:10; 2Ti. 2:11; He. 5:7-9; 1Pe. 2:21, 24; 1Jn. 3:16).

Scripture Interprets Itself

Often in Scripture, two statements are made side by side that together shed greater light on a given theme. Consider 1Co. 1:19; Ro. 2:12; 14:15, 20-21. "I will destroy [*apollumi*] the wisdom of the wise; I will bring to nothing ["set aside"—NAS] the understanding of the prudent" (1Co. 1:19).

Here *apollumi* is used in the same sense as "set aside" or "bring to nothing." "For as many as have sinned without law will also perish [*apollumi*] without law, and as many as have sinned in the law will be judged by the law" (Ro. 2:12). Scripture is clear that all are judged including unbelievers who have sinned without law (Re. 20:12-13). Thus, to "perish" here cannot be utter annihilation, for judgment must follow. Consider also Ro. 14:15: "If your brother is grieved because of your food, you are no longer walking in love. Do not destroy [*apollumi*] with your food the one for whom Christ died" (Ro. 14:15). Do you think *apollumi* here means we can cancel out another's eternal redemption paid by Christ by our diet? Or consider 1Co. 8:11 where Paul asks, "because of your knowledge shall the weak brother perish [*apollumi*] for whom Christ died?" Can we really annihilate others for whom Christ died by our knowledge?

Note how Paul defines *apollumi* by his comments regarding his use of it in Ro. 14:15. "Do not tear down the work of God for the sake of food" (Ro. 14:20 NAS). "It is good neither to eat meat nor drink wine nor do anything by which your brother stumbles or is offended or is made weak" (Ro. 14:21). He contrasts *apollumi* (v. 15) with "tear down," "stumble," "offend," and "make weak" (v.20-21).

In all the above, whatever is meant by death and destruction, it cannot be unending torment or utter annihilation. Could Jukes be right in saying death for man is an end or separation from some given form of life in which he has lived? What did our Lord mean when He said in order to save our life, we must lose *apollumi* it? Is this not to end living a self-centered life and instead to live for God—to stop being ruled by sin, but instead by righteousness?

Did you realize the very ones Christ came to save are the "destroyed" ones? "For the Son of Man has come to seek and to save that which was lost [*apollumi*]" (Lu. 19:10). *Apollumi* is the very condition qualifying us for salvation. Are the *apollumi* the annihilated ones or those not yet found? At what point does *apollumi* become so permanent it exceeds

> *God has given man a 'measure' of free will, but certainly not to the degree that He would allow him or her to damn themselves forever in torment.*

God's power and will to save? What justifies us to put limits on Him who is able to turn stones into worshippers (Lu. 3:8)?

In conclusion then, even were God to utterly annihilate someone, has He not the power to restore (De. 32:39; 1Sa. 2:6; Mt. 3:9)? What gives God greater glory: annihilation or restoration? Do we deny that with God "all things are possible" (Mt. 19:26)? Popular theology claims God is able to do all things except restore the destroyed for whom Christ died. Really?

Free Will

What father holding his little daughter's hand while crossing a busy street would ever let it go? The more she pulls, the tighter her dad squeezes. There's no way she is going anywhere! Is God any different? The argument that a person can choose hell by rejecting God as a result of "free" will is in effect saying a little girl has more strength than her father. God has given man a "measure" of free will, but certainly not to the degree He would allow him or her to damn themselves forever in torment. Is God less of a parent than we are (Mt. 7:11)? We extend increasing freedom to our children as they mature. Too much too soon is disastrous. He knows just how much freedom we need for our development.

God, as Creator, is owner of all things (Ps. 2:8; Ez. 18:4; Col. 1:16; He. 1:2), and that includes you and me. He has never relinquished that title. Only He has absolute "free" will over His property. Should we be forever lost, He would be the loser. Many say hell is locked on the inside. But how? Christ has the keys! (Re. 1:18). Many believe God's hands are tied; as much as He would like to keep us, He is unable. But, is our power to destroy His property really greater than His power to preserve or restore it? How "free" and powerful are we? What role did we play in controlling our life experiences that have made us what we are? Will we deliberately choose what sufferings we will undergo in the future that inevitably will affect what we become? What intricacies of our reasoning processes, which determine our decisions, do we fully control?

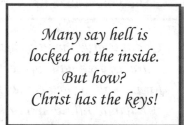

Many say hell is locked on the inside. But how? Christ has the keys!

Is the Bible right in saying no one seeks after God, that our natural mind is at odds with Him and not subject to His law? "Indeed it cannot be subject," said Paul (Ro. 3:11; 8:7). How can a naturally hostile mind, that "indeed" cannot subject itself to God, of its own "free" will do so? Isn't there a contradiction here? Only God can give us faith and draw us to Himself; we cannot muster it up (He. 12:2; Ro. 12:3; Jn. 6:44; 15:16; Ph. 1:29; Mt. 11:27; 16:16-17; Jn. 1:13; Ac. 13:48; 1Co. 4:7; Ep 2:8-9; 3:16-17; Ph. 1:6; 2:13; Col. 1:12; 2 Th. 3:2; 1Ti. 1:14; Tit. 1:1; Ez. 36: 26-27; Jer. 24:7; 31:33-34; 32:39-40). To idolize "free" will as though it were the crux of our salvation contradicts the Bible and fosters a boastful attitude! (1Co. 1:26-31; 4:6-7).

What are we implying when we infer God is helpless in the face of man's "free" will? It intimates our salvation depends on human power, not divine. Thus God is stripped of His power and glory leaving the blood of Christ powerless to save those for whom it was shed (all sinners). In fact, it negates the very definition of God as "The Almighty," leaving us with no real God at all. In *Exploring the Attributes of God* Dr. Robert Morey, author of over 40 books, stated:

> God's sovereignty was viewed as an essential attribute by the early Church and anyone who dared to deny it was called an atheist. This is one of the most misunderstood and maligned attributes of God. Yet, it is an essential attribute that makes God GOD. The Scriptures always describe God as actively controlling and guiding the entire creation. It is never viewed as bare potential. Where should we begin when studying God's sovereignty and man's responsibility? Should we begin with man and establish his free will and then define divine sovereignty in such a way it

does not conflict with man? Or, should we begin with God and His free will and then develop our understanding of man from that viewpoint? We must begin where Scripture begins....The Bible begins with GOD. He is the great I AM, the Alpha...Omega, the Beginning...End.[25]

The story of Joseph pictures God powerfully working behind the scenes influencing the wills of men. Who of these men thought their will was not solely their own? Yet God, in His infinite power, was at work accomplishing His purposes through their decisions (Ge. 45:5). While the king of Egypt decreed all male Hebrew babies should die, God was all the while orchestrating His plan for putting Moses at the head of the kingdom! Even while Pharaoh resisted Moses, God was at work according to His plan. Where was Pharaoh's "free" will? Consider what Isaiah wrote about Assyria:

> *Woe to Assyria, the rod of My anger...I will send him against...the people of My wrath...will give him charge....* ***Yet he does not mean so, nor does his heart think so....****For he says: "By the strength of my hand I have done it....Shall the ax boast itself against him who chops with it?"* (Is. 10:5-7, 13).

Assyria was being used by God and had no clue. In all these cases we see men doing, but God orchestrating. Please carefully reflect on these passages.

+ *God will circumcise your heart to love the Lord your God with all your heart and soul* (De. 30:6).
+ *I know that thou canst do all things, and that no purpose of Thine can be thwarted* (Job 42:2 RSV).
+ *Blessed is the man You choose, and cause to approach You* (Ps. 65:4).
+ *A man's heart plans his way, but the Lord directs his steps* (Pr. 16:9).
+ *The lot is cast into the lap, but its every decision is from the Lord* (Pr. 16:33).
+ *There are many plans in a man's heart, nevertheless the Lord's counsel—that will stand* (Pr. 19:21).
+ *A man's steps are of the Lord; How then can a man understand his own way* (Pr. 20:24)?

- *The king's heart is a stream...in the hand of the LORD; He turns it wherever He will* (Pr. 21:1).
- *You will establish peace for us, for You have also done all our works in us* (Is. 26:12).
- *I will do all my pleasure,...indeed...I will bring it to pass. I have purposed it; I will do it* (Is. 46:10-11).
- *None who seeks for God....Where is boasting* (Is.53:6; Ro. 3:11, 19b, 27)?
- *The way of man is not in himself; It is not in man who walks to direct his own steps* (Jer. 10:23).
- *I will give them a heart to know Me...for they shall return to Me with their whole heart* (Jer. 24:7).
- *I will put My fear in their hearts so that they will not depart from Me* (Jer. 32:40).
- *I will...cause you to walk in My statutes, and you will keep My judgments and do them....* (Ez. 36:27).
- *He does according to His will among the inhabitants of the earth. No one can restrain His hand* (Da. 4:35).
- *Those...were born...nor of the will of man, but of God* (Jn. 1:12, 13).
- *No one can come to Me unless the Father...draws [drags] him* (Jn. 6:44).
- *Without Me you can do nothing* (Jn. 15:5).

> *It does not depend on the man who wills or the man who runs but on God who has mercy.* (Ro. 9:16 NAS)

- *You did not choose Me, but I chose you* (Jn. 15:16).
- *Creation [people] was subjected to futility, not willingly, but because of Him who...subjected it in hope....* (Ro. 8:20).
- *It does not depend on the man who wills or the man who runs but on God who has mercy* (Ro. 9:16 NAS).
- *You will say to me then, "Why does He still find fault? For who has resisted His will?"* (Ro. 9:19).
- *God chose the foolish...God chose the weak...He chose the lowly...so that no man may boast...* (1Co. 1:27-29 NIV).
- *Predestined man...to the purpose of Him who works all... according to the counsel of His will* (Ep. 1:11).
- *God works in you both to will and to do for His good pleasure* (Ph. 2:13).
- *He is able even to subdue all things to Himself* (Ph. 3:21).

- *God has put it into their hearts to fulfill His purpose, to be of one mind* (Re. 17:17).

Who is in control here? Man or God? Whose will prevails? In his article titled, "The Work of the Cross", Ken Eckerty commented, "How ironic it is that those who believe that God will not violate the "free" will of men have no problem believing that God will force men—against their will—to confess and bow to Christ."[26] The director of Bread of Life Frontier Missions, David Nuckols, said it this way, "How ironic that those who believe God will not violate the 'free' will of man have no problem believing He will violate His own free will—that all men should be saved!"

What are we saying to God in deifying the will of man? "Oh well, Lord, it is a sad thing that...

- You cannot have what is yours (Ro. 11:36).
- You cannot find what you have lost (Lu. 15:4).
- Isaiah was wrong about your hand not being so short it cannot save (Is. 59:1).
- The Bible exaggerates in saying nothing is too difficult for you (Jer. 32:17).
- Man has robbed the keys of death and of Hades from You (Re. 1:18).
- He who is in the world is ultimately stronger than You (1Jn. 4:4; 1Jn. 3:8).
- Your propitiation for the whole world is really only for a few (1Jn. 2:2).
- Your promises to reconcile all things are just exaggerated hopes (Ac. 3:21).
- Your hands are tied and you cannot accomplish all your will (Is. 55:11).
- All creatures will not really worship you like you hoped" (Re. 5:13; Phil. 2:10-11).

What has happened to GOD? Our tradition has pawned His power off to man in the myth of "free" will. Are we better than the fools Paul referred to in Ro. 1:20-21? Why were they called fools? For failing to glorify God "as GOD." Do we do the same?

God's Will

Given Bible translators are human, they are naturally inclined to conform the text to their world view. Since most believe in the sovereignty of man's will, they must weaken the sense of phrases such as "to will" and "to purpose" with "to desire" and "to wish" when referring to God. Thus God is seen as merely "desiring" things instead of "willing" them into existence.

> *This is good and acceptable in the sight of God our Saviour; Who **will** have ["desires"–NKJV] all men to be saved, and to come unto the knowledge of the truth. For there is one God, and one mediator between God and men, the man Christ Jesus; Who gave himself a ransom for all, to be testified in due time* (1Ti. 2:3-6 KJV).

God "will" have all men to be saved. Does this mean God purposes with intent to accomplish His will, or that He merely desires it with no power to make it happen? The Greek word "will" here is *thélō* (Strong's 2309) which *The Complete Word Study Dictionary New Testament* defines at (**I**) (**C**) 'To will as the equivalent of to purpose, to be decided upon, seeing one's desire to its execution..."(**V**) "*Thélō* indicates not only willing something, but also pressing on to action."[27] Of more importance than what any lexicographer would say, is how the apostles understood Christ when He used the word.

> *Jesus said to him, "If I **will** [thelo] that he remain till I come, what is that to you? You follow Me." Then this saying went out among the brethren that this disciple would not die. Yet Jesus did not say to him that he would not die, but, "**if** I will [thelo] that he remain till I come, what is that to you?* (Jn. 21:22-23).

The apostles evidently understood Jesus statement, "I will" as the equivalent of "to purpose," "to be decided upon," and to "seeing one's desire to its execution." That is why they went out and proclaimed this disciple would not die. To believe such a statement is especially revealing as all men die. Did Paul's hearers understand 1Ti. 2:4 differently? I don't think so. And for the sake of argument, even if the text read "desire" instead of "will," it still does not change a thing, for Isaiah says: "My counsel shall stand, and I will do all My pleasure ["delight"—YLT]" (Is. 46:10).

Tradition has taught that God will not save a person against their will. I agree. However, He has the power to orchestrate whatever circumstances are necessary to effect one's will to change.

> *He has the power to orchestrate whatever circumstances are necessary to effect one's will to change.*

Quillen Hamilton Shinn, Civil War soldier, teacher, and acclaimed Vermont minister wrote,

> He does not save men by arbitrary force. He saves by their wills, through moral influence. God has resources in his universe, the all conquering agencies of love, to make the unwilling soul willing! He has light enough to make the blind see, and love enough to melt the hardened heart."[28]

Pastor and author of *The Outcome of Infinite Grace*, Loyal F. Hurley, pointed out:

> Again and again, when trouble stalks his path, a man turns back to the God he has despised. When his wife dies, or his children go wrong; when loss and disaster fall upon him, again and again he will seek the God he has neglected. That is not because God coerces the man, but because God brings upon him such experiences as change his attitude. And God brings such experiences upon men, not in anger, but in love. For love is the only ultimate power that is not coercive.[29]

> *"For love is the only ultimate power that is not coercive."*[29]

The Myth of "Eternal" Rejection

We know in part...we see...dimly.
(1Co. 13:9-12)

No one has complete or perfect knowledge of God. So when a person "rejects" a given concept of God, they are not in truth rejecting the true God, but only their partial or flawed understanding of Him. Only Christ truly knows Him, and he to whom He wills to reveal Him (Mt. 11:27; Lu. 10:22; Jn. 6:46). If Christ has not "revealed" the Father in truth to someone, can that person be held accountable for rejecting what was not really made known?

Once a "full" revelation of God is received in the ages to come (Ep. 2:7), men will bow and confess Jesus Christ is Lord, just as Isaiah and Paul prophesied (Is. 45:21-25; Ro. 14:11; Ph. 2:9-11). Who would want to continue in active and persistent rebellion knowing God only wants what is best for them? Knowing the great goodness and love of God, along with the Holy Spirit working in their hearts, these hardened hearts must melt before His glorious being. It is impossible that an omnipotent God can fail in His purpose, and some would forever resist unconditional love opting for everlasting pain. This would be totally irrational. And even if one were that irrational, such resistance would not arise out of a "free" will, but an "enslaved" will, a will in bondage to an insane mind.

Martin Luther declared:

> I frankly confess that, for myself, even if it could be, I should not want free-will to be given me....But now that God has taken my salvation out of the control of my own will, and put it under the control of His, and promised to save me, not according to my working or running, but according to His own grace and mercy, I have the comfortable certainty that He is faithful and will not lie to me, and that He is also great and powerful, so that no devils or opposition can break Him or pluck me from Him.[30]

John Wesley claimed that everyone in the world could be saved without the loss of liberty, according to a sermon entitled, "The General Spread of the Gospel," he preached on April 22, 1783. He said a city, nation, or the whole world could become Christian, and it could take place without difficulty if only we suppose God acts irresistibly. "Now in the same manner as God has converted so many to Himself without destroying their liberty, He can undoubtedly convert whole nations, or the whole world. And it is as easy to Him to convert a world as one individual soul."[31]

"Free" will? Have you really thought it through? Are God's hands really tied by it? Your belief or disbelief in "free" will must inevitably be determined by your view of God's sovereign will and His power. I would like to leave you with this question to ponder: Why is it that our tradition can only accept man's will as "free" if it leads our race to destruction, but cannot accept it as "free" if it leads it to life (Ph. 2:9-11; Ro. 14:11)? Does God place a higher value on man's freedom than He does His own kind intentions for him? Such a freedom is in effect an illusion, for such absolute freedom would be bondage of the worst kind imaginable.

Appendage

Dr. Helena Keizer, may be the world's greatest authority on the definition of *aiōn* in ancient Greek literature, including the Bible in the time of Christ. Keizer published a 315-page doctoral dissertation titled: "Life, Time, Entirety – A Study of *Aion* in Greek Literature and Philosophy, the Septuagint and Philo." Presented on September 7, 1999 in Holland, at Amsterdam University. Keizer states:

> "*Olām* and hence *aiōn* in the Biblical sense is time constituting the human temporal horizon."[32]

> "Our study has led to the conclusion that infinity is not an intrinsic or necessary connotation of *aiōn*, either in the Greek or in the Biblical usage ('*olām*)."[33]

> "To speak of 'this *aiōn*', its 'end,' and 'the *aiōn* to come' clearly lends to *aiōn* the meaning of a limited time."[34]

> "The following description of Gregory of Nyssa's interpretation of *aiōn* makes a good finishing point for now: '*Aeon* designates temporality, that which occurs within time.'"[35]

Because of the emphasis defenders of everlasting punishment have placed on the word "eternal" (*aiōn*) in Scripture, no effort is too extensive to prove its accurate meaning. Thus, if you would like to pursue this further, I refer you to my website, under the sections titled "Eternity" and "Church History."

◆ ◆ ◆ ◆ ◆

In this chapter, we have examined the foundational pillars upon which belief in infinite punishment is based and found them wanting. How many Christians including pastors and theologians have critically examined these pillars in light of the evidence presented here? I would venture to say very few. Given this evidence, let us explore with a fresh and open mind, unshackled by a flawed system, and study the following chapters in sincerity and truth. Is there hope beyond *Gehenna* and the lake of fire? Might these judgments also have a positive purpose in God's unfailing plan for man? The answer lies in the very nature of God Himself. Would a truly all-powerful and all-loving Creator bring into existence billions of people knowing full well they would suffer for eternity as a result? Would He really pay such a price to get a few to love Him forever? This is what our tradition has taught. Is it true?

CHAPTER TWO

GOD'S NATURE

I will sing of Your power...
I will sing aloud of Your mercy.
(Ps. 59:16)

What is God really like? Is the ultimate destiny of the majority of the human race tragic? Our only hope as a race and as individuals lies in the nature of God, and more specifically, in His power and love. In this chapter, we will focus on the Scriptures relating to His nature—His power, love, fatherhood, and will. Does He have all power to do what He wills? Does He truly love all mankind impartially, or does He have favorites? Is He, as the Creator of all, also Father of all? What is the difference? What is His will for mankind? Will His will be accomplished?

Of all these questions, the most critical to our hope are those relating to His power and love. What is the extent of His power? Can He really do what His heart would like to do? If God is not in truth Almighty, then there is no God, and we are destitute of all hope. Yet, even if we believe Him to be Almighty, what hope does that bring us if we doubt His love for any of His creatures?

His Power

Ye do err, not knowing the Scriptures, nor the power of God.
(Mt. 22:29 KJV)

Notice the importance of knowing the Scriptures in relation to the power of God. It is a serious error to not respect this relationship. Without a firm belief in God as the "Almighty" (the one who can do all His will), the knowledge of Scripture is of little value. We must be convinced, like Paul was, that what He promises, He is able to accomplish (Ro. 4:21). This is what credited Abraham as righteous (Ro. 4:22). Have you taken to heart what Scripture declares regarding the power of God?

- *Is anything too hard for the Lord (Ge. 18:14)?*
- *Whatever His soul desires, He does (Job 23:13).*
- *You can do everything...no purpose of Yours can be withheld from You (Job 42:2).*
- *He does whatever He pleases (Ps. 115:3).*
- *Whatever the Lord pleases He does, in heaven, earth, sea, and in all deep places [heart] (Ps. 135:6).*
- *Surely, as I have thought, so it shall come to pass, and as I have purposed, so it shall stand (Is. 14:24).*
- *The Lord has purposed, who will annul it? His hand is stretched out, who will turn it back (Is. 14:27)?*

> *Ye do err, not knowing the Scriptures, nor the power of God.*
> *(Mt. 22:29KJV)*

- *Through Your power Your enemies shall submit to You.... All the earth shall worship You (Ps. 66:3-4).*
- *Is my hand shortened at all that it cannot redeem? Or have I no power to deliver (Is. 50:2)?*
- *My word shall not return to Me void, but it shall accomplish what I please (Is. 55:11).*
- *You made the heavens and earth by Your great power. There is nothing too hard for You (Jer. 32:17).*
- *Is there anything too hard for Me (Jer. 32:27)?*
- *He does according to His will in heaven and earth; no one can restrain His hand or say to Him, "what have You done?" Who can be saved?...with men it is impossible, but not with God; with God all things are possible (Da. 4:35; Mk. 10:26-27;). (See also: Mt. 19:26; Lu. 1:37; 18:27).*
- *Predestined according to the purpose of Him who works all things according to the counsel of His will (Ep. 1:11).*
- *He is able even to subdue all things to Himself (Ph. 3:20-21).*
- *God's purpose is unchangeable [immutable—NKJV] (He. 6:17 NAS).*
- *He is also able to save to the uttermost those who come to God through Him (He. 7:25).*
- *I will put my laws into their minds and hearts...for all shall know Me (He. 8:10).*
- *Jesus the Author and Finisher of our faith (He. 12:2).*

God Can Change Anyone

Does God merely do the "best He can for every man" as our tradition implies? Thomas Allin asserted:

> If the best an Almighty Being can do for countless myriads of His children is to force on them whether they will or not, an existence stained with sin from the womb, knowing that in fact this sin will ripen into endless misery—then such phrases are but dust thrown in our eyes. They are as argument beneath refutation. To force on me the gift of life, is to do for me not the best, but the worst possible.[1]

At the heart of my understanding of God's power is the conviction He can change anyone. This is His best! If He can change you and me, why not all? If God can take Paul, the chief of sinners (1Ti. 1:15), and make him the chief of Apostles and a world changer, is there anyone He cannot transform?

Please reflect on the following passage—Ez. 36:23-36.

> 23 *"And I will sanctify My great name, which has been profaned among the nations, which you have profaned in their midst; and* **the nations shall know that I am the LORD**,*" says the Lord GOD, "when I am hallowed in you before their eyes....*
>
> 26 **"*I will give you a new heart and put a new spirit within you*;** *I will take the heart of stone out of your flesh and give you a heart of flesh.*
>
> 27 *"I will put My Spirit within you and* **cause** *you to walk in My statutes, and* **you will keep** *My judgments and do them....*
>
> 29 *"I will deliver you from all your uncleanness....*
>
> 31 *"Then you will remember your evil ways and your deeds that were not good; and you will loathe yourselves in your own sight, for your iniquities and your abominations.*
>
> 32 *"***Not for your sake** *do I do this," says the Lord GOD, "let it be known to you. Be ashamed and confounded for your own ways, O house of Israel!"* For whose sake? The nations in verse 23 and 36.

35 *"So they will say, 'This land that was desolate has become like the garden of Eden; and the wasted, desolate, and ruined cities are now fortified and inhabited.'*

36 *"Then **the nations which are left all around you shall know that I, the LORD**, have rebuilt the ruined places and planted what was desolate. I, the LORD, have spoken it, and **I will do it**."*

In this passage (vs. 27) God causes unfaithful Israel to walk in His statutes. In verse 26, He will even give Israel a new heart and spirit. Wow, just think of it! Is there anyone on earth in due time God is unable to change? And as 1,000 years is as a single day to God (2Pe. 3:8), I have complete confidence He will accomplish all His purposes for every individual. Time is not a problem. He has the ages in which to operate. If He will do it for Israel, then He will do it for the nations as well, for He is not partial(see page 56). In fact, in verse 32, He even states it is not for their sakes He will do this. Then for whose? Who else but for the nations on His heart in verses 23 and 36! This shows God blesses Israel in order to be His channel of blessing to the whole world (Ge. 12:3). (See also Ge. 18:18; 22:18; 26:4; 28:14; Ac. 3:25-26; Ga. 3:8).

Is it really possible? Can God change people so they will do His will? Absolutely! But the question should not be, "Can God change people?" but rather, "Why does He?" Why? Love. Love that holds nothing back. Love itself became the propitiation for the sins of the whole world (1Jn. 2:2).

Love paid the ultimate price and redeemed the world. These promises to Israel should bring us much hope. God's plan has always been to reach the nations. It will yet be fulfilled, for the gifts and the calling of God are irrevocable (Ro. 11:29). Can God fail?

He Will Do It!

◆ *I will give them a heart to know Me...for **they shall** return to Me with their whole heart (Jer. 24:7).*

◆ *I will put My law in their minds, and write it on their hearts;...**they all shall** know Me, from the least of them to the greatest of them (Jer. 31:33-34).*

◆ *There is **nothing** too hard for You (Jer. 32:17).*

♦ *I will give them one heart and one way, that they may fear Me forever....I will put My fear in their hearts so that they will not depart from me* (Jer. 32:39-40).
♦ *He will again have compassion on us, and will subdue our iniquities* (Mic. 7:19).

It is most important to realize that God can and will change the hearts of men so they will repent and serve Him. What He does for a few, He does for all! Abraham did not waver at God's promise through unbelief, but was strengthened in faith. In this he gave

> *God can and will change the hearts of men so they will repent and serve Him.*

God glory. Abraham was fully convinced that God was able to do what He promised. Thus Abraham was accounted righteous (Ro. 4:20-22). Will we give Him glory and be accounted righteous too—or are we only partially convinced He is willing and able to do what He promised? Let us repent for not acknowledging God's power as it is set forth in Scripture (Mt. 22:29).

His Love

Does God love all mankind or only some? Many believers do not realize that there exists a whole theological stream in Christianity that actually believes God does not in fact love all men. They believe God has only destined the "elect" or "firstfruits" to be saved from hell. This belief system (also known as "Calvinism," or "Reformed") is becoming more and more embarrassing for pastors and theologians to outwardly profess. For example, my daughter had to directly ask her college chaplain (a Calvinist) to share frankly what he believed about predestination. You could not tell simply through his Sunday sermons. His sermons led her to think God's grace extended to all mankind, when in reality he did not believe it did. Thank God this is not the majority view of the Christian world. In order to understand God's love for all mankind, we must first understand that God, as Creator, is the Father of all humanity.

Fatherhood* of God

"Adam, the son of God" (Lu. 3:38). The genealogy of Jesus recorded in Luke goes back to Adam, the "son" of God. Can anyone deny Adam was God's son? When has God ever disowned Adam, Israel, or the nations? When has He ever ceased to be the Father of all creation?

If God is truly a "Father" as we understand fatherhood, then it further confirms He would only discipline His children for their good, as loving earthly parents do. To be made in God's image (Ge. 1:26) is an affirmation we are His children. In the strongest possible way, He, as "Creator," is also "Father." Allin wrote:

> We are told God is not the Father of all men; He is only their Creator! What a total misapprehension these words imply. What do we mean by paternity and the obligations it brings? The idea rests essentially on the communication of life to the child by the parent. Paternity is for us largely blind and instinctive; but creation is Love acting freely, divinely; knowing all the consequences, assuming all the responsibility involved in the very act of creating a reasonable immortal spirit. It seems, then, very strange to seek to escape the consequences of the lesser obligation, by admitting one still greater; to seek, in a word, to evade the results of a divine universal fatherhood, by pleading that God is only the Creator.[2]

In Adam, we all are children of God. If our sin and rebellion has caused our Father to disown us, how could He have said, "Return, you backsliding children, and I will heal your backslidings" (Jer. 3:22)? Or what was Jesus saying in His parable of the prodigal son in Lu. 15:11-32? Does the prodigal son not represent all the Father's wayward children? Though he had fallen into sin in all its degradation, he never ceased being a son. And if Paul could say to fail to provide for one's own is to be worse than an unbeliever (1Ti. 5:8), what does that say of God? "Behold, all souls are mine" (Ez. 18:4). All God has created is His own. It is inconceivable that God would be worse than an unbeliever. Allin stated:

> The essence of Christianity perishes in the virtual denial of any true Fatherhood of our race on God's part. Follow out

this thought, for it is of primary importance. We lose sight of the value of the individual soul, when dealing with the countless millions who have peopled this earth and passed away. What is one among so many? [But] each soul IS of infinite value, as if it stood alone in the eyes of God its Father. And more than this, we are altogether apt to forget whose the loss is, if any one soul perishes. It is God's loss: it is the Father Who loses His child. The straying sheep of the parable is the Great Shepherd's loss: the missing coin is the Owner's loss. In this very fact lies the pledge that He will seek on and on till He find it.[3]

"Our" Father, is also "a" father to all men. God has never stopped being the Father of His creation. His love and purpose toward all endures forever. However, men have left their Father's house to serve another. This severance came from the human side, not the divine. So, in one sense, and in one sense only, men have disowned their Father to become the children of another, by doing the deeds of the prince of this world (Jn. 8:41). But it is because of this, Jesus came. He came to restore this broken relationship (Ro. 5:10), and to destroy the works of the devil (1Jn. 3:8). The Father has never disowned His children. The cross is proof of that. Note carefully these texts:

+ *God created man in His **own image**....* (Ge. 1:27; 9:6).
+ *I said...**all of you are children** of the Most High* (Ps. 82:6).
+ *You are **our Father**...our potter; and **all we are the work of Your hand*** (Is. 64:8).
+ *Have we not **all one Father**? Has not one **God created us*** (Mal. 2:10)?
+ *Seeing the **multitudes**.... in this manner pray: **our Father**...* (Mt. 5:1; 6:9).

> *God has never stopped being the Father of His creation. His love and purpose toward all endures forever.*

+ *Jesus spoke to the **multitudes** and to His disciples....one is **your Father*** (Mt. 23:1, 9).
+ *Men of **Athens**....For we also are **His children**. Being then the **children of God**...* (Ac. 17:22, 28-29 NAS).
+ *I bow to the **Father**...from whom the **whole family in...earth** is named* (Ep. 3:14-15).

- *Be in subjection to the **Father of spirits** and live* (He. 12:9)?

The expressions of Fatherhood used in these passages encompass unbelievers: "All of you," "all we," "we all," "multitudes," "people," "men of Athens," "whole family in earth," and "of spirits."

"*My son*, give me your heart...observe my ways" (Pr. 23:26). It seems to me, if this passage also refers to the Lord and not only to Solomon, then God regards us as sons and daughters even before we give Him our hearts.

"If *you being evil*...give good gifts to your children, how much more *your Father*..." (Mt. 7:11). Note this passage is in the context of the "multitudes" which includes unbelievers (Mt. 5:1; 8:1). To these whom He termed "evil," He calls God "your Father." Will God do less for His children than we who are "evil"? Do we disown our kids as a result of rebellion? Do we not patiently and persistently do all we can to help them mature and amend their ways? Are we better parents than God?

The fatherhood of God over all creation is incontestable evidence that His love extends to all humankind. In spite of what some mistaken theologians and reformers have claimed, to acknowledge God is a "faithful" Creator who always does what is "right" (1Pe. 4:19 NAS), and then deny His impartial love for all men by claiming He considers some merely as "creatures" as opposed to "children" is preposterous. It contradicts all that Christianity and the Bible stand for.

* See my website "Book Updates" p. 52 regarding our adoption.

God Loves All People

The love of God is evident in the Scriptural references of God as "Father of all," and in countless other passages as well. In fact, the evidence of God's love for all is so abundant in Scripture, it is beyond my comprehension that a whole system of Christian theology could have been built around its denial. Consider just these few:

- *He is **good to all**. His tender **mercies are over all*** (Ps. 145:9).
- *Look to Me, and be saved, **all** you ends of the earth* (Is. 45:22)!
- *God so loved the **world*** (Jn. 3:16).
- *I came...to save the **world*** (Jn. 12:47).

- *God gives to **all life**....He has made from one blood every nation of men* (Ac. 17:25-27).
- *I was sought by those who did not ask for Me; I was found by those who did not seek Me. I said, "Here I am, here I am," to a nation that was not called by My name* (Is. 65:1).

His will is for all people to find Him, even those who are not presently seeking Him. A time will come when they will, for God can orchestrate whatever circumstances are needed to change their hearts; for love never fails (1Co. 13:8).

- *His goodness and longsuffering...leads to repentance* (Ro. 2:4).
- *God demonstrates His own love toward us, in that while we were still sinners Christ died for us* (Ro. 5:8). "Us" here includes all people. (See Jn 1:29; 6:51).
- *God was in Christ reconciling the world to Himself* (2Co. 5:19).
- *God our Savior...**will have all** men to be saved* (1Ti. 2:4 KJV).
- *The grace of God has appeared, bringing salvation to all men* (Tit. 2:11 NAS).

God our Savior...will have all men to be saved.
(1Ti. 2:4 KJV)

- *And this is love, not that we loved God, but that He loved us and sent His Son to be the propitiation for our sins* (1Jn. 4:10).
- *He...is the propitiation for our sins, and **not for ours only** but also for the **whole world*** (1Jn. 2:2).
- *The Lord is...longsuffering...not willing that **any** perish* (2Pe. 3:9).
- *The **longsuffering** of our Lord **is salvation*** (2Pe. 3:15).

The longsuffering of our Lord "is" salvation. What a thought! When does the longsuffering of our heavenly Father for His children ever end? Does it end sooner than yours toward your children? The love of God expressed in His longsuffering will do what His brute power could never do—win the hearts of His enemies (Ps. 66: 3-4) and make them His friends (Jer. 31:34; Jn. 15:15; Ro. 5:10).

His Love Is Not Partial

Some people receive many chances to get saved, others receive a few, but billions have never received one! If the opportunity to receive Christ were given in this life only, then God could be accused of being partial. The only way He would not be partial is if He lacked the power to give all the opportunity. But God is neither weak nor partial. All have the same access to salvation, for God's will, power, and love guarantee it. And furthermore, Jesus paid the price for all. If all did not have equal access, it would especially be unfair to Him. Scriptural support abounds for God's impartiality. God loves all men equally. For example:

+ *He is good to all* (Ps. 145:9).
+ *In truth...God shows no partiality* (Ac. 10:34).
+ *There is no partiality with God* (Ro. 2:11).
+ *There is no distinction between Jew and Greek* (Ro. 10:12).
+ *God shows personal favoritism to no man* (Ga. 2:6).
+ *There is no partiality with Him* (Ep. 6:9).
+ *There is no partiality* (Col. 3:25).
+ *God...wills [KJV] all men to be saved* (1Ti. 2:3-4).
+ *Wisdom...from above...is without partiality and without hypocrisy* (Ja. 3:17).
+ *The Father...without partiality judges...* (1Pe. 1:17).

But, you may ask, "Why was Esau hated and Jacob loved (Mal. 9:13), isn't this showing favoritism?" This was a play on words similar to Christ's command to hate our family (Lu. 14:26). Jesus wants us to love our families, but in our heart of hearts our deepest love should be for God. This is hyperbole—something very common in ancient eastern writings. God's hate regarding Esau relates to something about Esau God disliked in a greater way than what God disliked about Jacob the "deceiver." When God elects someone over another, it does not mean He loves him or her more. Rather, He is delegating to them a greater responsibility in His service.

The same goes for God's chosen people: the Jews. He did not choose them because He was partial to the rest of humanity. On the contrary, He wanted a nation through which He could bless all peoples of the earth! "In you all the families of the earth shall be blessed" Ge. 12:3. (See also Ge. 18:18; 22:18; 26:4; 28:14; Ac.3:25, 26; Ga. 3:8).

God Is Love "But"

When we say, "God is love, but He is also just and must punish sinners forever," we demean God's greatest expression of love in His Son's sacrificial death for all mankind. Talk about justice!? How unjust this is to Him who propitiated the sins of the whole world, who gave His life as a ransom for all! (1Jn. 2:2; 1Ti. 2:6). To recognize hell's remedial purpose in no way contradicts His holiness, justice, or sacrifice. To the contrary, it magnifies them. How dare we qualify or limit a Love "that never fails" (1Co. 13:8a).

Scripture straightly declares God to "be" love (1Jn. 4:8, 16), but never to be vengeance itself. God is one, and He is not divided within Himself. Augustinian theologians have pitted His love against His attributes of holiness and justice not realizing His very essence is Love. He "is" Love. When referring to God as love, they immediately qualify it with "but," as though His love were not compatible with holiness and justice. Thus they deny His love to maintain their idea of judgment. They claim His ways are not ours (Is. 55:7-9) to justify themselves. They miss what Isaiah really wished to reveal in chapter 55—God's unlimited mercy. Allin wrote:

> God is not anger though He can be angry, God is not vengeance though He does avenge. These are attributes, love is essence. Therefore, God is unchangeably love. In judgment He is love, in wrath He is love, in vengeance He is love—"love first, and last, and without end." Love is simply the strongest thing in the universe, the most awful, the most inexorable, while the most tender.[4]

God's righteous judgments, like His acts of mercy, are a manifestation of His love—a love with no "buts." Both His mercy and His judgments serve His one holy and loving purpose to draw (drag) all men to Himself. Scripture abounds with passages of God's great love and mercy. Here are just a few to ponder:

- *The Lord is merciful and gracious, slow to anger, and abounding in mercy...* (Ps. 103:8).
- *He is good! For His mercy endures forever* (Ps. 136:1). (Repeated 26 times).
- *The Lord is gracious and full of compassion, slow to anger and great in mercy* (Ps. 145:8).

- *The Lord upholds all who fall, and raises up all who are bowed down* (Ps. 145:14).
- *You open your hand and satisfy the desire of every living thing* (Ps. 145:16).
- *Through the Lord's mercies we are not consumed, because His compassions fail not. They are new every morning; great is Your faithfulness* (La. 3:22-23).
- *I know that You are a gracious and merciful God, slow to anger and abundant in lovingkindness, One who relents from doing harm* (Jon. 4:2).
- *He delights in mercy....will again have compassion on us, and will subdue our iniquities* (Mic. 7:18-19).
- *He is kind to the unthankful and evil. Be merciful, as your Father* (Lu. 6:35-36).
- *Love suffers long and is kind...endures all....never fails* (1Co. 13:4-8).
- *Blessed be the Father of mercies and God of all comfort* (2Co. 1:3-4).
- *The Lord is very compassionate and merciful* (Ja. 5:11).
- *God...only does wondrous things* (Ps. 72:18)!

God truly loves all mankind unconditionally, and if we should doubt this, even for a moment, we need only look at His Son, the radiance of His glory and the exact representation of His nature (He. 1:3). Erasmus Manford, 19th century minister, publisher, and author wrote,

> Jesus appeared on earth in the character of a Savior, not of a destroyer....When persecuted, He retaliated not; when reviled, He reviled not; when reproached and scoffed at, He did not curse His foes. His whole life was one continued exhibition of love, benevolence, and compassion. It is emphatically and truly said of Him, "He went about doing good."...He gave health to the sick, feet to the lame, ears to the deaf, speech to the dumb, sanity to the lunatic, bread to the hungry, forgiveness to the sinful, salvation to the lost, and life to the dead....He wept at the grave of Lazarus, His friend, and also over the approaching woes of Jerusalem, where resided His bitterest foes; and even for His bloody and cruel murderers He prayed on the cross, and in the agonies of death at their unfeeling hands, besought His Fa-

ther for their forgiveness....The character, then, of Christ is the character of God; the tenderness and compassion that Jesus possessed for all men, the good, the evil, is that which God possesses for all mankind.[5]

To sum up the theme of God's love, I encourage you to read Lu. 15:11-32. Please note carefully verse 20: "When he was still a great way off, his father saw him and had compassion, and ran and fell on his neck and kissed him." Jesus gave us this story so we would get a glimpse of the Father heart of God for all His wayward children. What a Father! The Psalmist also writes, "His anger is but for a moment, His favor is for life" (Ps. 30:5a). Why is it on earth God's anger lasts but a moment and His favor is for life, but after death His favor is not even a moment and His anger is forever? How is it possible God's love can change so drastically in a heart beat?

His Will [Purpose]

(This is an expansion of what was said near the close of the previous chapter). Most people believe God wills the best for every person on earth, but unfortunately, like us, He cannot get what He wants. We have brought God down to our level. Because we cannot always get our will, it must be the same with Him. We make His will out to be something merely hoped for or desired. In this section, we will consider what Scripture declares is His will for all mankind, and also, what it says relative to His power to accomplish it.

> He **purposed**...that in...**fullness of the times** He might gather together in one all things in Christ....who works all things according to the counsel of His **will** (Ep. 1:9-11).

This is a very deep and revealing passage. It shows God purposing His will to be done, and not merely hoping it so. Job confirmed this when he wrote that no purpose of His will be thwarted (Job 42:2 RSV). What is His purpose? To gather together in one all people in Christ. Paul also expressed it this way: "that God may be all in all" (1Co. 15:28).

In order for God to be "all in all," all must first be subjected to the Lordship of Jesus Christ (1Co. 15:28a). This cannot happen without Christ being formed in each person (Ga. 4:19; 1Jn. 3:2; 2Pe. 1:4).

Thankfully, He has not left us on our own. He is committed to its realization and intimately involved in the process (Ep. 2:10; Ph. 1:6; 2:13). He has assured us His purpose for all will be fulfilled, for He cannot fail (Job 42:2). It will all take place in the context of the ages— the "fullness of the times" (Ac. 3:21; 1Ti. 2:6).

Christ's Purpose
(Reflection of His Father's will)

The Son of Man has come to seek and to save that which
was lost. For this purpose the Son of God was manifested, that
He might destroy the works of the devil.
(Lu. 19:10; Mt. 18:11; 1Jn. 3:8)

Christ came to save "that which was lost." "That" includes all the lost. God sent Him so the world would be saved (Jn. 3:17). The world is not a few only. The few whom our Lord refers to in Mt. 7:14 are His elect firstfruits who labor with Him now and in the coming ages to bring in the whole harvest. (More on this in Chapter 5). The Father sent His Son as the Savior of the whole world, and not merely some out of it (1Jn. 4:14). He whose very name

> *The Son of Man has come to seek and save that which was lost.*
> *(Lu. 19:10)*

means Savior, came to save, not merely to "offer" salvation. He is the Good Shepherd who seeks those who are lost until He finds them (Lu. 15:4, 20).

Our Lord's sacrifice on the cross was His supreme act in destroying the devil's work, but not His only act. In addition, He works in men's hearts and intercedes for them throughout all ages to draw them to Himself and conform them into His likeness. Jesus' purpose on earth included modeling before a sinful world a holy and righteous life. At the very outset of His ministry, in His very first public address, He laid down exactly what a model Christian life must be. In so doing, Christ revealed His heart of compassion for suffering humanity.

Observe what He said quoting from Is. 61:1-2a:

> The Spirit of the LORD is upon Me, because He has
> anointed Me to preach the gospel to the poor; He has sent
> Me to heal the brokenhearted, to proclaim liberty to the

captives and recovery of sight to the blind, to set at liberty
those who are oppressed; to proclaim the acceptable year
of the LORD... (Lu. 4:18-22; Is. 61:1-2a).

Reading from the original passage in Is. 61 from where Jesus
was quoting, we read further and glimpse an even deeper part of His
heart:

> *"...to comfort all who mourn, to console those who mourn
> in Zion, to give them beauty for ashes, the oil of joy for
> mourning, the garment of praise for the spirit of heaviness;
> that they may be called trees of righteousness, the planting
> of the LORD, that He may be glorified"* (Is. 61:2b-3).

This is a glimpse into the heart of our God and Savior. We see
His deep concern for the anguish all people experience. He desires to
deliver us from sorrow, heaviness of spirit, blindness, captivity, and
oppression. But one thing seems to be lacking. Do you see it? He
seems more concerned about our momentary sufferings in this life,
than with eternal sufferings just a heart beat away! Consider another
text further revealing His heart.

> *When He saw the multitudes, He was moved with com-
> passion for them, because they were weary and scattered,
> ["distressed and dispirited"—NAS] like sheep having no
> shepherd. Then He said to His disciples...."pray the Lord...
> to send out laborers into His harvest"* (Mt. 9:36-38).

Why are we asked to pray for laborers for the harvest? Why are
they needed? Doesn't the text say it is because people are weary,
scattered, distressed, and dispirited? But what has our tradition led
us to believe? Answer: To pray because all people are on their way to
hell! Isn't there an inconsistency here?

What are earthly pains compared to eternal woe? Yet, the temporal pains weighed heavy on our Lord's heart, not those of the life
beyond. How can we explain His focus on the temporal pains and
seeming lack of concern for eternal damnation? Along with the
Gehenna study in Chapter 1, Lu. 4:18-19 and Mt. 9:36-38 further
suggest our Lord did not believe in everlasting punishment, and thus
He did not mention it.

We must take into account another key piece of evidence. Note where Christ ended His quotation in Lu. 4:19: "proclaim the acceptable year of the LORD." Now look at Is.61:1-2. What had the Lord not repeated? He left out, "and the day of vengeance of our God" (Is. 61:2b). Why might He have left this out? Could it be the day of vengeance is just that, "a day"? For, if it were days without end of vengeance, how can we explain His silence? Should He not have at least finished the sentence? Yes, and much more! He should have warned them in the strongest possible way to snatch them all out of the everlasting fire! If there was ever an appropriate time to lay the foundation of eternal torment, this was it. He was sitting on a proof text. Did He not care some in His audience might die that night and go straight to hell? What kind of precedent would this set for His followers who would thereafter follow His example?

One final point regarding His first public address. Did you notice the response of the people? "All marveled at the gracious words that proceeded out of His mouth" (Lu. 4:22). Gracious words—the people marveled!

◆ ◆ ◆ ◆ ◆

What is God really like? Is the destiny of the human race tragic? I hope in this chapter you have come to see God's nature more clearly—that all is not lost for mankind.

Does God really love every single human being impartially? YES

Can He really do what His heart would like to do? YES.

The God of all the earth is truly GOD, not god. He has all the power of the universe at His disposal, and His very essence is love—pure, unadulterated, impartial love for all His creation. Knowing Him in Spirit and in truth—who He really is—will fill our hearts with peace and hope in spite of any fearful thing He has created. We can face whatever might lie before us, when we know Him in all His power and love. Our only hope as a race and as individuals lies in His very nature. Can we trust Him with our eternal destiny? Can we trust Him with the eternal destiny of each of our loved ones? We can! Let us sing aloud of His power and of His mercy (Ps. 59:16)!

CHAPTER THREE

PURP⊙SE-DRİVEN
jUDGMENT

We went through fire...
but You brought us out to rich fulfillment.
(Ps. 66:12)

*I*s there any positive purpose to God's *Gehenna* judgment? What purpose does it serve? According to the prevalent theology, its only purpose is to inflict pain. It refuses to acknowledge it has any remedial effect, and presents it merely as a perpetual prison from which its victims can never escape. I intend to show in this chapter the following facts: First, this view is simply unjust, and Scripture does not support unjust punishment of any kind. Second, Scripture affirms death is no obstacle to God in accomplishing His purposes in any life. Third, God is just and His justice satisfies even our God given human understanding of justice. Fourth, the Bible provides clear examples that all His judgments are driven by a positive purpose.

Justice vs. Infinite Penalty

Tradition has taught us that finite sins merit infinite penalty because they are committed against an infinite God. This may seem right to some minds, but how would it seem to a God who "is" love? How can justice require infinite penalty from creatures born in sin through no fault of their own, prone to sin by an inherited weakness (Adam's curse), created with imperfect knowledge, surrounded by demons tempting on every side, and all in light of Christ's propitiation for the sins of the whole world (1Jn. 2:2; Jn. 1:29)?

- What Scripture teaches such a travesty of all justice?
- Whose conscience is not violated at the thought?

- Would not a single sentence of infinite penalty outweigh the guilt of the whole race?
- What purpose would it serve once its retributive requirements are met?

Infinite penalty cannot satisfy justice by definition. For at the point at which it satisfies justice, the penalty must end. Because what is infinite cannot end and Scripture affirms just penalty (Col. 3:25; He. 2:2), "just infinite penalty" is self-contradictory. If justice requires infinite penalty, then the following passages are senseless:

- *Speak comfort to Jerusalem...for she has received from the LORD double for all her sins* (Is. 40:2) (See also Jer. 16:18). How can what is infinite be doubled? Whatever led God to double this penalty, one thing is clear: the penalty is measurable and limited.
- *His anger is but for a moment, His favor is for life; weeping may endure for a night, but joy comes in the morning* (Ps. 30:5). What possible comfort could "a moment" and "a night" offer anyone tormented by the threat of infinite penalty? It would be a mere mockery. This further suggests that just penalty is for a limited time.

> *Infinite penalty cannot satisfy justice by definition. For at the point at which it satisfies justice, the penalty must end.*

- *You render to each according to his work* (Ps. 62:12; Ro. 2:5, 6). Penalty "according to his work" is something measurable and unquestionably just. How does infinite penalty accommodate varying levels of guilt? "It shall be more tolerable for Sodom than for you" (Mt. 11:24; Lu. 10:14). Such wording implies the penalty referred to is measurable.
- *You laid affliction on our backs....We went through fire...but You brought us to rich fulfillment* (Ps. 66:10-12). This penalty was given to bring the sufferer to rich fulfillment; that is, it had a positive purpose. What positive purpose is served by infinite punishment? In addition, would God, the epitome of all justice and impartiality, inflict purposeful penalty for some and only purposeless for others?

> ◆ *The Lord will not cast off forever. Though He causes grief,* ***yet*** *He will show compassion according to the multitude of His mercies. For He does not afflict willingly, nor grieve the children of men* (La. 3:31-33). Though He causes grief, "yet" there is purpose. What happens to "yet," when you contemplate infinite penalty? It becomes a meaningless word. "Yet" assures us the penalty is not infinite.

> *Though He causes grief, yet He will show compassion....*
> *(La. 3:32)*

Hope Beyond Death

Is one's state after death absolutely final as we have been led to think? Tradition maintains that God's judgment has no remedial purpose—it is eternal, and as a result, we can have no hope beyond death or hell. What mysteriously happens at death making it impossible for God to bring someone to repentance? Has He been stripped of His power? Where does Scripture declare His impotence in the face of death? Many quote Hebrews 9:27 thinking it bars all hope. "It is appointed for men to die once, but after this the judgment" (He. 9:27). How does this passage address the issue? The point in question is not the fact of judgment, but whether or not it is infinite. This reference does not offer us any information.

Does judgment have a remedial or restorative element to it, or is it solely retributive? What is the evidence? A number of passages have led me to conclude it cannot be solely retributive. We will see these later under "Examples of Purpose-Driven Judgment." However, I would first like to demonstrate scriptural support for the conviction that death in and of itself is not a hopeless condition for anyone.

> *What mysteriously happens at death making it impossible for God to bring someone to repentance? Has He been stripped of His power? Where does Scripture declare His impotence in the face of death?*

Twenty-Five Texts Testify

Classic Texts—Ignored, Denied, or Explained Away...Why?

- *I kill and make alive; I wound and heal* (De. 32:39).
- *The Lord kills and makes alive; He brings down to the grave [Sheol] and brings up* (1Sa. 2:6). He brings down to *Sheol* (translated "hell" in some Bibles) and brings up. How can one be brought up from what is supposed to be an irremediable state?
- *We must die. But God does not take away life; instead, He devises ways so that a banished person may not remain estranged from Him* (2 Sa 14:14 NIV). Nothing stops God!
- *Thou wilt not leave my soul in hell [Sheol]* (Ps. 16:10 KJV). (See also: Ps. 30:2-3; 49:15; 86:13; 116:3-8). One is not left in hell forever. This is not an isolated text.
- *All who go down to the dust shall bow before Him...* (Ps. 22:29b). "All" who die will bow. Can what is annihilated bow? Bowing stems from a genuine and not a "forced" worship as discussed in Chapter 6.
- *He will swallow up death forever and will wipe away tears from all faces* (Is. 25:8). Death is swallowed up with tears wiped from all faces. Note the word "all."
- *For men are not cast off by the Lord forever. Though he brings grief, he will show compassion, so great is his unfailing love* (Lam 3:31-32 NIV). "For men" refers to all people. Death is no barrier to a God whose love cannot fail.
- *When I bring back their captives, the captives of Sodom and her daughters, and the captives of Samaria and her daughters, then I will also bring back the captives of your captivity among them* (Ez. 16:53; read entire chapter). God restores the destroyed of Sodom and Samaria. (See also Jer. 49:6, 37-39; 2Pe. 2:6).
- *I will ransom them from the power of the grave [Sheol]; I will redeem them from death. O Death, I will be your plagues! O Grave [Sheol], I will be your destruction* (Hos. 13:13-14)! God ransoms from the power of hell, redeems from death, and is death's destruction! Only if we do not believe God is all-powerful, impartial, and all-loving can we remain hopeless.

- *God is able to raise up children to Abraham from these stones* (Mt. 3:9). If God can do this, can He not raise the lost from death? Is this too hard for Him (Jer. 32:27)?
- *You will by no means get out of there **till** you have paid the last penny* (Mt. 5:26).
- *His master delivered him to the torturers **until** he should pay all. So My Father also will do to you* (Mt. 18:35). Does "till" and "until" support the concept of an unending hell?
- *Every sin and blasphemy will be forgiven, but blasphemy against the Spirit will not....either in this age or in the age to come* (Mt. 12:31-32; Mk. 3:29-30). "Every sin and blasphemy will be forgiven...in the age to come!" What else could this imply except that there is hope after death? If no sin can be forgiven in the next age, it would be pointless to single out one particular sin as an exception. Because a particular sin will not be forgiven does not require the penalty be infinite. It means a just penalty will be exacted, whatever that may be (He. 2:2). Either the just penalty of blasphemy will be exacted, or its forgiveness must await a subsequent age beyond the next one. (Scripture alludes to more than one future age—Ep. 2:7). We can rest assured that the Father's legal penalty for this sin will be just, righteous, and in character with His loving heart for all men.
- *He is not the God of the dead but of the living, for all live to Him* (Lu. 20:38). If all the dead live to Him, then we can have hope beyond death unless there is no hope in God Himself!
- *If their [Israel] being cast away is the reconciling of the world, what will their acceptance be but life from the dead* (Ro. 11:15)? Life from the dead for the world? That is what it says! Would this "life" be given merely as a prelude to further death?
- *Christ died, rose, and lived again, that He might be Lord of both the dead and the living* (Ro. 14:9). These "dead" are apparently those who once lived on earth. At some point they exist again under Christ's Lordship. It would be senseless to say He is Lord of the annihilated ones. For Christ to be "Lord" implies hope, not hopelessness, especially in light of Ph. 2:10-11. Once their subjection is made complete, God becomes all in them (1Co. 15:28).

- *The last enemy that will be destroyed is death* (1Co. 15:26). If death is destroyed, what is left? Life.
- *Jesus tasted death for everyone* (He. 2:9). If Christ tasted death for everyone, then hope beyond death must be for all! If it does not at least mean this, what is the point?
- *Death is swallowed in victory. O Death, where is your sting? O Hades, where is your victory* (1Co. 15:54-55)? What words could be brighter, or more hopeful than these? Who would dare place limits on such a promise? Do we forget what has made this possible? Nothing but the blood of Jesus shed for all!
- *What will they do who are baptized for the dead, if the dead do not rise at all? Why then are they baptized for the dead* (1Co. 15:29)? Why were some New Testament believers baptized for the dead if they believed the lost dead were in a hopeless state?
- *Christ abolished death* (2Ti. 1:10). Who did Christ not abolish death for according to Is. 53:6; Jn. 1:29; 6:51; Ro. 5:6, 8; 1Ti. 2:6; He. 2:9; 1Pe. 3:18; 1Jn. 2:2? In light of this, how can death possibly be hopeless for anyone?
- *He destroys him who had the power of death* (He. 2:14). If the one who had the power of death is destroyed, then there must be hope.
- *Jesus Christ the same yesterday, today, and forever* (He. 13:8). He does not change or fail! Once a Savior, always a Savior. "Jesus" means "Savior." As long as a Savior is needed, He remains such.
- *Fear not, I... have the keys of Hell and of Death* (Re. 1:17-18 KJV). Christ holding Hell's keys is our assurance that He will release its captives at the proper time. If not, the words "fear not," would be a mockery.
- *There shall be no more death* (Re. 21:4). How can death be a hopeless condition if it will cease to exist?
- *Christ...went and preached to the spirits in prison, who formerly were disobedient, when once the Divine longsuffering waited in the days of Noah....the gospel was preached also to those who are dead, that they might be judged according to men in the flesh, but live according to God in the spirit....He ascended on high...led captivity captive....descended into the lower parts of the earth...that He might fill all things* (1Pe. 3:18-20; 4:6-7; Ep. 4:8-10).

William Barclay wrote:

> If Christ descended into Hades and preached there,
> there is no corner of the universe into which the mes-
> sage of grace has not come. There is in this passage the
> solution of one of the most haunting questions raised
> by the Christian faith—what is to happen to those who
> lived before Jesus Christ and to those to whom the gos-
> pel never came? There can be no salvation without re-
> pentance but how can repentance come to those who
> have never been confronted with the love and holiness
> of God? If there is no other name by which men may be
> saved, what is to happen to those who never heard it?
> This is the point that Justin Martyr fastened on long
> ago: "The Lord, the Holy God of Israel, remembered his
> dead, those sleeping in the earth, and came down to
> them to tell them the good news of salvation." The doc-
> trine of the descent into Hades conserves the precious
> truth that no man who ever lived is left without a sight
> of Christ and without the offer of the salvation of God.
> Many in repeating the creed have found the phrase, "He
> descended into hell" either meaningless or bewildering,
> and have tacitly agreed to set it on one side and forget
> it. It may well be that we ought to think of this as a pic-
> ture painted in terms of poetry rather than a doctrine
> stated in terms of theology.[1]

Thoughts to Ponder

Most Christians do not believe infants or the mentally handicapped go to hopeless death. If hope is extended to these, then God
(if He is truly impartial and just) will extend hope to all. If not, then
these privileged few are given an unfair advantage. Who in their right
mind would want to live beyond the age of accountability if an
eternal hell is their destiny? Or who would want to be born with a
sound mind, if a mental handicap would keep them out of hell?

Martin Luther had hope for all. In his letter to Hanseu Von Rechenberg in 1522, he wrote: "God forbid that I should limit the time
of acquiring faith to the present life. In the depth of the Divine mercy
there may be opportunity to win it in the future."[2]

It is amazing to me that a passage such as He. 9:27 has been
used to deny the substance of these numerous passages! How could

we have allowed ourselves to believe death is an insurmountable barrier to an Almighty God? We simply assumed our tradition handed down from the time of Augustine was correct. I urge you to prayerfully re-evaluate the Scriptural evidence in support of hope beyond death and hell. (Ge. 18:14; Job 23:13; 42:2; Ps. 115:3; 66:3-4; 135:6; Is. 14:24, 27; 50:2; 55:11; Jer. 32:17, 27; Ez. 36:23-36; Dan. 4:35; Mt. 19:26; Mk. 10:26-27; Lu. 1:37; 18:27; Ep. 1:11; Ph. 3:20-21; He. 6:17; 8:10).

A Just Judge

What kind of a judge is God? Can we count on Him to do what is right and fair for everyone? Absolutely! "Shall not the Judge of all the earth do right" (Ge. 18:25)? Scripture abounds with references to His just and righteous judgments. Please reflect on these:

- *Beaten...according to guilt....forty blows...no more* (De. 25:2-4).

> *God renders to each according to his deeds.*
> (Ro. 2:5-6)

- *All His ways are justice, a God...without injustice* (De. 32:4).
- *As he has done, so shall it be to him—fracture for fracture, eye for eye, tooth for tooth* (Le. 24:19).
- *The judgments of the Lord are true and righteous altogether* (Ps. 19:9).
- *Your judgments are a great deep; O Lord, You preserve man and beast* (Ps. 36:6).
- *To You belongs mercy; You render to each one according to his work* (Ps. 62:12).
- *He shall judge the world with righteousness* (Ps. 96:13; Ac. 17:31).
- *I know that Your judgments are right, and that in faithfulness You have afflicted me* (Ps. 119:75).
- *Though He causes grief, yet He will show compassion according to the multitude of His mercies. For He does not afflict willingly, nor grieve the children of men* (La. 3:31-33).
- *He does not retain His anger forever, because He delights in mercy* (Mic. 7:18).
- *Every transgression and disobedience received a just reward...* (He. 2:2).

- *Woe to you...you will receive greater condemnation* (Mt. 23:14). Greater than what?
- *It shall be more tolerable for Sodom in the day of judgment than for you* (Mt. 11:20-24; Lu. 10:14). What kind of everlasting punishment would be "more tolerable" than another?
- *God renders to each according to his deeds* (Ro. 2:5-6).
- *He who does wrong will be repaid for what he has done, and there is no partiality* (Col. 3:25).

A generic infinite punishment for everyone contradicts all that Scripture declares about God's just and righteous judgments. Statements like, "to each one according to his deeds" and "fracture for fracture—eye for eye," fly in the face of infinite punishment. Each punishment fits its crime. God's idea of justice is not different than ours. Yes, His ways are not our ways, but only because He has more mercy than we have, not less! (See Is. 55:7-8). These numerous passages demonstrate what is right for the Judge of all the earth to do in judgment.

God's Wrath

What is God's "wrath" [Greek—*orgee*]? The KJV translators translate this one Greek word by four English words: "wrath," "anger," "indignation," and "vengeance." Which is it? They don't all mean the same thing. The literal translations, most often translate it as "anger." Rotherham, Weymouth, and Young's Literal translations all translate *orgee* as "anger" in the following passages.

- *Jesus...delivers us from the wrath [orgee—anger] to come* (1Th. 1:10).
- *Because of these things the wrath [orgee—anger] of God is coming upon the sons of disobedience* (Ep. 5:6; Col. 3:6).
- *Wrath [orgee—anger] has come upon them [Jews] to the uttermost* (1Th. 2:16-25). Note: "God's anger in its severest form has overtaken them" (Weymouth). Anger in its "severest form," yet all Israel will be saved (Ro. 11:25-26).
- *Beloved, do not avenge yourselves, but rather give place to wrath [orgee]; for it is written, "vengeance is Mine, I will* **repay***," says the Lord* (Ro. 12:19). Notice Scripture interprets itself in this passage.

Orgee is interchanged with the idea of "vengeance," "I will repay." To "repay" signifies to recompense what is due, no more—no less. It is in total harmony with the many texts stating God will righteously judge each one according to their works. "He who does wrong will be repaid *for what he has done*, and there is *no partiality*" (Col. 3:25). "God renders to each *according to his deeds*" (Ro. 2:5-6). (See also: De. 32:2-3; Le. 24:19; Ps. 62:12; He. 2:2).

> God's wrath is His passionate displeasure and just recompense of sinful conduct, which He deals with fairly according to deeds.

Being the most common word used by the literal translations, how does the dictionary define the simple word "anger"? "Extreme or passionate displeasure."[3] In brief, God's wrath is His passionate displeasure and just recompense of sinful conduct, which He deals with fairly according to deeds. This is all that can be said about God's wrath. How tragic that images of innumerable multitudes being cast into an eternal furnace of fire have been falsely associated with this word.

Examples of Purpose-Driven Judgment

Scripture makes it clear God exhibits no variation or shadow of turning. He does not change (Ja. 1:17; Mal. 3:6). If God's past and present judgments are just, righteous, and purposeful, we can rest assured they will continue to be so in the future. Reflect on the following passages which demonstrate His positive purposes in judgment.

- *You laid affliction on our backs....You brought us out to rich fulfillment* (Ps. 66:10-12).
- *When Your judgments are in the earth, the inhabitants of the world will learn righteousness* (Is. 26:9).
- *And if by these things you are not reformed by Me, but walk contrary to Me, then I also will walk contrary to you, and I will punish you yet seven times for your sins* (Le. 26:23-24). "These things" refer to a whole list of judgments, starting at verse 14. God states the purpose for these judgments is reformation. And He goes on to say if they continue to resist reformation by "walking contrary to Me," He will yet punish seven times for their sins. (If punishment can be quantified

(seven times), then by definition it is not infinite). Here is a God whose love for His wayward children knows no end.

♦ *Behold, happy is the man whom God corrects; Therefore do not despise the chastening of the Almighty. For He bruises, but He binds up; He wounds, but His hands make whole* (Job 5:17-18). Happy! What more can be said in response to "happy"? Does the thought God's judgments might have a wholesome purpose make you happy?

♦ *In trouble they visited You, they poured out a prayer when Your chastening was upon them* (Is. 26:16). Is not "prayer" purposeful?

♦ *If they break My statutes and do not keep My commandments, then I will punish their transgression with the rod, and their iniquity with stripes. Nevertheless My loving-kindness I will not utterly take from him, nor allow My faithfulness to fail* (Ps. 89:31-33).

♦ *Your judgments are right...in faithfulness You have afflicted me* (Ps. 119:75). Even in the midst of His rod, stripes, and afflictions, His loving-kindness is present and His faithfulness does not fail. For it is in faithfulness He afflicts. We expect "loving-kindness and faithfulness" from good parents in their disciplines, do we not? Do not these terms indicate God also has a good purpose in His punishments?

♦ *Those who sat in darkness and in the shadow of death, bound in affliction and irons—because they rebelled against the words of God, and despised the counsel of the Most High, therefore He brought down their heart with labor....Then they cried out to the LORD in their trouble, And He saved them out of their distresses* (Ps. 107:10-13). Bound in affliction because they rebelled, therefore He loads them down in labor. The result? They cried to the Lord in their trouble. The final outcome? They were delivered from their distress! Is this not purpose?

♦ *Before I was afflicted I went astray, but now I keep Your word....It is good for me that I have been afflicted, that I may learn Your statutes* (Ps. 119:67, 71). What is the fruit of affliction? Keeping His word and learning His statutes. What purpose!

♦ *When the Lord has washed away the filth of the daughters of Zion, and purged the blood of Jerusalem from her midst, by the spirit of judgment and by the spirit of burning"* (Is. 4:4). He washes filth by the spirit of judgment and burning.

♦ *You have stricken them, but they have not grieved; You have consumed them, but they have refused to receive correction....They are foolish; for they do not know...the judgment of their God* (Jer. 5:3, 4). They were stricken so they would repent and consumed to receive correction. But they were foolish and did not understand His judgments. Have we also been foolish?

♦ *Through deceit they refuse to know Me....therefore...I will refine them and try them* (Jer. 9:6-7). Those who refuse to know Him will go through a process of refining and testing. Is purpose not evident in the word refine?

♦ *The fierce anger of the LORD will not turn back **until** He fully accomplishes the purposes of His heart. In **days to come** you will understand this* (Jer. 30:24 NIV). God's judgment is proven to be measured and purposeful by the simple phrase, "until He fully accomplishes the purposes of His heart." Can it be clearer? Are we now in those "days"?

♦ *I have **driven** them in My anger;...I will bring them back....for the good of them* (Jer. 32:37-39). He drove them away, which ultimately was for their good. Was this not purpose "driven"? No pun intended.

♦ *You have appointed them for judgment; O Rock, You have marked them for correction* (Hab. 1:12). Can it be clearer?

♦ *All the earth shall be devoured with the fire of My jealousy. For then I will restore to the peoples a pure language, that they all may call on the name of the LORD, to serve Him with one accord* (Zep. 3:8-9). When His judgments have achieved their purpose, the people will be united. They will then call on God and serve Him!

♦ *Who can endure the day of His coming...stand when He appears? For He is like a refiner's fire and like launderer's soap...He will purify... and purge them as gold and silver, that they my offer to the Lord an offering in righteousness* (Mal. 3:2-3). His judgments are a refiner's fire, like launderer's soap that may offer an offering in righteousness.

♦ *Judgment to the nations....till He put forth judgment to victory, in his name shall nations hope* (Mt. 12:18-21 YLT).

"Judgment to victory" with "nations hoping [trusting] in His name" speaks of great purpose!

♦ *Now is the judgment of this world; now the ruler of this world will be cast out. And I, if I am lifted up from the earth, will draw [drag] all peoples to Myself* (Jn. 12:31-32). When judgment comes, the enemy is cast out, and all peoples are dragged to Christ. Is this not judgment with a grand and glorious purpose?

♦ *Concerning the faith have suffered shipwreck, of whom are Hymenaeus and Alexander, whom I delivered to Satan that they may learn not to blaspheme* (1Ti. 1:19b-20).

♦ *Deliver such a one to Satan for the destruction of the flesh, that his spirit may be saved in the day of the Lord Jesus* (1Co. 5:4-5). Here are two examples of judgment with purpose; learning not to blaspheme and saving the spirit. Note how even Satan unwittingly plays into God's hand. God is always in control.

♦ *Wrath has come upon them [Israel] to the uttermost* (1Th. 2:16). *"And so all Israel will be saved....He will turn away ungodliness from Jacob..."* (Ro. 11:26). Wrath to the uttermost, yet salvation with ungodliness turned away. The purpose of this judgment is Israel's salvation in its appointed time.

♦ *We shall all stand before the judgment seat of Christ.* **For** *it is written..."every knee shall bow to Me, and every tongue shall ['give praise'—NAS] to God."* **So then** *each of us shall give account of himself to God* (Ro. 14:10-12). (See also Ph. 2:9-11; Is. 45:22-25). Note "for" and "so then" link judgment (both before and after) with worship. Is this not evidence there is a glorious purpose in judgment? See "Every Knee," Chapter 6.

♦ *My son, do not despise the chastening of the Lord, nor detest His correction; for whom the Lord loves He corrects, just as a father the son in whom he delights* (Pr. 3:11-12). God chastens to correct, the same as human parents do. For whom He loves He corrects. Who does He not love according to John 3:16?

♦ *If you endure chastening, God deals with you as with sons; for what son is there whom a father does not chasten? But if you are without chastening, of which* **all have become partakers,** *then you are illegitimate and not sons. Furthermore, we have had human fathers who corrected us, and we* *paid them respect. Shall we not much more readily be in subjection to the Father of spirits and live? For they indeed for a few days chastened us as seemed best to them, but He for our profit, that we may be partakers of His holiness. Now no chastening seems to be joyful for the present, but painful; nevertheless, **afterward it yields the peaceable fruit** of righteousness to those who have been trained by it"* (He. 12:5-11).

The Lord loves all people and we can rest assured all will be chastened in the same spirit exemplified here. "Afterward" it yields fruit (vs.11). That is purpose! But there can be no "afterward" with infinite penalty. Kalen Fristad, a United Methodist minister and author of *Destined For Salvation*, wrote regarding Jer. 3:12-13, 22; 9:13-16; 32:37-38:

> God allowed the Babylonians to conquer and enslave the Israelites for the purpose of getting them to return to Him....The purpose of biblical punishment is to make a wrongdoer a right-doer. If hell is endured without end, the experience would be of no value to an individual because there would be no chance of his embracing good, repenting and attempting a new beginning....Suffering from which nothing can be learned or gained is meaningless, and the one who brought it about would be a fiend, not a father. We as parents discipline our children, not for the sake of punishment, but in order to encourage change. Surely God is at least as honorable as any parent in this regard.[4]

> *"The purpose of biblical punishment is to make a wrongdoer a right-doer."*[4]

> *"No chastening seems to be joyful for the present, but painful; nevertheless, **afterward** it yields the peaceable fruit of righteousness to those who have been **trained** by it"* (He. 12:11).

An illustration from Christ:

> Then Peter said to Him, "Lord, do **You speak** this parable only **to us**, or to all people?" And the Lord said, "Who then is that faithful and wise steward, whom his master will make ruler over his household, to give them their portion of food in due season? Blessed is that servant whom his master will find so doing when he comes. Truly, I say to you that he will make him ruler over all that he has. But if that servant says in his heart, 'My master is delaying his coming,' and begins to beat the male and female servants, and to eat and drink and be drunk, the master of that servant will come on a day when he is not looking for him, and at an hour when he is not aware, and will cut him in two and appoint him his **portion with the unbelievers**. And that servant who knew his master's will, and did not prepare himself or do according to his will, shall be beaten with **many stripes**. But he who did not know, yet committed things deserving of stripes, shall be beaten with few. For everyone **to whom much is given,** from him **much will be required**; and to whom much has been committed, of him they will ask the more. I came to send **fire** on the earth..." (Lu. 12:41-49)

This passage is a warning to believers. What is the threat? To be cut in two and appointed our "portion" with unbelievers. Unbelievers and unfaithful believers receive the same judgment! Why should we be shocked? Does not the judge of all the earth do right?

What is this "portion" to be meted out to believers and unbelievers alike? Many stripes! Not unending stripes. This is confirmed moreover by the use of the word "portion." To have a "portion" of something fits with a measured judgment (Mt. 7:2), not with an eternal one. This is exactly how judgment in the lake of fire is expressed, "shall have their part in" (Re. 21:8).

Finally, these "stripes" are associated with "fire" the symbol of God's purification process (See pages 217-220). "For everyone will be seasoned with fire..."(Mk. 9:49). Fire is something positive that everyone will experience to one degree or another.

Is this parable the only text where we see believers being appointed their "portion" in judgment with unbelievers? Re. 21:8 list eight categories of sinners with unbelievers singled out separately. This naturally infers that the others include believers. That agrees with this parable and the opening words, "He who overcomes." How many of us have glossed over this list feeling quite smug about ourselves? Should we be so confident? Reflect on them a moment.

> *He who overcomes shall inherit all things, and I will be his God and he shall be My son. But the cowardly* [Are you courageous?], **unbelieving** [Do you believe all God's promises?* Ro. 4:21], *abominable* [Are you ever proud? Pr. 6:16-17], *murderers* [Are you ever angry? Mt. 5:21-22], *sexually immoral* [Do you ever look with lust? Mt. 5:28], *sorcerers, idolaters* [Do you ever covet? Col. 3:5], *and all liars* [Do you always tell people what you really think?] *shall have their **part** in the lake which burns with fire and brimstone, which is the second death* (Re. 21:7-8). *Let him who thinks he stands take heed lest he fall* (1Co. 10:12).
> *Especially proclamation chapters 6 & 7.

Let us stop sweeping under the carpet the fearful parts of Scripture and denying the obvious. We who believe have been given much, and thus much will be required (Lu. 12:48). The warnings are very real. Neglect them to our peril. But let's keep this in mind:

In ancient Eastern literature, exaggerated expressions and metaphors to accentuate concepts are intended to grab the reader's attention and not meant to be taken literally. This is typical oriental style (See page 33). But the most critical thing to remember in this strong language is the character of the Judge and the purpose of His judgments. He "is" Love with no "buts" attached. All His judgments are exacted in love with a just, righteous, and remedial purpose. This is the key that unlocks our understanding and brings about a true harmonization of the Scriptures.

◆◆◆◆◆

In this chapter we have seen that infinite penalty is unjust and not supported by Scripture, that death is no obstacle to God in accomplishing His purposes for mankind, and that God is just in every sense of the word. Numerous biblical examples were set forth to exemplify God's purpose-driven judgments. Though we do not understand many things about God and His judgments (Ro. 11:33), His nature and justice are not mysteries. Now consider with me how God's purpose-driven judgments relate to the bigger picture of God's unfailing plan for man.

CHAPTER FOUR

BLESSED H⦿PE
PART ⦿ΠE

Looking for the blessed hope....
(Tit. 2:11-15)

*I*n the next two chapters, I will attempt to present a comprehensive understanding of the big picture—God's unfailing plan for man—as I perceive it through my dim mirror of understanding. I have called this "big picture" the "Blessed Hope" to facilitate comparison with the Augustinian tradition of everlasting punishment.

Hope for the World

Let us begin at the close of our Lord's earthly ministry: the night of His arrest. His whole life had led up to this climactic moment. He knew exactly what was to befall Him (Jn. 18:4). In the midst of a time like this, please reflect on the cry of His heart:

> *Lifting up His eyes to heaven, He said, "Father, the hour has come....Holy Father, keep them in your name...that they may be* **one** *even as we are one....that they may all be* **one***...that the* **world may believe***....that they may be* **one***...that they may be* **perfected in unity***, so that the* **world may know** *that You sent Me"* (Jn. 17:1, 11, 21-23 NAS).

Just think of it! Our Lord could have been completely paralyzed with fear with only His execution in mind. On the contrary, His thoughts did not dwell on Himself, but instead on all humanity. His heart went out to the whole world. And what does the world need? To witness Christians loving one another—walking in unity. The world has yet to see it. It is my conviction that the Blessed Hope has the potential to tear down the highest walls that have divided believers over the centuries, and restore the fullness of joy into the hearts of God's people. "You greatly rejoice with joy inexpressible and full of glory" (1Pe. 1:8 NAS). Then the world will believe! Then the world will know who sent Christ and why!

Babes

"It shall be more tolerable for the land of Sodom in the day of judgment than for you." At that time Jesus answered and said, "I thank You, Father, Lord of heaven and earth, that You have hidden these things from the wise and prudent and have revealed them to babes"
(Mt. 11:24-25; See also 1 Co. 1:26-29)

I am grateful that the discovery of God's truth is not the exclusive domain of the religious "elite." In this passage, God has hidden "things" pertaining to His judgments from the wise and has revealed them to "babes." Oh, that we would all be babes! Many "babes" today, I believe, long for the day when the dark cloud veiling God's judgments is lifted from the Church. Oh what joy, peace, and unity of purpose will envelop His Body on that day! Then the world will know Jesus Christ is Lord! (Jn. 17:23). This is the glory of the Blessed Hope I cherish.

Reason

God expects us to think through what we believe and not to simply accept what men teach. Christ commands us to judge for ourselves what is right (Lu. 12:57). Paul exhorts us to test all things (1Th. 5:21) and to judge for ourselves what he says (1Co. 10:15). From the outset of biblical revelation, we are challenged to think for ourselves—"Shall not the judge of all the earth do right" (Ge. 18:25)? Does not such a question require thinking? Our Lord always expected His hearers to think. "What do you think, Simon" (Mt. 17:25)?

> *God expects us to think through what we believe and not simply accept what men teach.*

"What do you think? If a man has a hundred sheep..." (Mt. 18:12). "What do you think? A man had two sons..." (Mt. 21:28). "What do you think about the Christ" (Mt. 22:42)? "If you then, being evil, know how to give good gifts to your children, how much more will your Father..." (Mt. 7:11)? Call to mind the Bereans who searched the Scriptures daily to find out whether the words preached to them were so (Ac. 17:11). They are said to have been "more noble-minded" (NAS).We have been endowed with great reasoning powers, and God expects us to use them. He even invites us to reason with Him! "Come...let us reason together, says the LORD" (Is. 1:18). It is our very capacity to reason that enables us to love and be like God.

Our hell tradition goes against all reason. In response to this; some will quote Is. 55:8: "His thoughts are not our thoughts, and His ways are not our ways." By this, they are inferring man's reasoning is flawed—what we think is cruel and unjust is really not. If this be true, then we are not made in His image and have nothing in common with God. It would be impossible to reason with Him on any level. But is this what Isaiah meant? If you check the context, you will see that His thoughts are different than ours in relation to mercy, not cruelty. What a travesty such a wondrous passage has been twisted out of context to say the very opposite about God. This is a prime example of invalidating the Word of God for the sake of tradition (Mt. 15:6)—a tradition fostering a fear toward God taught by the commandment of men (Is. 29:13).

> Though man a thinking being is defined,
> Few use the great prerogative of mind.
> How few think justly of the thinking few!
> How many never think, who think they do!
> —Jane Taylor

Question of Questions

How can a good God create creatures He knows will be tormented forever? Answer one: According to the prevalent view, this is the price He had to pay to get a few into Heaven. Answer two: According to the Blessed Hope, He does not face this dilemma at all, but reconciles all to Himself in the fullness of time. Which most glorifies the Father of our Lord Jesus Christ? Which conforms with an all-knowing, all-powerful, and all-loving Creator?

How can we believe God is good, while at the same time believe infinite penalty is the lot of most of mankind? We cannot unless we have a perverted sense of what "good" is, or we do not believe God has the power to prevent it, or we have not thought long and hard enough about the horror of what infinite penalty entails. However, if we believe God is "good" in the normal sense, and His penalties are finite and just, there are no conflicting issues. This is the theology of the New Testament, the early Church, and a remnant of believers throughout the centuries since. It is a theology honoring God, satisfying God's moral witness in men's hearts (see Chapter 8), satisfying reason, and most importantly harmonizing the Scriptures. This is the Blessed Hope.

Power *vs.* Love or Power *and* Love?

I look at it simply. Jesus said we must receive the kingdom of God as a child (Mk. 10:15). If one and one equals two, it cannot be three. The following two points add up to a final glorious sum, and not a tragic one.

A. God is all-powerful and always accomplishes His will (Calvinist/Reformed theology).
B. God loves all people and wills the reconciliation of everyone (Arminian theology and everyone else's).

Since He wills the reconciliation of all and has all power necessary to accomplish His will, is it too much to believe He will accomplish it? For if He does not, which part of the equation is flawed? "A" or "B"? Calvinists say "B" is flawed, while Arminians say "A" is flawed. But if we accept "A" as the Calvinists do, and "B" as the Arminians do, then we would, like a child, conclude that every person must ultimately be reconciled. This is the Blessed Hope.

POWER	+	love =	Calvinism/Reformed
power	+	**LOVE** =	Arminianism/Majority
POWER	+	**LOVE** =	Blessed Hope

The key to unlock the mystery as I see it, is Calvinists are right about God's power, and Arminians are right about His love. The tragedy is both adhere to Augustine's theory of judgment which forces them to reject (or explain away) the glorious side of each other's theology. But if instead, they both embraced the Blessed Hope, they would become one and the world would soon know Jesus Christ is Lord! (Jn. 13:35; 17:21, 23). There would be nothing to reject or explain away. The greatest theological controversy and division in the body of Christ would vanish. Might this not be the key to set the captives free, harmonize the Scriptures of judgment and mercy for all, and unite the body of Christ?

Which of these three perspectives most glorifies God, harmonizes the Scriptures, and has the potential to change the world? Which is the truth?

Paradigm Shift

If you are facing disturbing questions in your faith, perhaps your underlying paradigm (the big picture) is flawed. How we understand God's plan for man affects how we understand all things. "But if your eye [paradigm] is bad, your whole body [understanding] will be full of darkness" (Mt. 6:23).

For 25 years I held the Arminian paradigm. Then, while a missionary in Senegal, the realization that I did not have complete assurance of my salvation unsettled me. I wrestled with this for months and finally concluded that salvation had to be the work of God. Thus, I made a paradigm shift. I began to understand God's power in the way our Calvinist and Reformed brethren do. I continued joyfully in this new perspective for about two years, until I no longer found comfort in my personal salvation. How could I in the midst of a world of lost people? Living in a Muslim country deeply affected me. It prepared the ground so I might consider a third paradigm—the "Blessed Hope."

Most of us are not aware of how powerfully our paradigms affect how we understand the Scriptures. They force us to conclude certain passages do not mean what they say. Unless we are keenly aware of this, and make a diligent effort to compare Scripture with Scripture, we cannot see truth staring us in the face. It has been a slow, hard process for me. But once I stepped out of the eternal hell paradigm and began seeing Scripture without that filter, I was freed to receive God's revelation in a fresh new way.

I believe God would have us embrace a more glorious paradigm. It must precede, override, and triumph over law and judgment. We should not be surprised that the predominant view has been the hard, cruel dogma of Augustine, for it conforms with the legalistic, hard, and cruel side of our fallen nature. Man's tendency has always been to see the hard side of God and His judgments, and our traditions are a reflection of that. They blind us from seeing God's mercy and love in judgment. Let us embrace the only paradigm worthy of our glorious God—God's inexhaustible grace, the Blessed Hope.

Salvation

What is meant by "salvation"? What does believing in Jesus save us from? In "Repentance and Salvation," Robert Wilkin, executive director of the *Grace Evangelical Society* stated:

> It would be difficult to find a concept which is richer and more *varied in meaning* than the biblical concept of salvation. The breadth of salvation is so *sweeping* and its intended aim so magnificent that in many contexts the words used *defy precise definition.*[1]

Joseph Dillow, Th.D. Dallas Theological Seminary and author of *The Reign of the Servant Kings*, explained:

> Salvation is a *broad term.* It commonly means "to make whole," "to sanctify," "to endure victoriously," or "to be delivered from some general trouble or difficulty." Without question, the common "knee-jerk" reaction which assumes that "salvation" always has eternal deliverance in view, has seriously compromised the ability of many to objectively discern what the New Testament writers intended to teach.[2]

In *A Generous Orthodoxy*, Brian McLaren, founding pastor of Cedar Ridge Community Church in Baltimore and author of *Finding Faith* and other titles, wrote,

> In the Bible, "save" means "rescue" or "heal." It emphatically does not automatically mean "save from hell" or "give eternal life after death."...Its meaning varies from passage to passage, but in general, in any context, "save" means "get out of trouble."[3]

In order to better understand salvation, we need to get a broad overview of what Christ came to do for us. He came to:

- ◆ Give rest (Mt. 11:28).
- ◆ Heal the brokenhearted, free the captives and oppressed, and give sight to the blind (Lu. 4:18).
- ◆ Comfort the mourning, give beauty for ashes, joy for mourning, and a garment of praise for the spirit of heaviness (Is. 61:2, 3).
- ◆ Save from sin and turn from iniquity (Mic 7:19; Mt. 1:21; Ac. 3:26; Ro. 11:26).
- ◆ Save from God's passionate displeasure (wrath) and just recompense of sinful conduct (Ro. 5:9). (See "God's Wrath," page 71).
- ◆ Set free from sin (Ro. 6:22).
- ◆ Rescue from this present evil age (Ga. 1:4 NAS).
- ◆ Bring hope and God to the hopeless and godless (Ep. 2:12).
- ◆ Redeem from every lawless deed and purify us (Tit. 2:11-15 NAS).
- ◆ Set free those who all their lives were enslaved to the fear of death (He. 2:14-15).
- ◆ Redeem from aimless conduct (1Pe. 1:18-19).
- ◆ Seeing the distressed and dispirited made Him command us to pray for laborers (Mt. 9:36-38 NAS).

If salvation is deliverance from eternal woe, why the emphasis on temporal deliverances? These passages speak of deliverance from being heavy laden, blindness, broken-heartedness, sorrow, mourning, heaviness of spirit, hopelessness, impurity, fear of death, aimless conduct, weariness, being distressed and dispirited, lawless deeds (sin) and their consequences, the present evil age. How can Scripture emphasize these comparatively insignificant temporal pains in the face of infinite pain? For life on earth is but a vapor (Ja. 4:14), and then we are hurled into eternal woe. How could James say pure religion is to visit orphans and widows (Ja. 1:27)? What a waste of time when we could be snatching the masses from hell! Why does Scripture not place the emphasis where it ought to be? Why the smoke screens? The only answer making any sense to me is that a flawed paradigm has veiled the truth of Scripture from us.

Salvation's Purpose

Having an idea of what we are saved "from," we must now consider what we are saved "unto." C. S. Lewis, twentieth century British teacher and prolific author, understood the purpose of salvation. He wrote, "Every Christian is to become a little Christ. The whole purpose of becoming a Christian is simply nothing else."4 Scripture reveals salvation to be a process as much as it is an event. It goes beyond a new birth experience. Consider these:

- *Warn...that we may present everyone perfect in Christ* (Col.1:28). Warn against what?
- *Boldness in the day of judgment; because we are like Him* (1Jn. 4:17). Christians facing judgment?
- *Work out salvation* (Ph. 2:12-13). Salvation by works?
- *Shall be saved by His life* (Ro. 5:10). Shall be saved? I thought I was saved already!
- *Take heed...in "doing" you will save yourself* (1Ti. 4:16). Saved by doing? Save yourself?

> *Scripture reveals salvation to be a process as much as it is an event. It goes beyond a new birth experience.*

How are such expressions reconciled with Paul's teaching on salvation by grace? They refer to salvation's "made complete" dimension (Col. 1:28)—the end goal of our salvation. Salvation always depends completely on the work of Christ on the cross. But, we must understand that God is going somewhere with our salvation. We are predestined to be conformed to the image of His Son (Ro. 8:29); "We shall be like Him..." (1Jn. 3:2); "Till we all come in the unity of the faith...unto a perfect man, unto the measure of the stature of the fullness of Christ" (Ep. 4:13 KJV; Ga. 4:19). Reconciliation (Ro. 5:10) is not salvation in that sense, but refers to what God has already done in Christ. It is a means to an end—our perfection (Col. 1:28). Once reconciled, God's purpose is for us to become transformed into the image of Christ. This is why believers are said to be "especially" saved (1Ti. 4:10) since they are presently submitting to God who is "working out" salvation in them (Ep. 2:10; Ph. 2:13). Salvation goes beyond deliverance from temporal things and from God's passionate displeasure in judgment, to actual deliverance from our sinful nature. Our perfection is the goal (See Ro. 6:3, 4, 11-12; 8:29; Ga. 4:19; Ph. 2:12-13; Col. 1:27-28; 2Ti. 2:11-13; Tit. 2:14; 3:8; Ja. 1:27; 1Jn. 3:3; 4:17).

This goal, to become Christ-like, comes only through the cross working in our lives. "God forbid that I should boast except in the cross of our Lord Jesus Christ, by whom the world has been crucified to me, and I to the world" (Ga. 6:14). It is only through dying to ourselves, sufferings, and trials can we develop spiritually (Mt. 16:24; Jn. 12:24; Ro. 5:3-5; 6:6; 2Co. 12:9, 10; Ga. 2:20; Ja. 1:2-4; 1Pe. 1:6-7; 2:21). Though sufferings and trials (our cross) are not redemptive (only the blood of Christ is), they are nevertheless essential to our training. Either we take up our cross willingly, or God will lay it on us in His own time. For the way of the cross is the only path to our "full" salvation— "to a perfect man" (Ep. 4:13).

Salvation goes beyond deliverance from temporal things and from God's passionate displeasure in judgment, to actual deliverance from our sinful nature. Our perfection is the goal.

There are no shortcuts. Even Christ "learned obedience by the things which He suffered" (He. 5:8). "The disciple is not above his teacher; but everyone who is *perfectly trained* will be like his teacher" (Lu. 6:40).

We all must be perfectly trained. Believers have the opportunity of crucifying themselves daily now, while unbelievers will have their opportunity in the coming age or ages as God brings the cross upon them through judgment.

Why faith then? What is its purpose? What does it mean to believe in the "name" of Jesus for salvation (Ac. 4:12; Ph. 2:9-11)? Faith is "trusting" in God's "Person"—His nature, character, and ways being fully assured that what He promises, He can and will do (Ro. 4:21). It is not a religious formula, but childlike trust in the true God (Mk. 10:15). Faith opens the channels of God's blessings into our lives. As we "trust" Him we begin to know His peace and subsequently yield to His Spirit working in us.

Many think because they have faith, they are a cut above the rest. Not so. Faith is God's gift and work in us : "Jesus...author and finisher of our faith"(He. 12:2). The following, I believe, will confirm this. Mt. 11:27; 16:16-17; Jn. 1:13; 6:44; 15:16; Ac. 13:48; Ro. 12:3; 1Co. 4:7; Ep. 2:8-9; 3:16-17; Ph. 1:6; 1:29; 2:13; Col. 1:12; 1Ti. 1:14.

Some even scorn the thought that unbelievers may be able to trust Christ beyond this life. How sad. "Of course they'll believe then," they say, "it will all be too obvious. There will be no merit to that!" Merit? Since when is faith meritorious? "Where is boasting then? It is excluded. By what law? Of works? No, but by the law of faith" (Ro. 3:27). Why must faith only be valid in this life? Can trusting God ever become obsolete? And what "if" faith were limited to this life? Would that paralyze an almighty, all-loving God from restoring life to whom He wants, when He wants, and where He wants? When did He stop being GOD? For more on faith, see website, "Book Updates," p. 87.

Mystery to Ponder

Somehow in God's infinite wisdom, He integrates both mercy (pardon) and judgment (chastisement). It is not simply "either/or " as our tradition implies. To give you an example of what I mean, consider the following texts.

- *To You...belongs mercy; **for** You render to each one according to his work* (Ps. 62:12; 101:1). Mercy, yet He renders according to work?
- *You were to them God-Who-Forgives, You took vengeance on their deeds* (Ps. 99:8). God forgives, yet takes vengeance?
- *Her iniquity is pardoned; she has received from the Lord...double for all her sins* (Is. 40:2). Sin pardoned, yet receives double for sin?
- *As the elect of God...Christ forgave you....**but** he who does wrong will be repaid for what he has done, and there is no partiality* (Col 3:12, 13, 25). Forgiven, yet repaid?
- *Judges according to work...redeemed...precious blood of Christ* (1Pe. 1:17-19). Judged according to work, yet redeemed?
- *We [believers] must all appear before the judgment seat of Christ, so that each one may be recompensed for his deeds...according to what he has done, whether good or bad....He made Him who knew no sin to be sin on our behalf, so that we might become the righteousness of God in Him* (2Co. 5:10, 21 NAS). Recompensed for bad deeds, yet righteous in Christ?

How do we reconcile these conflicting statements? In addition to these, have you noticed the extensive number of warnings in Scripture directed to believers—to those redeemed and washed in the blood? The dangers warned about are very real. (See Appendix II).

The answer, I believe, lies in simply accepting that God integrates both mercy and judgment as He sees fit. But is there a verse that says it plainly? Yes! "Judgment is without mercy to the one who has shown no mercy" (Ja. 2:13). If judgment is without mercy to the merciless, it must be with mercy to the merciful! So here it is in black and white.

Along with this, might there be further light offered if forgiveness, like salvation, has more than one dimension? Could there be a legal and relational side to it? All humankind receives pardon from our inherited sin in Adam through Christ's redemption as the last Adam (Ro. 5:11-21; 1Co. 15:22,45; 1Jn. 2:2). This is "legal" pardon based solely on the merits of Christ. Note the legal/financial term involved – "redeem" (1Pe. 1:18; Ep. 1:7). Yet relational forgiveness rest on each person's individual responses to God's truth revealed in each heart. "To whom much is given (revealed), much is required" (Lu. 12:48). God is absolutely fair and just with each person (Le. 24:19). In all the universe no one is more fair and just than Him (De. 32:4; Ps. 19:9). "If we confess our sins, He is faithful and just to forgive us our sins and to cleanse us from all unrighteousness" (1Jn. 1:9). This passage refers to relational forgiveness, as it is linked to confession—a relational action. Notice 1Jn. 1:9 says God will forgive because He is "just". Why is that a factor? Because Christ legally paid the penalty for the sins of the whole world (1Jn. 2:2)! Since the bill has been paid, God must forgive. But that does not exclude Him from doing it on His terms and for our correction (Pr. 3:11-12). Remember, He's a loving Father to all.

> *All mankind receives legal forgiveness in Christ for their inherited sin in Adam. Yet, in relational forgiveness, forgiveness depends on each person's individual responses to God's truth revealed in each heart.*

We need to recognize that God merges both mercy and judgment together. This realization is a crucial piece of the puzzle helping us better understand the big picture. By integrating His mercy with His judgments, He accomplishes what is good and just in the lives of all people.

Charles Pridgeon, president and founder of the Pittsburgh Bible Institute, argues:

> There is an erroneous idea that, when one accepts forgive-ness of his sins, he thereby escapes all the consequences of his sins. This is by no means the case, as every one may know by experience. The consequences last until there is no longer need of their warning and judging lesson. Some of them continue to the end of this life, and even extend much further.[5]

Does this throw a wrench in our theology? Did we think we had God or even salvation all figured out? Did we forget how deep are the riches of God's wisdom and knowledge? Or that His judgments are unsearchable? Or that His ways are unfathomable (Ro. 11:33)? Did we forget even Paul only knew in part (1Co. 13:9-12)? How could we have expected Paul to make things clear when he did not even know? Is it any wonder myriads of Christian denominations abound in the world—all fiercely adhering to their conflicting tenets?

Let us humble ourselves before God's power and wisdom, and accept that He is infinitely greater than we can imagine (Ep. 3:20). Let us accept that we do not have all the answers. Let us cease being so dogmatic in our doctrines and humble ourselves before the mighty hand of God. Consider what God said to Daniel: "Do not fear, Daniel, for from the first day that you set your heart to understand, and to humble yourself before your God, your words were heard...." (Da. 10:12). The key to understanding is a humble heart.

"Oh, the depth of the riches both of the wisdom and knowledge of God! How unsearchable are His judgments and His ways past finding out" (Ro. 11:33)! "For we know in part....For now we see in a mirror, dimly....Now I know in part..." (1Co. 13:9-12). "Now to Him who is able to do exceedingly abundantly above all that we ask or think, according to the [His] power..." (Ep. 3:20).

In order to grasp the vital role God has given His just and right-eous judgments in His unfailing plan for man, we must understand salvation's depth and purpose – the grandeur of what salvation encompasses; salvation's relationship to faith and the cross; and recognize that God integrates pardon with chastisement. Lacking any of these elements will compromise our ability to make sense of it all.

Thoughts and Prayers

Ephesians 3:20 states God is able to do exceedingly abundantly above all we ask or think. Do we believe it? Can we dare believe, hope, and pray for something this grand and wonderful—that God can and will accomplish all His will for mankind? Is His hand so short it cannot redeem all people (Is. 50:2)? Is the redemption of all not good and acceptable to Him (1Ti. 2:3)? John Wesley believed God can convert a world as easily as one individual.[6] Was he mistaken?

> *I [Paul] exhort...that...supplications, **prayers**, intercessions, and giving of thanks, be made for **all men**...for this is **good and acceptable** in the sight of God our Savior; who **will have all men to be saved**....Christ Jesus...gave himself **a ransom for all**, to be **testified in due time**....I will therefore that men pray everywhere, lifting up holy hands **without...doubting*** (1Ti. 2:1-6, 8 KJV). (See also: Mk. 11:22-4; Ro. 4:20; Ja. 1:6-8).

Does God not call us to pray and thank Him for the salvation of all, and to do so without doubting? Is He not willing and able to save all people? If we err by praying in such a lofty way, would this dishonor or displease Him? Our only sin would be taking His Word to heart. If I am to err, I prefer it be for expecting too much of Him than too little. Let us dare to think and believe the very highest of thoughts! What can be higher than thanking God for the salvation of all people?

Scope of the Gospel

*Scripture, foreseeing God would **justify** the Gentiles **by faith**, preached the **gospel** to Abraham beforehand, saying, **"In you all the nations shall be blessed**."*
(Ga. 3:8)

The Gospel is defined in eight simple words! "In you all the nations shall be blessed." These words are the very Gospel Paul preached—justification by faith. This Gospel was first revealed to Abraham and is repeated five times in Genesis! (Ge. 12:3; 18:18; 22:18; 26:4; 28:14). God did not want us to miss it. Notice it does not say "some" nations, but "all." The important question in all this is: Does the term "nations" include every person? Peter makes it clear:

"And in your seed all the *families* of the earth shall be *blessed*. To you *first*, God, having raised up His Servant Jesus, sent Him to bless you, in turning away *every one* of you from your *iniquities*" (Ac. 3:25-26).

According to Peter, the blessing of all nations includes all the "families" of the earth. But he does not stop there. He goes on specifying that the blessing includes every member of the family. Notice his words, "every one of you." For years as a missionary, I have heard and read that God was merely interested in a token representative from every nation, tribe, and tongue. That has always troubled and perplexed me. As I re-evaluate the Scriptures, I see a totally different picture of God.

> In your seed **all** the families of the earth shall be blessed. To you **first**, God, having raised up His Servant Jesus, sent Him to bless you, in turning away **every one** of you from your iniquities (Ac. 3:25-26).

Acts 3:25-26 establishes four critical points.

- The Gospel comes to the elect first (not exclusively), and in "due time" it will bless every one of your family members, regardless of what you think their present spiritual state is.
- What is the blessing? It is turning away from sin.
- It is the same gospel Paul preached—justification by faith. This is established in Galatians 3:8 via God's promise to Abraham (Ge. 12:3) and repeated here (Ac. 3:25).
- It confirms that justification by faith, as marvelous as it is, is not an end in itself; it is the prerequisite to turning from sin, the "working out" of our salvation.

Think about the term "family." What does it mean to be a member of a family? It means one is part of a cohesive whole. If one is hurting, all are hurting. It can be accurately compared to the Body of Christ. We are *"members individually,"* and the members should have the same care for one another. If one member suffers, all the members suffer with him or her (see 1Co. 12:25-27). Now ponder this: How can these "blessed ones" spoken of by Peter in the above passage—all individual members of families—experience the "great joy" of the Gospel (Lu. 2:10; Ro. 10:15) if they are vexed and tormented over the destiny of any of their lost family members? Could you "greatly rejoice with joy inexpressible"(1Pe. 1:8 NAS), knowing that your son, daughter, dad, mom, wife, or husband are suffering in an eternal hell?

If we do not provide, love, and care for our own household, we have denied the faith and are worse than unbelievers (1Ti. 5:8). We must love our family members and neighbors "as" ourselves (Ro. 13:8-9). If we so loved in truth, we could not have peace and joy unless we knew all our loved ones were eternally safe. This simple truth alone confirms the unlimited scope of the Good News.

Paid in Full

One of the last things Christ said while hanging on the cross was, "Father, forgive them" (Lu. 23:34). Did God not answer His prayer? In John's gospel, His last recorded words were, "It is finished" (Jn. 19:30), which *The Bible Knowledge Commentary* says means, "paid in full."[7] What is the significance of this? Consider the commentary John provides on Christ's redemption. What better commentary could we have than the author? He says, "Behold! The Lamb of God who takes away the sin of the world" (Jn. 1:29)! "He Himself is the propitiation for our sins, and *not for ours only* but also for the whole world" (1Jn. 2:2). The sins of the whole world have been paid for in full! I would not dare place any limitations on the power of the blood of Christ to save all for whom it was shed—the world. Perhaps no passages are more precious and essential than these. I entreat you to prayerfully meditate on each one.

+ *Behold! The Lamb of God who takes away the sin of the world"* (Jn. 1:29)! The world!
+ *It is finished* (Jn. 19:30). Paid in full!
+ *He is the propitiation for our sins, and not for ours only but also for the whole world* (1Jn. 2:2). The world!

> *Behold! The Lamb of God who takes away the sin of the world!*
> *(Jn. 1:29)*

+ *The LORD has laid on Him the iniquity of us all* (Is. 53:6). Everyone!
+ *My flesh...I...give for the life of the world* (Jn. 6:51). The world!

- *Christ died for the ungodly* (Ro. 5:6). That includes everyone!
- *When we were enemies we were reconciled...through [His] death* (Ro. 5:10). If you and I, why not all?
- *Justification...to all men* (Ro. 5:18 NAS). All men!
- *For it pleased the Father...by Him to reconcile all things to Himself...through the blood of His cross* (Col. 1:19-20). All!
- *He...tasted death for everyone* (He. 2:9). Everyone!
- *Christ...suffered once for sins, the just for the unjust* (1Pe. 3:18). Everyone!
- *He gave Himself a ransom for all, to be testified in due time* (1Ti. 2:6). Everyone!

Christ gave Himself a ransom for all (1Ti. 2:6) and not merely some. He propitiated not only our sins, but also those of the whole world! (1Jn. 2:2). That includes the ungodly (Ro. 5:6), the unjust (1Pe. 3:18), and even His enemies (Ro. 5:8). In fact everyone (He. 2:9). The ransom for their sins has been paid in "full" (Jn. 19:30). Thus all are reconciled through His blood (Col.1:20). I accept these passages as they read. Moreover, because I do, I am confident that God will reveal Himself to all men in His ordered (due) time (1Ti. 2:6).

What "Paid in Full" Implies

Christ did not suffer in vain for anyone. For sooner or later, all will come to faith and obedience. All are washed in the blood. "And I, when I am lifted up from the earth, will draw [drag] all men to myself" (Jn. 12:32 RSV). See Chapter 6, "Drags All."

Why is "all coming to faith" so hard to believe in light of what Scripture teaches about Christ's death and God's power? Just think of your own faith and obedience. You were blessed enough to experience it in this age, perhaps in your youth, or later in life. In any case, it happened. To whom do you give credit for your faith and obedience? Do you credit yourself for being lucky enough to have been at the right place at the right time? Or wise enough to have seen the opportunity and grabbed it (Lu. 10:21; 1Co. 1:26-31)? Or righteous enough to carry your cross and remain faithful to the end? If you do not credit yourself, then you credit another—Christ and His "paid in full" redemption.

If you believe you have faith and are obedient, do you think God arbitrarily selected you over others? No one is any less deserving than you to receive God's mercy. The only way you can believe you are eternally "in" and others are not, is to believe that God arbitrarily selected you over others. Sadly, that clashes head on with the above passages and with all those verses speaking of God's impartiality. It would mean Christ died for all, yet He only chooses some (all equally undeserving) to receive the benefits of His sacrifice. This possibility would dishonor the precious blood shed for all. The words, "He died for all" would become a mockery or cruel lie. You can scratch this possibility off your list (that Christ only chooses some) if you believe the Father of our Lord Jesus Christ is neither arbitrary, cruel, nor deceptive—**unless**, our tradition has missed something about "election." That will be discussed in the next chapter.

◆ ◆ ◆ ◆ ◆

In this chapter, I attempted to lay a solid foundation upon which our hope can stand. I showed that the burden of our Lord's heart was for the whole world. Christian unity is the essential ingredient necessary in God fulfilling His plan for His world. It is important we understand that education, wisdom, and status are not the prerequisites for spiritual revelation. We must be "babes" before Him. We are called to judge for ourselves what is right and to face squarely the question of all questions: "How can a good God create people He knows will be tormented forever?"

The two major views of salvation in Christianity were contrasted with each other. This set the stage to show the Blessed Hope to be the key to Christian unity. Veiled behind the traditional paradigms, we saw the truth about salvation for all mankind— becoming like Christ and the integration of both pardon (through Christ's death) and chastisement. The challenge is to embrace God's promise for the world. This wondrous scope of salvation was traced to God's promise to Abraham, and confirmed by Peter, Paul, and ultimately by Christ on the cross as the sins of the whole world were "paid in full."

Thus, we started with Christ facing the cross with the world on His heart, and closed with His very last words while suspended between heaven and earth: "Father, forgive them....It is finished." Yes, it is finished, and what He finished made the Blessed Hope a reality. In the next chapter, we will address several themes essential to a fuller appreciation of this hope.

CHAPTER FIVE

BLESSED HOPE
PART TWO

*...the bringing in of a better hope, through which
we draw near to God.*
(He. 7:19)

What role has God given the Church in His unfailing plan for man? How do the "ages" or "time" fit into His economy?

Election

Election, to many, is a theological term meaning God has decided in advance who He will save. Its roots go back to Augustine.[1] The Augustinian view of election holds that God has chosen to save a select few—His "elect." Many pastors have been taught this in seminary, particularly those of the Baptist and Reformed persuasions. Fewer and fewer are openly professing it today. One prominent theologian who has exerted a profound influence in Calvinist circles (and on my life 30 years ago), was Arthur Pink. He wrote:

> Faith is God's gift, and "all men have not faith" (2Th. 3:2); therefore, we see God does not bestow this gift upon all. Upon whom then does he bestow this saving favor? We answer, upon his own elect—"As many as were ordained to eternal life believed" (Ac. 13:48) hence it is that we read of "the faith of God's elect" (Tit. 1:1). But is God partial in the distribution of his favors? Has he not the right to be? Are there still some who "murmur against the good man of the house?" Then his own words are sufficient reply—"Is it not lawful for me to do what I will with mine own" (Mt. 20:15)? God is sovereign in the bestowment of his gifts....[2]

Pink frankly stated that God is partial when the testimony of Scripture says He is not (See Nu. 16:22; Ps. 145:9; Ac. 10:34; Ro. 2:11; 10:12-13; Ga. 2:6; Ep. 6:9; Col. 3:25; 1Ti. 2:3, 4; Ja. 3:17; 1Pe. 1:17). The truth in Pink's understanding of election lies in his acceptance of all that the Bible teaches regarding God's power and sovereignty. In this, I agree. God does have the power to draw any one to Himself whom He chooses. The point on which Pink has erred is not in election itself, but in its purpose. Had he understood that, he would not have been forced to draw the conclusion that God does not love all men impartially. The following passages lend support for election: (Mt. 11:27; Mk. 4:12-23; Ac. 13:48; Ro. 8:28-30; 9:4, 11-26; 10:20; 11:5-12; 1Co. 1:23; 2Th. 2:13; 1Ti. 6:12; 2Ti. 2:25; Tit. 1:1; He. 3:6; 9:15; 12:2; Ja. 2:5; 1Pe. 1:2, 3; 2:12).

Purpose of Election

Like Pink, most who believe in election view it solely as deliverance from infinite punishment. However, infinite punishment is not a biblical teaching. God has called a people in election, choosing them for a particular purpose. It has nothing to do with God playing favorites. This has been His way from the time of Abraham and the Israelite nation, down through the centuries to the Church of the firstborn (He. 12:23).

> The Lord said to Abram: "Get out of your country...to a land that I will show you. I will make you a great nation; I will bless you and make your name great; you shall **be a blessing**...in you all families of earth shall be blessed." God...preached the gospel to Abraham beforehand, saying, "In you all the nations shall be blessed." (Ge. 12:1-3; Ga. 3:8). (See Ge. 18:18; 22:18; 26:4; 28:14; Ac. 3:25).

God promised Abraham and his seed that they would be the heirs of the world! (Ro. 4:13). With this comes purpose and great responsibility. We, the "elect," are called to "be" a blessing, and not merely to be "blessed."

"He saved us and called us with a holy calling, not according to our works, but according to His own purpose and grace which was given to us in Christ Jesus before time began" (2Ti. 1:9). "In the exercise of His will He brought us forth by the word of truth, so that we would be a kind of first-fruits among His creatures" (Ja. 1:18 NAS).

We as a "kind of firstfruits" among His creatures share this distinction with Christ who is the "firstborn over all creation" (Col. 1:15). We labor with Him to implore all people to be reconciled with God (2Co 5:20). We are preparing now to rule and reign with Him in the coming ages (2Ti. 2:12; Re. 20:6), to govern five or ten cities (Lu. 19:17, 19), to sit on thrones governing the tribes of Israel (Mt. 19:28; Lu. 22:30), even to rule over all He has (Lu. 12:43-4). Our Lord is preparing leaders for that time, and it all depends on our faithfulness now (2Ti. 2:12-13). The phrase "firstfruits," naturally implies there are "second" fruits. Who are they? They are those whom God will reach in "due time," who are not part of the firstfruits. Christ will draw [drag] all to Himself (Jn. 12:32).

"For if the firstfruit is holy, the lump is also holy" (Ro. 11:16). In God's eyes, all are holy (set apart for Himself) including the lump from which the elect are derived and worthy of His wondrous salvation. Why? Because He is the Father of all creation, and Christ died for everyone. However, you might think the lump refers to the elect Gentiles only. But consider the immediate context of the preceding verses. "Now if their transgression is riches for the world and their failure is riches for the Gentiles, how much more will their fulfillment be!...For if their being cast away is the reconciling of the world, what will their acceptance be but life from the dead" (Ro. 11:12, 15)? As well, James writes, "In the exercise of His will He brought us forth by the word of truth, so that we would be a kind of firstfruits among His creatures" (Ja. 1:18 NAS). "Riches for the world," "reconciling the world," and "firstfruits among His creatures," refer to all men.

> He chose us...before the foundation of the world...predestined us to adoption...according to the good pleasure of His will....having made known to us the mystery of His will, according to His good pleasure which He purposed in Himself, that in the dispensation of the **fullness of the times** He might **gather together in one all [things]** in Christ, both which are in heaven and which are on earth—in Him....predestined according to the purpose of Him who works all things according to the counsel of His will, that we who **first trusted** [firstfruits] in Christ should be to the praise of His glory (Ep. 1:4-12).

Please read this passage carefully noting the words I have emphasized.

> *To what purpose are the elect chosen? To demonstrate an honorable conduct before the lost who may also glorify God on the day of visitation.*

"He made us sit together in the heavenly places in Christ Jesus, that in the *ages to come* He might *show* ["display" WEY/DBY] the exceeding riches of His grace in His kindness toward us in Christ Jesus" (Ep. 2:6-7). To whom does God plan to display the exceeding riches of His grace if not to those in greatest need of it? Why display it to those who have already known and experienced it?

"The household of Stephanas...the *firstfruits* of Achaia...have devoted themselves to the ministry of the *saints*" (1Co. 16:15). As firstfruits, our ministry is both to those within the elect family of God, and to those yet outside. For unless the firstfruits themselves receive the nurture they need, they will lack the brightness of God's reflection before the world (Mt. 5:13-16; Ga. 6:10).

[**Please read Ro. 8:19-23.**]

The creation also will be delivered from corruption. Of course, this includes people. Who groans more than suffering humanity for whom Christ died? The focus here is not the animal kingdom. For all people (as second fruits) in due time, are dragged into Christ (Jn. 12:32). and thus delivered from corruption and brought into the liberty of the firstfruit company. Notice how the phrase "firstfruits" is introduced in the immediate context of the "whole creation"(vs. 22 - 23). Truly, this has great significance.

[**Please read 1Pe. 2:9, 12.**]

To what purpose are the elect chosen? To demonstrate an honorable conduct before the lost that they may glorify God on the day of visitation. Is it not the salvation of the lost that most glorifies God? Those who glorify Him on that day will have come to know Him through the elect! What a responsibility we have!

+ *Do you not know that the saints will judge the world? And...angels* (1Co. 6:2-3)?
+ *Jesus Christ...has made us **kings** and **priests*** (Re. 1:5-6).
+ *These...were redeemed from among men, being **firstfruits** to God...* (Re. 14:4-5).

We are the firstfruits—the priests and kings who will judge the world and intercede for the ungodly (lost) in this age and the ages to come. Note, we are not "exclusive" fruits. We are only "first" fruits among many to come. Andrew Jukes explained:

> To say that God saves only the first-born would be, if it may be said, to make Him worse than even Moloch, whose slaves devoted only their first-born to the flames. But Scripture never says that these only shall be saved, but rather that "in this seed," whose portion as the first-born is double, (De.21:17) "all kindreds of the earth shall be blessed." I fear that the elect, instead of bearing this witness, have too often ignored and even contradicted it. [3]

God does not merely settle for the firstfruits. They are but the pledge for the whole. As a royal priesthood (1Pe. 2:9), we are to labor with Christ in gathering in the whole crop—the remaining fruits. We are to shine as lights in a dark world, and not merely form Christian country clubs. We must guard against exclusiveness toward those "yet" outside the fold.

Is the organized church today much different than the Israelites who stoned Paul and Steven for merely mentioning that the Gentiles were included with them? True, as believers, we have a legal adoption status (See website "Book Updates" p.52 re. adoption.) However, we are nevertheless wild olive shoots grafted in (Ro. 11:17) and as such are not special above the rest of men. We are of the same stock.

For if the firstfruit (elect) is holy, the lump (mankind) is also holy (Ro. 11:15-16). We easily forget that "while" we were enemies we "were" reconciled to God (Ro. 5:10). While "still" sinners Christ died for us (Ro. 5:8; 5:6). We need to keep in mind one principal difference between an "us" and "them" mentality: to whom much is given, much is required (Lu. 12:48).

Plan B

I would like to now address those steeped in Arminian theology (those who do not recognize the role of election in God's plan). Contrary to Arminian beliefs, God never had a "plan B." Christ was "indeed" foreordained before the foundation of the world (1Pe. 1:18-20) "God saved us...before time began..." (2Ti. 1:8-9). "The Lamb was slain from the foundation of the world" (Re. 13:8). "He chose us in

> *The Trinity is not God, the Devil, and the Will of Man!*

Him before the foundation of the world" (Ep. 1:4). God did not do the best He could; He did the best He would! Augustine's idea of infinite penalty was never part of God's plan. For the God of the Universe is GOD, not god. The Trinity is not God, the Devil, and the Will of Man! This is polytheism. But God Is One! To say God had to change His plans due to man's unpredictability does grave injustice to God's absolute sovereignty over His creation, His power, His wisdom, His knowledge, and His victory over all evil. In truth, it does nothing less than strip Him of His DEITY.

As I look closely at the Scriptures, I see a God who knows where He is going; a God who knows the future. God has but one plan and the following passages bear this out.

- *And I will put enmity between you and the woman, and between your seed and her Seed; He shall bruise your head, And you shall bruise His heel* (Ge. 3:15).
- *Then He said to Abram: "Know certainly that your descendants will be strangers in a land that is not theirs, and will serve them, and they will afflict them four hundred years. And also the nation whom they serve I will judge; afterward they shall come out with great possessions"* (Ge. 15:13-14).

> *Before I formed you in the womb I knew you.*
> *(Jer. 1:5)*

- *But I am sure that the king of Egypt will not let you go, no, not even by a mighty hand* (Ex. 3:19).
- *I am God, and there is none like Me, declaring the end from the beginning, and from ancient times things that are not yet done, saying, "My counsel shall stand, and I will do all My pleasure....Indeed I have spoken it; I will also bring it to pass. I have purposed it; I will also do it"* (Is. 46:9-11).
- *Before I formed you in the womb I knew you* (Jer. 1:5).
- We are *"predestined according to the purpose of Him who 'works all things' according to the counsel of His will"* (Ep. 1:11).

For more examples, you may consider these: Ex. 9:30; 11:9; 1K. 13:1-5, 32; 21:20-22; 2K. 8:12; Ps. 147:5; Is. 41:21-26; 44:11, 28; 65:24-

25; Mt. 10:17, 18, 21, 22; 11:14, 21; 12:45; 13:35; 24:2, 33-41; Mk. 14:30; Lu. 14:28-32; Jn. 6:64; 8:20; 21:18-19; Ac. 2:23; 15:8, 18; 17:26; Ro. 4:17; 8:29-30; 11:2, 33; Ga. 3:8; 2Ti. 1:9; Tit. 1:2; He. 4:13; 1Pe. 1:2, 19-20; 1Jn. 3:20; 5:14; Re. 13:8; 17:18. (In addition, consider all the Messianic Prophecies). Incidentally, this is not an exhaustive list.

Due Time

According to Andrew Jukes, three principles solve the great riddle of mercy for all (Ro. 11:32) and of the few finding the way (Mt. 7:14): the biblical understanding of God's judgments, His purposes in election, and His appointed times. Jukes wrote, "These truths throw a flood of light on Scripture, and enable us at once to see order and agreement, where without this light there seems perplexing inconsistency."[4]

We need to take seriously the many references to God's appointed times. How do they relate to God's loving purposes in bringing salvation to all men (Tit. 2:11 NAS)? When will it take place? Let us see.

♦ *God...will have all men to be saved, and to come unto the knowledge of the truth. For...Christ...gave Himself a ransom for all, to be testified in **due time** (1Ti. 2:3-6 KJV). Christ gave Himself a ransom for all, which will be testified [or proved TEV, NEB] in its proper time or era.*

♦ *He has made everything beautiful **in its time** (Ec. 3:11).*

♦ ***At that time** Jerusalem shall be called the Throne of the LORD, and all the nations shall be gathered to it, to the name of the LORD....No more shall they follow the dictates of their evil hearts (Jer. 3:17).*

♦ *The fierce anger of the LORD will not turn back **until** He fully accomplishes the purposes of His heart. In **days to come** you will understand this (Jer. 30:24 NIV).*

♦ ***Seventy weeks** are determined for your people and for your holy city, to finish the transgression, to make an end of sins, to make reconciliation*

> *God... will have all men to be saved, and to come unto the knowledge of the truth.... For... Christ ...gave Himself a ransom for all, to be testified in due time.*
>
> *(1Ti. 2:3-6 KJV)*

for iniquity, to bring in everlasting righteousness... (Da. 9:24).

♦ *Whom heaven must receive **until the times** of restoration of all things, which God has spoken by the mouth of all His holy prophets since the world began* (Ac. 3:21).

♦ ***To you first**, God, having raised up His Servant Jesus, sent Him to bless you, in turning away every one of you from your iniquities* (Ac. 3:26).

♦ *At **this present time** there is a remnant according to the election of grace* (Ro. 11:5).

♦ *Do not... be ignorant of this mystery...blindness in part **has happened** to Israel **until** the fullness of the Gentiles has come in. So **all Israel will be saved**....The Deliverer will come...He will turn away ungodliness from Jacob; for this is My covenant with them, **when** I take away their sins* (Ro. 11:25-27) (See also Ro. 11:8). Note Paul does not distinguish between Jew and Greek (Ro. 10:12-13).

♦ *In the dispensation of the **fullness of the times** He might gather together in one all things in Christ, both which are in heaven and which are on earth—in Him* (Ep. 1:9-10).

♦ *In the **ages to come** He might show [display WEY—DBY] the exceeding riches of His grace in His kindness toward us in Christ Jesus* (Ep. 2:7).

[Please read 1Co. 15:22-28.]

♦ ***For as** in Adam **all** die, **so also** in Christ **all** will be made alive* (1Co. 15:22 NAS).

♦ *But each in his own order: Christ the **firstfruits**, **after** that those who are Christ's at His coming. **Then** comes the end, **when**...* (1Co. 15:23-24 NAS).

When what? "When all things are subjected to Him...that God may be all in all" (1Co. 15:28 NAS). Notice the four critical time references used here: "firstfruits," "after," "then...when." These time words seem to relate to three separate time periods (orders) and three categories of persons.

Christ the **"firstfruits"** .... **Christ** .... 1st **order**

"After" those who are
Christ's at His coming................. **Elect** .... 2nd **order**

"Then" comes the end
"when"...all things
are subjected to Him................... **Mankind** .... 3rd **order**

What is the goal of all being subjected to Christ? That God may be all in all. "*When* all things [people] are subjected to Him, *then* the Son Himself also will be subjected to the One who subjected all things to Him, so *that God may be all in all*" (1Co. 15:28 NAS).

What is the meaning of "God may be all in all" for those who submit to Christ? This is a most critical question. It means those who have submitted acknowledge the Lordship of Jesus Christ as evidenced by their sincere submission. Should we be surprised? Once all ignorance and rebellion are abolished (1Co. 13:12; He. 2:8), what is left to prevent faith and trust? In addition to all becoming subjected to Christ, the last enemy (death) no longer exists (1Co. 15:26). The significance of death destroyed can be none other than life restored, or the statement is meaningless. Now, with no more death and rebellion, God becomes all in all. This points to a glorious transformation and culmination of human experience into the very nature of God Himself—the complete realization of what we were meant to be.

> You **have put** [past tense] *all* things in **subjection** under his feet. For in that He put [past tense] all in subjection under Him, He left **nothing** that is not put under Him. **But now** we do not **yet** see all [things] put under Him (He. 2:8).

This is a very revealing passage. It assures us that though all have not "yet" made Christ their Master, they will! "You *have put* all in subjection." Christ works in every life toward this goal and cannot fail. All in "due" time will come to a place of genuine repentance. "He left *nothing* that is not put under Him." Nothing! God can refer to future events as past—"God...calls those things which do not exist as though they did"(Ro. 4:17b); for He is the eternal "I AM" (Ex. 3:14) who transcends time (Ps.90:4; Ep. 1:4, 10; 2:7; He. 13:8; 2Pe. 3:8).

The Greek word for "subjected," here is *hupotasso* (Strong's # 5293)[5], which applies to both Christ and man. "Now, whenever all may be subjected [5293] to Him, then the Son [as the Son of Man—Man's representative Head] Himself also shall be subjected [5293]..." (1Co. 15:28 CLT). Paul uses this same word in the context of the righteousness of faith: "They being *ignorant* of God's righteousness... *have not submitted* [5293] to the righteousness of God... righteousness to everyone who believes" (Ro. 10:3, 4).

Once God lifts the veil covering all eyes, and His righteousness in Christ is revealed, what will stop all from submitting to Christ? A submitted and believing heart brings glory and honor to God, and conforms to such an awesome thought as "God all in all." That is precisely why submission will take ages to achieve. Sure, God could cause all creation to bow to Him instantly by brute force. He could have done that ages ago. But this is not the submission worthy of a God who "is" love. "He is able even to subdue [win the hearts of] all things to Himself" (Ph. 3:21). "Christ...seated...above all...not only in this age but also in that which is to come. And He put all things under His feet...Him who fills all in all" (Ep. 1:20-23).

What a God! He has a plan for man that transcends everything Augustinian theology has ever taught us. I now know He makes everything beautiful in its time. Unfortunately, many of Scripture's critical time statements have been veiled to us by the mistranslation of the Greek word *aion*. (See Appendix V: Disturbing Facts).

Last Things

Biblical truth is not always presented in chronological order. The truths regarding the end of the ages and the restoration of all things take place beyond the scope of the book of Revelation. For at no time in Revelation do we see an end to all rule, authority, and power. For Christ must reign until He has put all enemies under His feet, including death. Only when all things are subjected to Him, will God be all in all (1Co. 15:28). At no point in Revelation does that take place. In verse 15 of the last chapter, we read of sorcerers, the sexually immoral, murderers, idolaters, and liars lurking outside the gates of the New Jerusalem.

The Holy City, if interpreted literally, will cover an area about the size of half the continental USA (Re. 21:16), and there will be no sea (Re. 21:1). Therefore, you can imagine how big the outside world is going to be. Scripture says kings will visit the city (Re. 21:24). It identifies them as those who have "washed their robes, (NAS), that they may have the right to the tree of life, and *may enter through the gates into the city*" (Re. 22:14). It is evident sinners will be outside the gates; they will come to repentance, do His commandments, and enter through the gates into the city. Why not?

Does God change? Ja. 1:17 refers to God as "the Father of lights, with whom there is no variation or shadow of turning." See also the following verses:

- *For I am the LORD, I do not change; therefore you are not consumed, O sons of Jacob* (Mal. 3:6).
- *God is love. Love never ends* (1Jn. 4:8, 16; 1Co. 13:8 RSV).
- *The same yesterday, today, and forever* (He. 13:8).

He pursues the lost sheep and will continue to do so until He finds them! We will labor with Him, as His joint heirs and fellow workers in His world harvest field!

Although the book of Revelation is the last book in the Bible, it was Paul, not John, who received the most far-reaching and profound revelations of Christ and God's purposes for the Church. Consider Col. 1:15-20 for example. He was entrusted with the task of completing the word of God, or making it fully known (Col. 1:25-26).

"I became a minister according to the divine office, which was given to me for you, *to make the word of God fully known, the mystery hidden for ages* and generations but now made manifest to his saints" (Col. 1:25-26 RSV). Darby & CLT read, "to complete the word of God."

Paul was named the "Apostle to the Gentiles" (Ro. 11:13). We can call him "our Apostle." To Him was given the truth regarding justification by faith and the law's purpose; Israel and the Church, with no distinction between Jew and Gentile; the fruits of the Spirit and the priority of Christian unity; the Bride of Christ and our freedom in Him; spiritual gifts with love as the more excellent way; Church government and the five-fold ministry; instructions pertaining to worship, the Lord's supper, family relationships, giving, diet, godly living, church discipline, spiritual warfare, civil government; and finally, the consummation of the ages (1 Corinthians fifteen) climaxing in the ultimate reconciliation of humanity – with God all in all. All this came through Paul.

♦ ♦ ♦ ♦ ♦

The Blessed Hope chapters were the most challenging for me to write. In them, I attempted to clearly present the Blessed Hope—a glorious hope encompassing a global view of God's plan for man that truly rejoices the heart. In this chapter, I have shown that God has called us, His "elect," to be lights in the world. We have been given a privileged status, not for ourselves, but for Him, in serving all people. God is truly sovereign over all creation, and has but one plan. His destiny for all men cannot be thwarted, and will come to pass in His due time. To see God's unfailing plan unfold in Scripture, we must understand the true meaning of key biblical words like *aion*. In addition, remember Paul (not John) was given the revelation of the consummation of the ages.

I challenge you to look at all Scripture from the viewpoint of God's absolute Sovereignty and infinite love. We must understand judgment in light of who God is, and not God from a flawed view of judgment. Judgment only serves God's unfailing purposes for all. I offer these thoughts, not as one with great knowledge, but merely as one who believes in a great GOD. I pray He imparts to you only what pleases Him. I invite you to take a journey with me through the passages that have sealed the Blessed Hope in my heart.

CHAPTER SIX

PROCLAMATIONS
PART ONE

The word...upon which You have caused me to hope.
(Ps. 119:49)

*T*he above verse says perfectly what the next two chapters are a-bout. Here, I submit to you over 35 texts that either directly confirm or indirectly support my conviction in the Blessed Hope. Truly, they are the word upon which He has caused me to hope. They speak powerfully to me. I have arranged them in alphabetical order with a few exceptions. Please pray for God's revelation as you read these precious passages.

All Is Possible

With God all things are possible.
(Jer. 32:17; Mt. 19:24-26; Mk. 10:27; Lu. 18:26)

With God all things are possible? Do we believe this statement? Is it possible that an all-powerful God who can do anything, and who loves everyone, cannot save whom He will, or will not save whom He can? I can accept one might admit they do not know if God can or would save those in hell. But, to say dogmatically "there can never be any hope" is a frank denial of this passage, God's power, and the many promises made in Scripture.

Beatitudes

Blessed are you poor, for yours is the kingdom of God.
Blessed are you who hunger now, for you shall be filled.
Blessed are you who weep now, for you shall laugh.
(Lu. 6:20-21)

Christ was not speaking only to believers here as seen in Lu. 6:19, 7:1; Mt. 5:1-2, 7:28-29; and Mt. 8:1. He addressed the crowd.

According to our tradition, the majority of mankind is hopelessly lost. Therefore, when will these lost ones receive the kingdom, be filled, and laugh? I no longer struggle with this passage, as I can simply accept it as it is. This is one more example of how the Scriptures are harmonized as a result of the Blessed Hope.

Creation Freed

For the earnest expectation of the creation eagerly waits for the revealing of the sons of God. For the creation was subjected to futility, not willingly, but because of Him who subjected it in hope because the **creation** *itself also* **will be delivered** *from the bondage of corruption into the glorious liberty of the children of God. For we know the whole creation groans and labors with birth pangs until now.*
(Ro. 8:19-22)

"Creation" in the above passage certainly includes people. Christ died for people. What part of creation groans and labors with birth pangs more than people? All people in God's appointed time will be delivered from the bondage of corruption and share in the blessings of the sons of God, the firstfruits (elect) of His creation. That is what this glorious passage says. Any other view demeans this precious promise into something insignificant. If people are not referred to here, how do we understand the following passages?

> *All people…will be delivered from the bondage of corruption and share in the blessings of the sons of God, the firstfruits.*

- ◆ *Go into all the world and preach the gospel to every creature* (Mk. 16:15).
- ◆ *If anyone is in Christ, he is a new creation* (2Co. 5:17).
- ◆ *In Christ, neither circumcision nor uncircumcision avails but a new creation* (Ga. 6:15).

"Creation" clearly includes people! Oh, if we would only see how central people are in this passage. We could then fully experience the great comfort and joy it was intended to impart to our hearts!

Death Destroyed

The last enemy that will be destroyed is death....
(1Co. 15:26)

German scholar and Bible translator A.E. Knoch said this re-garding the last enemy:

> Death at any time is an enemy. We are agreed on that. The second death is an enemy. One of these is the last enemy. Is it the first or second? Can the first death be the last en-emy? No enemy can be last if it has another coming after it. Hence the single word last is all the proof needed to estab-lish the fact that it must be the second death which will be abolished.[1]

If death, the last enemy, is destroyed, then life is the result. If this is not so, the statement is void of meaning. For what is the opposite of death? For the process of dying is not the greatest or last enemy, it is the state of death itself. Whether death be the first, second, or tenth, nothing changes because "death" in 1Co. 15:26 is not qualified. Scripture includes any types there may be. All death is an enemy. "O Death, where is your sting? O Hades [hell], where is your victory? The sting of death is sin....But thanks be to God, who gives us the victory through Christ" (1Co. 15:55-57). Only life re-mains—life more abundant! (Jn. 10:10).

Drags All

Now is the judgment of this world; now the ruler of this world will be cast out. And I, when I am lifted up from the earth, will draw all men to myself.
(Jn. 12:31-32)

Once the judgment of this world has run its full course and the ruler of this world is cast out, Christ will drag all men to Himself. A little further (vs. 47), He states that He came "to save the world" (not merely "some" out of it). The word "draw" (*helkouo*) is literally "to drag."[2] It does not depend on the resistance of the one being pulled, but on the power of the one pulling.

See the following passages:

- *Peter, having a sword, **drew** it and struck ...(Jn. 18:10).*
- *Peter went up and **dragged** the net to land, full of large fish* (Jn. 21:11).
- *They seized Paul and Silas and **dragged** them into the market place* (Ac. 16:19 NAS).
- *Taking hold of Paul, they **dragged** him out of the temple* (Ac. 21:30 NAS).
- *Is it not the rich who...**drag** you into court* (Ja. 2:6)?

As the "sword," "net," "Paul," "Silas," and the poor were not able to resist the powers that overcame them, neither can men resist Christ's power to drag them. No one can come to God unless the Father drags them in (Jn. 6:44). The stress of the power is placed on God who drags, and not a person's resistance to being dragged.

Especially Believers

This is a faithful saying and worthy of all acceptance.
For to this end we both labor and suffer reproach, because we trust in
the living God, who is the Savior of all men, especially of those who
believe. These things command and teach.
(1Ti. 4:9-10)

This must be a very important passage to warrant such a powerful introduction and closing. Notice Paul exhorts us to view these faithful words as worthy of all acceptance, and tells us to command and teach these truths. Understand the importance of this critical passage. If God is the Savior exclusively of those who believe during their earthly existence, as our tradition teaches, why is this passage saying something different? The difference between "exclusively" and "especially" is significant; to interchange these two concepts is to contradict Scripture.

What does "especially of those who believe" mean? The immediate context sheds much light: "Set the believers an example....practice these duties....so that all may see your progress. Take heed to yourself and teaching; hold to that, for *by so doing you will save* both yourself and your hearers" (1Ti. 4:12-16 RSV).

Is this salvation by works? No, it is "working out" salvation (Ph. 2:12). God's purpose in salvation is not to save us in our sins (Mt.

1:21), but from them. Christ saves us from our sinful nature and transforms us into His image (Ga. 4:19) so we may shine as lights in the world (Mt. 5:13-16). Thus, believers are "especially" saved because they have been justified by faith, and are presently working out their salvation as God empowers them (Ph. 2:13). Their salvation is being perfected (made complete) for all to see (1Ti. 4:15-16).

None of this changes the fact that God is still the Savior of those who do not yet believe. Once His righteous, just, and purpose-driven judgments have run their course, death will be destroyed, all will be made alive, and all will be subjected to Christ. Then God will be all in all (1Co. 15:22-28). He is, in an ultimate sense, the Savior of all men, (unbelievers and believers) but especially, at present, of believers.

The key word is *malista*, translated "especially." Could it also mean "exclusively"? The only way to know is to observe how it is used in Scripture. This is a good example of how useful *The Word Study Concordance* can be. It occurs 12 times. As you read the references below, try substituting the word "exclusively" and see how it fits.

- *They wept and fell on Paul's neck sorrowing **most of all** for the words which he spoke* (Ac. 20:38).
- *I have brought him out before you, and **especially** before you* (Ac. 25:24-27).
- *King Agrippa...**especially** because you are expert* (Ac. 26:2-3).

> *God… is the Savior of all men, especially [not exclusively] of those who believe.*
> *(1Ti. 4:10)*

- *Let us do good to all, **especially** to those who are of faith* (Ga. 6:9-10).
- *All the saints greet you, but **especially** those who are of Caesar's household* (Ph. 4:20-23).
- *If anyone does not provide for his own, and **especially** for those of his household…* (1Ti. 5:3-8).
- *Elders be counted worthy of double honor, **especially** those who labor in the word and doctrine* (1Ti. 5:16-18).
- *Bring the cloak…and the books, **especially** the parchments* (2Ti. 4:13).
- *There are many…deceivers, **especially** those of the circumcision…* (Tit. 1:10-11).

- *But more than a slave—a beloved brother, **especially** to me but how much more to you (Phil. 16).*
- *Reserve...for the day of judgment, and **especially** those who walk according to the flesh (2Pe. 2:9-11).*

Could you accurately substitute "exclusively" for "especially" in these passages? If you could not here, on what grammatical or contextual grounds can you do it in 1Ti. 4:10? This text, rightly understood in light of the other proclamations in this section and the evidence presented elsewhere, offers solid ground to believe what it says. God is the Savior of "all men," especially (and not exclusively) of those who believe. Let us command and teach this!

Every Knee

At [in] the name of Jesus every knee will bow, of those who are in heaven and on earth and under the earth, and that every tongue will confess that Jesus Christ is Lord, to the glory of God the Father.
(Ph. 2:10-11 NAS) See also Ps. 66:3-4; Is. 45:22-25; Ro. 14:11; Re. 5:13

It is tragic that our hell theology has forced us to deny the glorious majesty of this great declaration. It has forced us to read into it a compelled submission, as one would give to a tyrant such as Hitler or Nero. Without such a prejudice, we would never have looked at it that way. A close examination of the context will show that only a genuine adoration is possible. I list 18 points to demonstrate this. (See Appendix VI).

Forgive Them

"Father, forgive them."
(Lu. 23:34)

Jesus prayed from the cross, "Father, forgive them" (Lu. 23:34). Who really nailed Jesus to the cross, a handful of Roman soldiers or all of us? Do you think those cruel and merciless soldiers were forgiven that day? I do. Why? Because Jesus prayed for them and sealed His request in His very own blood. I cannot believe God would forgive the soldiers who actually tortured Christ while the mass of mankind, for whom He was so tortured, are forever barred from forgiveness. Do you?

Fullness of Times

*Having made known to us the mystery of His will, according to His good pleasure which He purposed in Himself, that in the dispensation of the **fullness of the times** He might **gather together in one all** things in Christ, both which are in heaven and which are on earth—in Him...who works all things according to the counsel of His will.*
(Ep. 1:9-11)

The good pleasure of God is to gather together in one all people, from every place. A time is coming when this promise will be realized in all its greatness. For God is truly GOD, a God who works all things out according to the counsel (purpose) of His will. This is not just "wishful" thinking on His part; it is His decree. What He decrees will take place and nothing—not even man's sin—or will can stop it (Job 42:2; Ez. 36:27; Da. 4:35). This passage says in God's good time, He will bring everyone into Christ. This is not hard to believe for those who know His nature and power.

For As...Even So

For as in Adam all die, even so in Christ all shall be made alive.
(1Co. 15:22)

Would the following statement sound strange to you? "For as in the pre-Civil War era **all** African Americans were slaves, **even so**, in the post-Civil War era, **some** African Americans were given liberty." Of course it sounds strange. It doesn't make sense.

+ In "For as **all**...even so **all**," the agreement makes grammatical sense.
+ In "For as **all**...even so **some**," the statement makes no grammatical sense because "all" and "some" do not agree in context: "for as...even so" requires agreement. Grammatically, you cannot say, "all" to mean "some." "All" means "inclusive;" "some" does not.

Some say that "made alive" simply means all are resurrected to judgment. The whole context argues against such a thought, for "made alive" is presented solely as something glorious and positive. (I discuss this next). Others claim "all" refers to two completely different groups of persons. Only those "in" Christ are made alive, inferring the majority of mankind is excluded. This would be tautology, for it is like saying, only the saved will be saved. Of even greater weight is the context: in such a glorious chapter as this, to say "only the saved will be saved" would seem a forced or strained interpretation. For in what way then would death be destroyed, swallowed up in victory, and its sting lost (See 1Co. 15:26-28, 54-55)? Do the magnificent words of these verses fit with a victory affecting just a small fraction of the earth's population?

The Jerusalem Bible states it this way: "Just as all men die in Adam, so all men will be brought to life in Christ" (1Co. 15:22).

Made Alive

For as in Adam all die, even so in Christ all shall be made alive.
(1Co. 15:22)

To some, "made alive" means merely to resurrect in order to annihilate. The word is *zōopoieō* (Strongs #2227). It is the verb form of *zōē* (#2222). Vine defines it as, "to make alive, cause to live, quicken" from *zōē*, "life," and *poieō*, "to make."[3] *Zōē* is the same word used in Jn. 3:16, and in more than 130 New Testament passages. "I am the way, the truth, and the life [*zōē*]" (Jn. 14:6). The phrase "made alive," (*zōopoieō*) is used only 12 times (Jn. 5:21a, 21b; 6:63; Ro. 4:17; 8:11; 1Co. 15:22, 36, 45; 2Co. 3:6; Ga. 3:21; 1Ti. 6:13; 1Pe. 3:18). Try to read the idea of annihilation or everlasting torment in these references and see if they fit. You will quickly see they refer only to a positive and glorious spiritual life.

Last Adam

"As through one transgression there resulted condemnation to all men, even so through one act of righteousness there resulted justification of life to all men. For as through the one man's disobedience the many were made sinners, even so through the obedience of the One the many will be made righteous."
(Ro. 5:18-19 NAS)

Let's take a moment to break down and discuss this text.

Clause 1. *"As through* **one** *transgression there resulted condem-nation* **to all** *men,*

Clause 2. **even so** *through* **one** *act of righteousness there resulted justification of life* **to all** *men.*

Clause 3. **For as** *through* **the one** *man's disobedience* **the many** *were made sinners,*

Clause 4. **even so** *through the obedience of the* **One the many** *will be made righteous"* (Ro. 5:18-19 NAS).

Why should "the many" in clause 4 refer to a different group than "the many" in clause 3, since nothing is said to indicate a difference? Only someone trying to support an agenda would try to read into it such an idea. In addition, it would contradict clauses 1 and 2. The point made in clauses 3 and 4 is singularity versus plurality.

Singular..................versus....................plural
the one...............**affecting**.............**the many**

Since everyone agrees all men were made sinners, clause 1 clearly refers to all men. Clause 2 argues from clause 1 and even states all men are in view. In clause 3, Paul expounds his thought further, he points out Adam, though only one person, has affected the lives of the multitudes of mankind (the many). No one will argue "the many" in clause 3 is not all men. So also, in clause 4, the exact comparison is being made except that "the One" affecting the lives of the multitudes of mankind (the many) is Christ. The "many" of clause 4 must be the same "many" as clause 3 because nothing is stated to the contrary. The "for as" followed by the "even so" requires the agreement. An honest seeker of truth must acknowledge these relationships. Basic grammar and ethics require it.

> *For as through the disobedience of the one individual the mass of mankind were constituted sinners, so also through the obedience of the One the mass of mankind will be constituted righteous.*
>
> *(Ro. 5:19 WEY).*

The Weymouth translation words it clearly.

> *It follows then that just as the result of a single transgression is a condemnation which extends to the whole race, so also the result of a single decree of righteousness is a life-giving acquittal which extends to the whole race. For as through the disobedience of the one individual the mass of mankind were constituted sinners, so also through the obedience of the One the mass of mankind will be constituted righteous* (Ro. 5:18-19 WEY).

Joseph Kirk, pastor, radio preacher, and former director of *Scripture Studies Concern*, said it this way:

> But someone will ask, Why does it say "the many" instead of "all" in verse 19? This is because the one disobedient man and the One righteous Man are put in a class by themselves. They are in contrast with "the many." We may put it as follows: The one disobedient man plus "the many" equals all mankind made sinners. The One obedient Man plus "the many" equals all mankind made righteous. That "the one" plus "the many" made sinners, includes all mankind, few, if any, attempt to deny. Even so, "the One" plus "the many" made righteous is all-inclusive and guarantees justification of life for all mankind.[4]

See also Richard H. Bell's "Romans 5:18-19," *New Testament Studies*, Vol. 48 (2002), pp. 417-432. This Tübingen scholar argues "that Paul does in fact support a universal salvation in Rom. 5.18–19. Such an understanding is supported by both the context and by a detailed study of these verses" (p. 417).[5]

Finally, to get the full sense of Paul's force of argument, we need to meditate on the whole context, especially verses 12 through 21. In the event Paul might be misunderstood, he spells it out clearly in his closing statement. "Where sin abounded, grace abounded *much more*" (Ro. 5:20)! How can a believer claim Christ gained back less than what Adam lost?

One phrase has been used to reduce the "many" in Christ to mean the "few": "For if by the one man's offense death reigned through the one, much more those *who receive* abundance of grace and of the gift of righteousness will reign in life through the One, Jesus Christ" (Ro. 5:17). Paul is comparing Adam to Christ. He refers to "those who receive [*lambanō*]" in a passive sense. Adam sinned, and as a result, all men have received (passively) the consequences of his action. The consequences of Christ's action must also be received in the same manner, or Paul's whole argument falls apart. Dr. Bell's exegesis confirms this. 5 Consider the following examples of Paul's use of the word, *lambanō*, in the very same letter:

+ *Through Him, we have received [lambanō] grace and apostleship for obedience to the faith among all nations for His name* (Ro. 1:5).
+ *We also rejoice in God through our Lord Jesus Christ, through whom we have now received [lambanō] the reconciliation* (Ro. 5:11).
+ *For you did not receive [lambanō] the spirit of bondage again to fear, but you received [lambanō] the Spirit of adoption by whom we cry out, "Abba, Father"* (Ro. 8:15).

In which of these cases is *lambanō* used in an active, qualifying sense? They are all examples of passively receiving something as a result of factors outside of ourselves. In the same way we have received (*lambanō*) the Spirit of adoption, or sin in Adam, we have received (*lambanō*) abundance of grace in Christ. See how this passage reads in the literal versions.

+ *For if by the offense of the one the death did reign through the one, much more those, who the abundance of the grace and of the free gift of the righteousness are receiving, in life shall reign through the one—Jesus Christ* (Ro. 5:17 YLT).
+ *For if, by the offense of the one, death reigns through the one, much rather, those obtaining the superabundance of grace and the gratuity of righteousness shall be reigning in life through the One, Jesus Christ* (Ro. 5:17 CLT).
+ *For, if, by the fault of the one, death reigned through the one, much more, they who the superabundance of the favour and of the free-gift of the righteousness do receive, in life, shall reign through the one, Jesus Christ* (Ro. 5:17 ROTH).

For your scrutiny, I submit this passage in the *Greek Interlinear New Testament*. It illustrates the exact relationship between the words of Scripture, incorporating the *Strong's Concordance* numbering system:

ei <1487> {**IF**} *gar* <1063> {**FOR**} *tw* <3588> {**BY THE**} *tou* <3588> {**OF THE**} *enov* <1520> {**ONE**} *paraptwmati* <3900> *o* <3588> {**OFFENCE**} *yanatov* <2288> {**DEATH**} *ebasileusen* <936> (5656) {**REIGNED**} *dia* <1223> {**BY**} *tou* <3588> {**THE**} *enov* <1520> {**ONE,**} *pollw* <4183> {**MUCH**} *mallon* <3123> {**MORE**} *oi* <3588> {**THOSE**} *thn* <3588> {**THE**} *perisseian* <4050> *thv* <3588> {**ABUNDANCE**} *caritov* <5485> {**OF GRACE**} *kai* <2532> {**AND**} *thv* <3588> {**OF THE**} *dwreav* <1431> *thv* <3588> {**GIFT**} *dikaiosunhv* <1343> {**OF RIGHTEOUSNESS**} *lambanontev* <2983> (5723) {**RECEIVING,**} *en* <1722> {**IN**} *zwh* <2222> {**LIFE**} *basileusousin* <936> (5692) {**SHALL REIGN**} *dia* <1223> {**BY**} *tou* <3588> {**THE**} *enov* <1520> {**ONE**} *ihsou* <2424> {**JESUS**} *cristou* <5547> {**CHRIST**} (Ro. 5:17)

If *lambanō* in this passage was meant to be understood in an active, qualifying sense in this age only, then it would restrict the "all" to those who were lucky or blessed enough to even have heard the Gospel in their earthly life; those who were intelligent enough to have understood it clearly; those who were wise enough to accept it; and those who were faithful enough to deny themselves, take up their cross, and endure to the end. If this is so, then the language Paul is using in verses 12-21 is very strange indeed! Only those forced to make Paul's argument fit their theology would insist *lambanō* in this context is the active sense.

Paul's argument is irrefutable: God, who is Love, sent Christ, "a life-giving spirit" as the last Adam (1Co. 15:45). In His eternal purpose—from before the foundation of the world (Ep. 1:4; Re. 13:8)—He sent Christ to undo all the harm committed by the first Adam.

Much More

Where sin abounded, grace abounded much more.
(Ro. 5:20)

"If the ministry of condemnation had glory, the ministry of righteousness exceeds *much more* in glory" (2Co. 3:9). Is Adam's work in destroying lives greater than Christ's work in restoring them? If, as a result of the first Adam's sin, infinite punishment reigns over the whole human race, then what the second Adam has accomplished in rescuing a few is infinitely "much less," not "much more." Consider how the Weymouth translation reads:

> *But God's free gift immeasurably outweighs the trans-gression. For if through the transgression of the one indi-vidual the mass of mankind have died, infinitely greater [much more] is the generosity with which God's grace, and the gift given in His grace which found expression in the one man Jesus Christ, have been bestowed on the mass of mankind* (Ro. 5:15 WEY).

God Changes People

I will...cause you to walk in My statutes, and...do them.
(Ez. 36:26-27)

Is God a respecter of persons? What He has done for these, will He not do for others? Sadly, our flawed tradition has kept us from knowing Him in His unlimited power and unstoppable will to change people. Scripture clearly teaches it. For God to sentence even one person to infinite penalty only proves He cannot or will not change that person, and it is a frank contradiction of who He is.

God Does Right

Shall not the Judge of all the earth do right?
(Ge. 18:25)

Is there a double standard? If something is wrong for God, is it not also wrong for His creation? How many people truly believe God would knowingly create a world of people who would suffer infinite punishment? Many Christians acquiesce to this belief because they think the standard of right and wrong for God is not the same as the stan-dard of right and wrong for His creation. They erroneously base this belief on Is. 55:8; "For My thoughts are not your thoughts, nor are your ways My ways." By simply quoting this one passage, they think they can justify an eternal hell. But they ignore the context. The phrase refers to God's mercy, not cruelty! Read the passage (Is. 55:7-12) for

> *God's ways are higher than ours relative to mercy, not cruelty!*

yourself. Those who have a right concept of morality, love, and justice, know a loving God could never inflict unjust (infinite) punishment.

God Wills All Saved

Who will have all men saved....
(1Ti. 2:4 KJV)

Consider this text in context:

> *I exhort first of all that supplications, **prayers**, inter-cessions,...be made **for all men**....this is **good and ac-ceptable** in the sight of God our Savior; **Who will have all men to be saved**, and to come unto the knowledge of the truth....Christ Jesus; Who gave himself a **ransom for all**, to be **testified in due time*** (1Ti. 2:1-6 KJV).

Our Lord rebuked His people for invalidating God's word for the sake of tradition (Mt. 15:6 NAS). Have we not done the same thing? Because we cannot accept that God is truly all-powerful to do His will, we have made His "will" into a mere "desire," thus negating the force of His words.

Have we not demeaned the power of prayer for all men? We deny Christ really ransomed all. What kind of a sovereign would not release the ransomed when the penalty has been paid in full?

We make the clause "testified in due time," meaningless. What is really good and acceptable in the sight of God our Savior? The majority of our race forever cursed?

The Blessed Hope glories in every dot and tittle of this passage! Nothing needs to be explained away. (See page 42, "God's Will").

◆ ◆ ◆ ◆ ◆

It is my hope that you will prayerfully reflect on the proclamations expounded in these two chapters. Please do not rush through them, but allow the Holy Spirit time to impart these glorious promises to your heart.

CHAPTER SEVEN

PROCLAMATIONS PART TWO

Good News

*Behold, I bring you good tidings of great joy
which will be to **all people**.*
(Lu. 2:10)

*T*he Christian message is a message of peace and glad tidings of good things! (Ro. 10:15) It is supposed to be good tidings of great joy which will be to **all** people. That includes the billions who have never heard of Christ in this life. However, our tradition has limited the Good News to only the following three small classes of individuals.

+ Those who have received Christ (in this life) and who are not yet truly burdened about any of their lost loved ones.
+ Those who have received Christ (in this life) and who care more about their own "personal" salvation than the rest of humanity—billions of their fellow human beings which Christ loves and died for, and whom they should be loving "as" themselves (Mt. 22:39).
+ Those who have received Christ (in this life) and who ignore or fail to take to heart the numerous warning passages addressed to believers. (See Appendix II)

Do you find yourself in one of these classes? I believe I can speak with some authority having personally experienced all three scenarios. According to the prevalent theology, "great joy" is reserved solely for these. Where does that leave the "all people" of Luke 2:10? Hopelessly lost. Not so! The angel was not lying. Great joy will become a precious reality for all people in God's due time.

But to be fair, how does the prevalent view interpret Luke 2:10? It must define the "all" to mean "all classes" of people. This allows it to harmonize with the idea that the whole world is riding on a train destined for an "eternal" hell with only a "privileged" few (from every class) being spared this horrific fate. (See Appendix III #2.)

A note about our attitude in this privileged status: We rejoice in our "personal" rescue operation. We sing, laugh, and are merry in worship. We thank God for our personal rescue while the rest of our human family race down the tracks to everlasting pain. Something just doesn't feel right to me. Is this how Jesus would be?

The only view that I believe leads to lasting, unselfish, and unwavering joy, is to believe what it clearly says – "**all** people." This is not a sentimental Christmas passage void of any real meaning.

Israel

All Israel will be saved, as it is written: "The Deliverer will come out of Zion, and He will turn away ungodliness from Jacob."
Ro. 11:26 (Is. 45:25; Jer. 31:33-34; 32:40; Ez. 36:26-27; Ro. 11:1-2; He. 8:10-11)

Why Israel? Did God create this world with only one race in

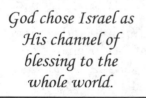

God chose Israel as His channel of blessing to the whole world.

mind? Or did He choose one particular people to affect all races? The following passages will show that God chose Israel as His channel of blessing to the whole world. And though they have failed in the past, as we all have to one degree or another, His purposes for the world will yet be realized through all His chosen ones. For the gifts and the calling of God are irrevocable (Ro. 11:29).

- *I will give You as a light to the Gentiles, that You should be My salvation to the ends of the earth* (Is. 49:6).
- *The nations shall know that I am the Lord...when I am hallowed in you before their eyes* (Ez. 36:23).
- *Then the nations which are left all around you shall know that I, the Lord...I will do it* (Ex. 36:36).
- *In the last days His house shall be established; and all nations shall flow into it* (Is. 2:2).
- *At that time Jerusalem shall be called The Throne of the Lord, and all the nations shall be gathered to it....No more shall they follow the dictates of their evil hearts* (Jer. 3:17).

- ♦ *All nations [families] of the earth shall be blessed* (Ge. 12:3; 18:18; 22:18; 26:4; 28:14; Ac. 3:25-26).
- ♦ *Scripture...preached the gospel to Abraham beforehand, saying, "In you all the nations shall be blessed"* (Ga. 3:8).

Does this people have a special distinction above all others? No, but they do have a great privilege. Paul writes, "The privilege is great from every point of view. First of all, because the Jews were entrusted with God's truth" (Ro. 3:2 WEY). But this is not the whole story. God has always had all nations in His heart and purposes. See the following passages:

- ♦ *God made no distinction between us and them, purifying their hearts by faith* (Ac. 15:9).
- ♦ *There is no distinction between Jew and Greek, for the same Lord over all is rich to all who call upon Him* (Ro. 10:12).
- ♦ *The Gentiles are fellow heirs, partakers of His promise* (Ep. 3:6).
- ♦ *He has made both one, and has broken down the middle wall of separation* (Ep. 2:14).
- ♦ *There is no partiality with God* (Ro. 2:11). (See also: Nu. 16:22; Ps. 145:9; Ac. 10:34; Ga. 2:6; Ep. 6:9; Col. 3:25; 1Ti. 2:3, 4; 1Pe. 1:17).

Will only Israel be saved?

- ♦ *All the ends of the world shall turn to Him, and all the families of the nations shall worship* (Ps. 22:27).
- ♦ *All flesh comes to Him....He provides atonement for transgressions* (Ps. 65:2-3).
- ♦ *Through the greatness of His power His enemies submit to Him. All the earth shall worship and sing praises to Him* (Ps. 66:3-4).
- ♦ *All kings shall fall down before Him: All nations shall serve Him* (Ps. 72:11).
- ♦ *All nations shall come and worship before Him and glorify His name* (Ps. 86:9).
- ♦ *He shall make for all people a feast...and will destroy the covering cast over all people, and the veil that is spread over all nations. He will swallow up death forever; and will wipe away tears from off all faces; and the rebuke of His people*

> *shall He take away from off all the earth: for He has spoken it* (Is. 25:6-8).

♦ *God has committed us all [Jews and Gentiles] to disobedience, that He might have mercy on all. Oh, the depth of the riches both of the wisdom and knowledge of God! How unsearchable are His judgments and His ways past finding out!...Of Him, through Him, and to Him are* **all** *things* (Ro. 11:32-33, 36).

These passages indicate Israel's salvation is not exclusive, but it precedes or heralds in the salvation of all.

Judge What Is Right

Why do you not even on your own initiative judge what is right?
(Lu. 12:57 NAS)

Our Lord calls us to judge for ourselves what is right. What is especially pertinent to our discussion is that these words are given in the very context of judgment! (See Lu. 12:42-49, 58-59 and Mt. 5:26; 18:34-35). Lu. 12:59 and Mt. 5:26 state that those judged are released when the last cent is paid. If this is true, then we have strong biblical grounds to question the teaching of infinite torment.

Have you critically examined its Scriptural basis for yourself? The Lord expects us to if we are to effectively proclaim the Gospel. Have you yet attempted to defend God's character to someone troubled with the thought of an eternal hell? Are you ready for that encounter? What passages has God given you? We cannot hope to be effective messengers of the Good News if we cannot answer the most basic of questions. We will be held accountable (Ro. 14:10; 2Co. 5:10) if we merely parrot the pat answers of tradition without checking the truth of the Scriptures for ourselves (Mt. 15:3, 6, 9; Mk. 12:24; Lu. 17:2; Ac. 17:11; 2Ti. 2:15; Ja. 3:1).

Keys

Fear not, I...have the keys of Hell and of Death.
(Re. 1:17-18 KJV)

Have you ever heard the cliché: "The gates of hell are locked on the inside"? This is to say sinners choose hell over heaven because they prefer to—even if given the chance to leave they would stay! This is pure twisted logic, and not at all based on Scripture; for we have only to think about it solemnly, and it falls apart. No, it is not we who have the keys of our judgment, but Christ. The fact that Christ holds these keys is intended to relieve our fear. To know His character, is to know He would never hopelessly lock anyone away. This text is of the strongest evidence against an everlasting hell. If it is not, what is the point of Christ holding the keys?

Kolasis

And all these will go away into everlasting [aionion]
punishment [kolasis].
(Mt. 25:46)

According to William Barclay, *kolasis* originally meant the pruning of trees to make them grow better. He wrote, "I think it's true to say that in all Greek secular literature *kolasis* is never used for anything but remedial punishment."[1] How ironic that the text most often used to support an eternal hell is, in fact, one that strongly opposes it when accurately understood. (See *Aion* in Chapter 1).

Love Never Fails

Love suffers long and is kind...does not behave rudely,
does not seek its own, is not provoked...bears all...endures all.
Love never fails ["ends"—RSV].
(1Co. 13:4-8)

Re-read this text substituting the word "love" with "God" because God "is" love (1Jn. 4:8, 16). When does Love that can never end or fail finally give up on us? If the prevalent theology is true, God has given up on or stopped loving billions of people He once loved. What is our brief life on earth compared to eternity? "It is just a vapor that appears for a little while and then vanishes away" (Ja. 4:14 NAS). Do you

> *Let us believe with the heart of a child God's word is true, and love never fails.*

really think God's love is as fleeting as vapor? We must believe with the heart of a child that God's word is true and His love never fails or ends. Let us stop ignoring, denying, and explaining away the most glorious declarations of God's word!

Mercy

Because He delights in mercy...
will subdue our iniquities.
(Mic. 7:18-19)

Is it conceivable that God delights in mercy towards people only until they die and then forever withholds mercy from them? Doesn't Scripture state His mercy reaches unto the heavens (Ps. 57:10)?

How can we put limits on it? Is He not merci**ful** (full of mercy)...abounding in mercy (Ps. 103:8)? What does it mean to be full of something and to abound in it? Psalm 145: 8-9 says the Lord is great in mercy and that His tender mercies are over all His works! Who is excluded from His tender mercies?

> *As long as there are people in need of mercy, we can rest assured God's mercy will reach them.*

"To You...belongs mercy; for You render to each one according to his work" (Ps. 62:12). Who does "each one" represent if not all people? Only a penalty that ends can be according to each one's work, especially in the presence of mercy. No judgment could be forever in a universe ruled by an infinitely merciful God (Ps. 136:1-26); a God full of compassion, gracious, longsuffering and **abundant in mercy** and truth (Ps. 86:15). For God has committed us **all** to disobedience, that He might have mercy on **all** (Ro 11:32)! As long as there are people in need of mercy, we can rest assured God's mercy will reach them. Is He not the same yesterday, today, and forever (He. 13:8)?

Overcoming Evil

Do not be overcome by evil, but overcome evil with good.
(Ro. 12:21)

Does God operate in a way opposite to what He expects of us? The question is its own refutation. "Love your enemies...that you may be sons of your Father; for He makes His sun rise on the evil and good; sends rain on the just and unjust....Therefore be perfect, just as your Father is perfect" (Mt. 5:44-48). "Do good to those who hate you" (Lu. 6:27).

Overcome evil with good? Be perfect, "just as" your Father is perfect? Notice the words "just as." The prevalent theology makes God out as one who hates His enemies, overcomes evil with evil, does evil to those that hate Him, and blesses His enemies for a season only to torment them forever. Is this what we are to model? Does loving our enemies merely mean we extend a token love while we envisage and plan their ruin?

Such theology falls apart at the seams, casting a dark shadow on God's character. Not so with the Blessed Hope, which is what we would expect from our loving Father.

Power in the Blood

*It **pleased** the Father...and by Him to reconcile **all** things to Himself, by Him, whether things on earth or things in heaven, having made peace through the **blood** of His cross.*
(Col. 1:19-20)

The reconciliation of all things in every place is the Father's pleasure. It is based solely on the power of Christ's blood shed for all people, and not on man's works (Tit. 3:4-5). Dare we place limits on what the blood of His cross has achieved, and on what pleases the Father? Wasn't it the Father's purpose to reconcile all to Himself from the beginning? He is the "Lamb slain from the foundation of the world" (Re. 13:8). (See also: Ep. 1:4; 1Pe. 1:18-20; 2Ti. 1:9). Notice Col. 1:20 reads "all" things and not "some" only. (See Ac. 3:21; 1Co. 15:28; 2Co. 5:19; Ep. 1:9-11; Ph. 3:21). To deny the extent of the power of our Lord's blood to restore all creation is a great disgrace and dishonor to His precious blood shed for all.

Rejoicing

You greatly rejoice with joy inexpressible and full of glory.
(1Pe. 1:8 NAS)

If the inexpressible joy Peter talked about is a true fruit of Christian experience, how can it co-exist in the presence of lost loved ones, or in the midst of an eternally lost world? How many Christians do you know are marked by that level of joy? To illustrate the depressing effect of traditional theology, I would like you to read the words of Albert Barnes, a respected Bible commentator and author of the popular, *Barnes Notes*. (In my early years as a believer, I used to refer to this commentary from time to time. So, when I came across this quote, it spoke strongly to my heart.)

> That any should suffer forever...that since God can save men, and will save a part, he has not purposed to save all; that, on the supposition that the atonement is ample, and that the blood of Christ can cleanse from all and every sin, it is not in fact applied to all....These are real, not imaginary difficulties. They are probably felt by every mind that ever reflected on the subject; and they are unexplained, unmitigated, unremoved. I confess, for one, that I feel them, and feel them more sensibly and powerfully the more I look at them, and the longer I live. I do not understand these facts; and I make no advances towards understanding them...for my whole soul pants for light and relief on these questions. But I get neither; and, in the distress and anguish of my own spirit, I confess that I see no light whatever. I see not one ray to disclose to me the reason why sin came into the world; why the earth is strewed with the dying and the dead, and why man must suffer to all eternity.
>
> I have never seen a particle of light thrown on these subjects that has given a moment's ease to my tortured mind; nor have I an explanation to offer, or a thought to suggest, which would be of relief to you....I confess, when I look on a world of sinners and of sufferers; upon death-beds and grave-yards; upon the world of woe, filled with hosts to suffer forever; when I see my friends, my parents, my family, my people, my fellow-citizens; when I look upon a whole race, all involved in this sin and danger, and when I see the great mass of them wholly unconcerned, and when I feel that God only can save them, and yet he does not do it, I am struck dumb. It is all dark, dark, dark to my soul, and I cannot disguise it. [2]

How sad! Here is a man who has dedicated His life to God and to the study of the Scriptures, and as a result of an Augustinian mindset, was brought to utter despair. He knew no joy. He saw no particle of light thrown on these subjects, nor a moment's ease to his tortured mind. He was struck dumb, saying "it is all dark, dark, dark" to his soul.

How many other sincere believers have experienced this same anguish— perhaps millions? I certainly have. This distress, anguish, and torture of mind are not the fruits of the true Gospel of Jesus Christ. Its source is in the lie of the enemy—the lie that God is a defeated God, and torments humanity forever. This lie is not the truth of the Gospel that fills the heart with joy inexpressible and full of glory (1Pe. 1:8), the glad tidings of great joy for all people (Lu. 2:10), or good news of good things (Ro. 10:15)! Albert Barnes' anguish is the opposite of the peace and joy the Lord would have us experience (Jn. 14:27; 15:11; Ga. 5:22).

If you believe in an eternal hell and think you have the joy Peter described above, how do you deal with the numerous warnings addressed to believers in Scripture (see Appendix II)? Do you simply ignore them or write them off as not

> *If we know God's judgments serve a positive and righteous purpose, we can rejoice knowing He works only good in those we love.*

applying to you? Are you 100 percent sure all your loved ones will finally be saved? If you're not sure, how can you experience a joy so wondrous, it can only be described as "inexpressible"? If however, you know that God's judgments, though painful, serve a positive and righteous purpose for all who experience them, you can then rejoice in God. For you know He will work only what is good in all those you love and with whom you are burdened. Inexpressible joy is possible for those who know God's true character and judgments! Only distress, anguish, and a tortured mind are in store for sincere thinkers in the prevailing view.

Rescued from This Age

*Christ gave Himself...in order to rescue us from the **present** wicked age.*
(Ga. 1:3-4 WEY)

If Christ came to rescue us from everlasting punishment, how could Paul have said Christ gave Himself to rescue us from the "present" wicked age?

Paul also wrote:

> *For the grace of God has appeared, bringing **salvation** to all men, instructing us to...live sensibly...in the present age, looking for the blessed hope and the appearing of...Christ Jesus, who gave Himself for us to **redeem us from every lawless deed*** (Tit. 2:11-15 NAS).

Note that in the context of salvation, Paul focused on the present age and redemption from every lawless deed with no mention of salvation from eternal flames.

Peter also says the same thing: "You were not redeemed with corruptible things...from your *aimless conduct*...but with the precious blood of Christ" (1Pe. 1:18-19). It is clear from passages such as these that our redemption is not from an infinite hell. If an infinite penalty was hanging in the balance just a heartbeat away, how could Paul and Peter have been so negligent to warn us?

True Religion

> *Pure and undefiled religion before God and the Father is this: to visit orphans and widows in their trouble, and to keep oneself unspotted from the world.*
> (Ja. 1:27)

A powerful subliminal message speaks loud and clear: If most of the world's people are on their way to an eternal hell, what could be more important than putting all our energies into preventing that? How can God ask us to divert our attention from eternal suffering to the temporal needs of orphans or widows, and call it pure and faultless religion? Would you rather be poor on earth or locked in hell forever? Something isn't lining up here.

Restoration of "All" Things

> *Heaven must receive [Christ] until the times of **restoration of all** things, which God has spoken by the mouth of all His holy prophets since the world began.*
> (Ac. 3:21)

The belief in infinite judgment compels its adherents to deny that "things" in this passage refers to persons. This is totally unjustified. The word "things" here does not have a strict Greek equivalent. The phrase, "of all things," is translated from the one Greek word— *pas* (Strong's #3956). [3] The KJV translates *pas*:

♦ "all"	748 times
♦ "all things"	170 times
♦ "every"	117 times
♦ "all men"	41 times
♦ "whosoever"	31 times
♦ "everyone"	28 times
♦ "whole"	12 times
♦ "all manner of"	11 times
♦ "every man"	11 times
♦ "every thing"	7 times
♦ "any"	7 times
♦ "whatsoever"	6 times[4]

The Concordant Literal reads, "restoration of all which God..."

The word "things" is added by translators to conform to English style. At times, this practice only muddies the waters when Scripture includes, or solely refers to persons. The safest method to determine the meaning of a word or phrase is to compare Scripture with Scripture. Consider the following texts.

♦ *Let no one boast in men. For all **things** are yours: whether Paul or Apollos or Cephas, or the world or life or death, or things present or things to come—all are yours* (1Co. 3:20-22). Are Paul and Apollos "things"?

♦ *He has put all **things** under His feet. However, when He says "all things are put under Him," it is evident He who put all things under Him is excepted* (1Co. 15:27). It would be pointless for Scripture to clarify God is exempted from the all "things" if He were not implied by it in the first place.

♦ *...to reconcile all **things** to Himself...made peace through the blood....And you...He has reconciled* (Col. 1:19-21). "And you," shows "things" refer to people.

♦ *Now we do not yet see all **things** put under Him. "But" we see Jesus...* (He. 2:8-9). Is Jesus a thing?

♦ *When all **things** are made subject to Him...that God may be all in all* (1Co. 15:28). Is God interested in being all in things?

Since "things" in these passages refer to persons, why should it not also refer to persons in Acts 3:21, especially in the context of such a major eschatological (relating to last things) event? All the prophets proclaimed it since the world began! To think such a glorious prophetic fulfillment could exclude the very part of creation created in the likeness of God Himself, and for which Christ died, is inconceivable. A time or "times" will come when all people will be restored to God. Acts 3:21 is not an isolated passage.

- *God was in Christ reconciling the world to Himself* (2Co. 5:19).
- *...The fullness of the times He might gather together in one all things in Christ* (Ep. 1:10).
- *He is able even to subdue all things to Himself* (Ph. 3:21).
- *It pleased the Father...to reconcile all things to Himself...through the blood...* (Col. 1:19-21).

YES! All are reconciled through the blood. The restoration of all in the fullness of times is His promise! It is clear "things" include people. However, if you think "all" here only means "some", see Appendix III, #2.

Satisfied

He shall see the travail of His soul, and shall be satisfied.
(Is. 53:11 KJV)

He suffered excruciatingly for the salvation of each person that ever lived. He paid in full the price for their sins. How could He ever be satisfied unless His travail has achieved its purpose? If you bought a hundred acres, and found your title only read 99, would you be satisfied? Neither is the Great Shepherd of the sheep. He will not be satisfied until the last sheep is found! (Lu. 15:4).

Unchanging

I do not change; therefore, you are not consumed....
(Mal. 3:6)

The fact that God is unchanging offers the greatest hope for all of us experiencing His chastisements. He will not utterly consume us!

We can count on His unchanging character. If He loves us today, we can know He will always love us.

I would like to share a true story recounted by Thomas Allin, author of *Christ Triumphant*:

> In a certain quarter of London, one of the many evangelists had gone forth to preach to the people. When he had concluded an eloquent address, he was thus accosted by one of his hearers:
>
> "Sir," said the man, "may I ask you one or two questions?"
>
> "Surely," said the preacher.
>
> "You have told us that God's love for us is very great and very strong."
>
> "Yes."
>
> "And that He sent His Son to save us, and I may be saved this moment, if I will."
>
> "Yes."
>
> "But, if I go away without an immediate acceptance of this offer, and if, a few minutes after I were to be killed on my way home, I should find myself in hell for ever and ever."
>
> "Yes."
>
> "Then," said the man, "if so, I don't want to have anything to do with a being whose love for me can change so completely in five minutes."[5]

Is this the way God really is? Does His love change in the twinkling of an eye or a heartbeat? Is He that fickle? Not so. God is called "the Rock" in De. 32:3-4 and many other passages (Ge. 49:24; De. 32:15, 18, 30, 31; 1Sa. 2:2; 2Sa. 22:2, 3, 32, 47; 23:3; Ps. 18:2, 31, 46; 28:1; 31:2, 3; 42:9; 61:2; 62:2, 6, 7; 71:3; 78:35; 89:26; 92:15; 94:22; 1Co. 10:4). The respected Old Testament scholars, Keil and Delitzsch, write, "God is called 'the Rock,' as the unchangeable refuge...by virtue of His unchangeableness or impregnable firmness."[6]

Author of over 40 books, Dr. Robert Morey in *Exploring the Attributes of God* wrote, "In the Christian view, God is immutable, changeless, consistent, faithful, dependable, the same yesterday, today, and forever in His existence, being, and attributes. God...the eternal I AM....["]7

God, who makes His sun rise on the evil and the good, commands us to be perfect, just as He is. How? By loving our enemies (Mt. 5:44-48). God loves His enemies while they walk on earth. Will He cease to love them after their last breath? Is He not immutable—unchangeable?

- His *longsuffering* "is" salvation! (2Pe. 3:15).
- God is not a man who changes His mind. He promises and fulfills. (Nu. 23:19 NIV; 1Sa. 15:29)
- *Who can make Him change (Job 23:13)?*
- *They will be changed. But You are the same....* (Ps. 102:26-27).
- *The Father of lights, with whom there is no variation or shadow of turning* (Ja. 1:17).
- *The gifts and the calling of God are irrevocable* (Ro. 11:29).
- *Jesus Christ is the same yesterday, today, and forever* (He. 13:8).
- *God, determining to show the immutability of His counsel [will] confirmed it by an oath...* (He. 6:17).

Scripture abounds with testimony of an unchanging God. As Malachi said above, "therefore" we are not consumed. It is not in God's unchanging nature to infinitely punish or annihilate His creatures, but rather to restore and transform them.

Until He Finds

*What man of you, having a hundred sheep, if he loses one, does not leave the ninety-nine...and go after the one **until he finds** it?*
(Lu. 15:4)

If we would do such for a mere animal (a sheep), how much more will God for His own children made in His image? (Mt. 7:11). "I am the good shepherd...(who) gives His life for the sheep" (Jn. 10:11). Since we humans leave the ninety-nine for the lost one, how much more will the Good Shepherd who gave His very life for the sheep? This passage assures me He will not give up the search until He finds all His missing ones! Note this very text is a prelude to the most touching passage in the New Testament: the parable of the wayward (prodigal) son.

Wayward Son

But when he was still a great way off, his father saw him and had compassion, and ran and fell on his neck and kissed him.
(Lu. 15:20 (See also Lu. 15:11-32).)

> *Our Father waits for His lost ones to realize their lost condition and need of reconciliation. When they do, He is there with eyes full of compassion and joy.*

Here is a grieving father, waiting, longing, and praying for his son's return. Day after day, he waits and he watches the distant fields. Finally the day came. "Is that him on the horizon? Could it possibly be? Yes! Yes! It is him!" His heart swells with compassion and joy. "My son is coming home!" He jumps to his feet. He does not merely walk, but he runs, yes, runs. He cannot wait to reach him. The party has already begun in heaven! (Lu. 15:7). Moreover when he gets to him, he falls on his neck, embraces him, and kisses him. Then he orders, "let's party!" What a picture of our heavenly Father!

The Christ I know and love is not a hired hand who does not care about the sheep, leaves the sheep, and flees when He sees the wolf coming (Jn. 10:12-13). No, a thousand times no. He does not turn and run, but He gives His life to destroy the wolf (He. 2:14). He destroys the works of the wolf (1Jn. 3:8), *"not"* the sheep for whom He came to rescue! (Lu. 9:56).

It is not by chance the Lord gave us this story in the context of the lost sheep and coin. He is revealing to us the heart of our heavenly Father. The lost son represents every lost person. It shows us how our Father waits for His lost ones to realize their lost condition and need of reconciliation. When they do, He flees to their side with comfort and blessing with eyes full of compassion. Meanwhile, He waits and works life's circumstances, be it in this age or in future ages, so His lost ones will come to themselves. A thousand years are as one day to Him (2Pe. 3:8). He does not give up. He is the Good Shepherd who goes after His sheep until He finds them.

Very Good

God saw everything that He had made,
*and **indeed** it was very good.*
(Ge. 1:31)

Does God know the future? Absolutely! Scripture abounds with testimony, telling us He knows the future from the beginning. So what? This is of paramount importance! For if God knew before He created the world what destiny awaited His creation, then He is responsible. There is no getting around it.

If you knew the ice was only ⅛″ thick and would not even support a cat, but yet you sent your son, little Johnny, across the lake to fetch firewood, and he drowned, you would be at fault. It does not matter what the boy knew or did not know. You are his parent, and you knowingly allowed it to happen!

At the outset of creation, God saw everything He had made, including how it related to the past, present, and future, since He transcends the time realm. What was His conclusion? It was all "indeed" very good. Notice the word "indeed." How is it possible that God could say all was "indeed very good" knowing eternal woe was the destiny awaiting the vast majority of humanity? Is that possible in a universe created by an all-powerful and loving God? That is impossible—unless of course God cannot know the future. Is that an option for us? If we doubt God knows the future, what do we do with the following passages: Ge. 3:15; 15:13-14; Ex. 3:19; 7:14; 9:30; 11:9; 1K. 13:1-6, 32; 21:20-22; 2K. 8:12; Ps. 94:8-9; 139:1-6; 147:5; Is. 41:21-26; 44:11, 21, 28; 46:9-11; 65:24; Jer. 1:5; 32:19; Ez. 11:5; Mt. 6:8, 10; 10:17, 18, 21, 22; 11:14, 21; 12:45; 24:2, 33-41; Mk. 14:30; Lu. 14:28-32; Jn. 6:64; 8:20; 21:18-19; Ac. 2:23; 15:8, 18; 17:26; Ro. 4:17; 8:29-30;11:2, 33; Ga. 3:8; Ep. 1:4-5, 11; 3:11; 2Ti. 1:9; Tit. 1:2; He. 4:13; 1Pe. 1:2, 20; 1Jn. 3:20; 5:14; Re. 13:8; 17:18; plus all the Messianic prophecies?

It is abundantly clear that God knows the end from the beginning. The fact that He sees everything as "indeed very good" brings me much comfort and peace. It confirms He has everything under control! It confirms the Blessed Hope.

What Moved Christ

Moved with compassion...because they were weary.
(Mt. 9:36-38)

One day, as I was meditating on the Scriptures, I thought about what moved Christ with compassion for the multitudes. It had nothing to do with the afterlife. The passage simply said, "because they were weary and scattered, [distressed and dispirited (NAS)] like sheep having no shepherd" (Mt. 9:36-38). The more I thought about this, the louder it spoke to me. Sometimes, an indirect statement speaks louder than one that states something directly:

> *But when He saw the multitudes, He was moved with compassion for them, because they were weary and scattered ["distressed and dispirited"—NAS], like sheep having no shepherd. Then He said to His disciples, "The harvest truly is plentiful, but the laborers are few. Therefore pray the Lord of the harvest to send out laborers into His harvest." (Mt. 9:36-38).*

The exhortation to pray laborers be sent to the harvest is especially pertinent. Of all places in Scripture, this would be "the place" to state, in the strongest possible terms, the danger of infinite punishment—our ultimate motivation for evangelism. Yet, the Lord does not utter a word about it. How do you explain this? Compare this with Christ's first recorded public address (Lu. 4:16-19; Is. 61:1-3).

World Purpose

He...gives life to the world.
(Jn. 6:33)

"For the Son of Man did not come to destroy men's lives but to save them" (Lu. 9:56). Christ has a world purpose. He came to give life to the world and not only a select few (Jn. 6:33). He gave His flesh for the life of the world in its entirety (Jn. 6:51). Neither did He come to condemn or even to judge the world, but to save it (Jn. 3:17; 12:47). Should not these "world" passages tell us something? They are totally consistent with who He is—the Savior of the "world"(Jn. 4:42; 1Jn. 4:14). How glorious these promises have become to me as I now understand them in their unlimited scope and power. Although destruction and judgment remain, they will not frustrate His ultimate purpose for the world. They are but the means to its fulfillment in the fullness of times.

- ◆ *God did not send His Son to condemn the **world**...* (Jn. 3:17).
- ◆ *My flesh, which I shall give for the life of the **world*** (Jn. 6:51).
- ◆ *Neither did He come to judge the **world** but to save it* (Jn. 12:47).

Yes, Christ came to save the world; that is His purpose, and nothing less than a world saved will satisfy Him.

◆ ◆ ◆ ◆ ◆

Many additional passages could be marshaled in support of the Blessed Hope. I list many of them in Appendix I. Taken as a whole, these proclamations offer powerful support for this Hope. As with all Scripture, unless God opens our hearts and minds, we will not see His truth even if it is staring us in the face.

Mercy Aiken, in *If Hell is Real* says, "Come Up Higher!" She writes:

> Traditional doctrines teach us to interpret the "victorious" scriptures in the light of the "judgment" scriptures. But what if God wants us to see it the other way around? Is not Christ's victory the greatest revelation in the Bible? Standing on this highest peak—that is, the finished work of the cross, causes us to see a much larger and far more beautiful panoramic view of God's plan throughout the ages. We do not throw out one set of Scriptures in favor of another. Rather, we seek to harmonize them... It is time to stop ignoring the parts of the Bible that do not fit in with our theology.[8]

It is my sincere prayer that you will rejoice in the full splendor of these precious proclamation passages, and no longer allow their glory to be stripped from your heart. I pray you will stand on the pinnacle of their glorious truth (emanating from Christ's victory) and understand God's purpose-driven judgment through them.

CHAPTER EIGHT

THE WİTΠESSES

By the mouth of two or three witnesses the
matter shall be established.
(De. 19:15)

*T*he case for the Blessed Hope stands on solid legal ground providing a strong basis upon which we can base our hope. Scripture declares by the mouth of two or three witnesses the matter shall be established (De. 19:15). In this chapter, I present six witnesses, more than doubling the legal requirement. Please weigh carefully the testimony you are about to hear from the Old Testament, the Apostles, the early Church, the Moral Witness, and the two opposing fruits of our theologies.

The Old Testament

Consider Adam and Eve, Cain, the Antediluvians (those prior to Noah's time), Sodom and Gomorrah, Pharaoh, and the Canaanites for example. Would you not have expected God to have warned them repeatedly of such a horrific judgment as everlasting torment? What was the very first warning given? "Of the tree of the knowledge of good and evil you shall not eat, for in the day that you eat of it you shall surely die" (Ge. 2:17). If death meant infinite punishment, why did not God say so? How about the Law of Moses with all its penalties and threatening? They all relate to earthly penalties. For example, read De. 28:15-68. For what are these in comparison with infinite punishment? What would you think of a government whose written legal code for petty theft stated three months incarceration, but in reality gave a life sentence? Is God guilty of infinitely worse?

Where does judgment refer to infinite penalty? After 3,455 years of biblical history, such a judgment is not pronounced. If *Sheol*, translated "hell," (KJV) meant punishment unending, how can the Psalmist be so confident he will be released from it? "You will not leave my soul in *Sheol*." (Ps. 16:10; 49:15; Ac. 2:27; also 1Sa. 2:6;).

[Please read Is. 19:21-25; Ez. 16:44-63.]

The Egyptians will know the Lord? Israel one with Egypt? "Blessed is Egypt My people and Assyria the work of My hands?" Sodom and Samaria are more righteous than Israel? The Lord brings back the captives of Sodom and Samaria, and He returns them to their former state? These whom tradition has led us to believe are lost forever are restored?

> *If Sheol, translated "hell," meant punishment unending, how can the Psalmist be so confident he will be released from it?*
>
> *(See Ps. 16:10)*

In *Hell Under Fire*, Daniel Block, answers, "very little."[1] to the question, "What does the Old Testament teach about hell?" "Very little" is indeed an overstatement because it does not teach it at all. He submits two "proof" texts he feels support the doctrine: Is. 66:24 and Da. 12:2.

> *And they have gone forth, and **looked on the carcasses** of the men who are transgressing against me, for their worm dieth not, and their fire is not quenched, and they have been an abhorrence to all flesh* (Is. 66:24 YLT)!

This Isaiah passage is not referring to an infinite spiritual state, but to earthly carcasses. The only reason it is offered in support of endless punishment is because it contains familiar metaphorical references to the worm and unquenched fire traditionally associated with hell. Those terms are examined in Appendix IV and do not at all require unending chastisement, only that it attain its goal.

> *The multitude of those sleeping in the dust of the ground do awake, some to life age-during, and some to reproaches—to abhorrence age-during* (Da. 12:2 YLT).

Regarding this Daniel passage, what has been said regarding Mt. 25:46 in Chapter 1 also applies here.

For argument's sake, assume Daniel 12 supports an eternal hell. Consider this. In my 842 page Bible, Da. 12:2 does not occur until page 791! Thus, we are not introduced to the idea of unending punishment until 94 percent of the Bible has been read! In a three year Bible reading plan, that would not occur until the 937th day, or before two years and seven months have passed! How many people have tried to read the Old Testament and have never got past Leviticus? If the doctrine was true, would God not have made it known from the very beginning?

Look at it this way. Daniel was written about 535 B.C. compared to 1450-1406 B.C. for the Pentateuch (the first five books of the Old Testament). Some say Adam was created about 2,000 years before Abraham who was born in 2166 BC. That means God's people did not have a 'proof' text on everlasting punishment until about 3,500 years from Adam or 900 years from Moses! Can you imagine? How can you explain such silence when the Old Testament is filled with warnings of temporal judgments?

The Apostles

Our example should be the lives and preaching of those who understood our Lord's teachings best, the Apostles. They were called to proclaim His Gospel to the whole world. If you would like to know what they taught regarding judgment, you need to read the book of Acts. Nowhere do they proclaim everlasting punishment. Neither is *Gehenna* mentioned by any of them anywhere except once by James who referred to it merely as a metaphor underlining the power of our words (Ja. 3:6). The following are the key references in Acts where the Apostles preach the Gospel: Ac. 2:14-40; 3:12-26; 7:2-50; 8:32-35; 10:34-48; 13:16-47; 16:30-31; 17:22-32; 20:18-35.

The strongest statement made is, "destroyed from the people" (Ac. 3:23 RSV). The Jerusalem Bible says, "cut off from the people." The Greek word translated "destruction" here is *exolothreúō*, Strong's #1842. It is used only once in the New Testament. Of it Spiros Zodhiates, in his *The Complete Word Study Dictionary*, says, "The word and its synonym never mean extinction, but a change of one's state involving retribution or punishment."[2] He bases this comment on the Greek usage of the word in the Septuagint—Ex. 30:33; 31:14; De. 7:10.

In addition, this "cutting off," whatever it entails, is not unchangeable. Though God is seen as severe in breaking off the natural branches in Ro. 11:21, He remains a God of goodness (v. 22). For He promises to graft them in again if they will change (v. 23).

When proclaiming the Gospel to the Gentiles, Paul says, "He has appointed a day on which He will judge the world in righteousness." (Ac. 17:31). That is all he says! If everlasting punishment was really in his mind, how could he not have warned them of it? Is this all that can be said about such an unimaginable and horrible judgment— "righteous judgment"?

If Paul believed God's judgments were everlasting, how could he claim in Ac. 20:27 that he had not shunned to declare the whole counsel of God, especially in light of Ez. 33:6-8?

> *I testify to you this day that I am innocent of the blood of all men. For I have not shunned to declare to you the whole counsel of God* (Ac. 20:27).

> *If the watchman sees the sword coming and does not blow the trumpet...his blood I will require...* (Ez. 33:6-8).

Paul does not mention God's everlasting judgments in any of his letters, nor does he do so in Acts. This is stunning, especially since Christ chose him as His apostle to the nations (Ac. 9:15). Who was a greater evangelist than Paul? "I labored even more than all of them." (1Co. 15:10). He who labored more never taught infinite punishment. Observe instead, what Paul does teach.

> *This is a faithful saying and worthy of all acceptance. For to this end we both labor and suffer reproach, because we trust in the living God, who is the Savior of all men, especially of those who believe. These things command and teach* (1Ti. 4:9-11).

The Apostle Peter as well, so far from supporting unending torments, offers us great hope! He proclaims the "times of restoration of all things" (Ac. 3:21), confirms all families (including each individual) of the earth shall be blessed (Ac. 3:25-26), declares God shows no partiality (Ac. 10:34), describes the Christian life as indescribable joy (1Pe.1:8), states Christ went and preached to the spirits in prison – specifying the dead (1Pe. 3:19; 4:6), affirms God's will to save all, and assures us that His longsuffering "is" salvation (2Pe. 3:9, 15).

Yes, the Apostles not only fail to proclaim everlasting punishment, but advocate instead, the Blessed Hope!

The Early Church

The early Church read the Scriptures directly from the Greek, and knew *aion* referred to a period of limited duration. For example, when they read Mt. 25:46, they did not understand it to mean infinite penalty like we do.

The theologian most responsible for establishing this teaching was Augustine in the 5ᵗʰ century. He was not a native Greek speaker. He said, "I have learned very little of the Greek language."[3] Is it surprising that a "non-Greek" speaker would misunderstand the Greek words of Scripture?

Charles Pridgeon, president and founder of the Pittsburgh Bible Institute, wrote:

> In these early centuries those holding the doctrine of endless punishment were in the minority and no one was counted unorthodox who believed in restitution and the ultimate and complete victory of Christ. In fact, the leaders in the early Church Councils and those who were chosen to establish orthodoxy were well-known believers in the beneficent side of future punishment. This is especially true of the second great Church Council which was held to perfect the Nicene Creed....There is no word in these early statements of creed in favor of endless punishment.[4]

"In these early centuries those holding the doctrine of endless punishment were in the minority and no one was counted unorthodox who believed in restitution and the ultimate and complete victory of Christ."[4]

Historian and scholar, Ethelbert Stauffer, author of *Christ and the Caesars*, and *New Testament Theology*, wrote: "The primitive church never gave up the hope that in His will to save, the 'all-merciful' and 'all-powerful' God would overcome even the final 'no' of the self-sufficient world."[5]

I would like to bring to your attention the testimony of the following early Church leaders regarding their beliefs: Irenaeus, Theophilus, Clement of Alexandria, Origen, Eusebius of Caesarea, Athanasius, Gregory Nazianzen, Ambrose, Didymus, Gregory of Nyssa, Jerome, Hillary,

Titus, Diodorus, Theodore of Mopsuestia, Cyril of Alexandria, Maximus of Turin, Theodoret, Peter Chrysologus. (See Appendix VII for a brief quotation from each).

Regarding Augustine (354-430 A.D.), Charles Pridgeon wrote "His influence probably more than that of any other of the Church Fathers brought forward and emphasized the doctrine of never-ending punishment. He spoke with greater consideration for those who differed with him than many of the moderns."[6] Pridgeon quotes Augustine:

> And now I see I must have a gentle disputation with certain tender hearts of our own religion, who are unwilling to believe that everlasting punishment will be inflicted, either on all those whom the just Judge shall condemn to the pains of hell, or even on some of them, but who think that after certain periods of time, longer or shorter according to the proportion of their crimes, they shall be delivered out of that state.—Augustine. (De Civ. Del, lib. 21, c.17).[7]

And in *Encheirid. ad Laurent*, c. 29 Pridgeon again quotes Augustine: "There are very many in our day, who though not denying the Holy Scriptures, do not believe in endless torments."—Augustine.[8]

Augustine admits that those who do not believe in endless torments are "very many," and that they do not deny the Holy Scriptures. It is also significant that he does not consider them "unorthodox." In fact he refers to them as "tender hearts of our own religion," with whom he must have a "gentle" disputation.

The above testimonies are only representative of what the early Church believed. In closing his chapter on the early Church, Pridgeon concluded:

> On account of the doctrine of Reserve which was held by so many of the Church Fathers, some who are quoted as holding to the doctrine of never-ending torment have other passages which teach quite the contrary. Many held the doctrine of the ultimate salvation of all for themselves...but felt that it was not safe for the multitude, and therefore taught them an endless perdition.
>
> When we remember the cruelty and militarism of the Roman Empire, and also the pagan teaching that was permit-

ted to enter on this great subject (because it was found in the pagan and barbarian religions of many who professed allegiance to Christianity), many of these we fear, judging from their actions, had not received a truly Christian spirit, and we are not surprised that "endless torment" was so largely incorporated in the western Church. Besides this, it took the dark ages and medieval ignorance to render this doctrine almost universal. It is time to return to the Bible and to the teaching of the early Church, which is not only Biblical but is sane and is also consistent with a God of love and the sacrifice of His Son who was a "propitiation for our sins and not for ours only, but also for the sins of the whole world" (1John 2:2).[9]

If you will look over these ancient writings carefully, you will notice that the early Church leaders, at times, made reference to *aionian* punishment when it is clear "eternity" is not what they had in mind. In reality, they taught the restoration of all in those very same contexts. Sadly, modern researchers of early Church documents, not taking this into consideration, simply assume that when they referred to *aionian* punishment they meant 'everlasting.'

I highly recommend you read Dr. Edward Beecher's *History of Opinions on the Scriptural Doctrine of Retribution*, published in 1878. Read it on our website: HopeBeyondHell.net "Church History." Having no agenda or denomination to defend, he honestly presents unbiased evidence and scholarly research. Dr. J.W. Hanson, a historical writer and contemporary of Beecher, referred to Beecher's work as "a most truthful and candid volume." Beecher wrote, "The more profoundly learned [in Scripture] any one was in Christian antiquity, so much the more did he cherish and defend the hope that the sufferings of the wicked would at some time come to an end."[10]

Another excellent source on church history is *Christ Triumphant* by Thomas Allin. A great part of his book is devoted to it.

In conclusion, the historical record shows that infinite penalty was not the predominant view held by the early Church.

The Moral Witness

Scripture everywhere appeals to our conscience. From the very beginning, the question is asked, "Shall not the judge of all the earth do right" (Ge. 18:25)? To what is such a question appealing? How can we know the difference between what is right or wrong if not for the moral witness God has placed in us? "Behold, the man has become like one of Us, to know good and evil." (Ge. 3:22). It begins with our God-given conscience. All subsequent and more complete moral understanding (such as the Bible provides) must build upon the foundation established by the witness of conscience. This completes the structure of God's revelation. It is critical we understand this.

"Why do you not even on your own initiative judge what is right" (Lu. 12:57 NAS)? Have you judged what is right? The primary means by which God speaks to us is through our conscience (moral witness). Without it, we would not have the capacity to receive any light from the Bible, or say "yes" to any of its truths. All we read is filtered through our conscience. This is how the Holy Spirit operates in our hearts to quicken His truth within us. "Come now, and let us reason together, says the Lord." (Is. 1:18). "Our sufficiency is from God...not of the letter but of the Spirit; for the letter kills, but the Spirit gives life." (2Co. 3:5, 6).

I looked up the 32 references to conscience in the New Testament to try to get an idea of its role. The texts, which I found most helpful, were in Romans. At the very outset, Paul establishes that conscience is God's initial revelation.

Why do you not even on your own initiative judge what is right?
(Lu. 12:57 NAS)

All men have the truth (Ro. 1:18). God has revealed Himself to all (Ro. 1:19). By not responding appropriately to the God they knew, their thoughts became futile, and their hearts became dark and foolish. Thus, God gave them over to a debased mind, to do the unfitting (Ro. 1:21, 28).

But, in spite of futile thoughts, a dark and foolish heart, and a debased mind to do the unfitting, men nevertheless know the righteous judgment of God—that 'such things' deserve death (Ro. 1:28-32). All men have a basic sense of morality and are without excuse before God (Ro. 2:1). "If you then, being evil, know how to give good gifts...." (Mt. 7:11). "The true Light...gives light to every man coming into the world" (Jn. 1:9).

Man has been made in the image of God (Ge. 1:26). Though marred or clouded by sin, that image has not veiled God's moral witness implanted in every heart. Our Lord commands us to let our light shine before men that they may see our good works and glorify God (Mt. 5:16). How can people appreciate our "good" works unless they have the moral capacity to recognize them as good? Our moral sense plays a primary part in God's revelation of Himself, and as a result, a central role in understanding His Word.

"[Have] your conduct honorable among the Gentiles, that when they speak against you as evildoers, they may, by your good works which they observe, glorify God in the day of visitation." (1Pe. 2:11-12). "Having a good conscience, that when they defame you as evildoers, those who revile your good conduct in Christ may be ashamed" (1Pe. 3:16). (See also: Ro. 13:3-5; Ph. 2:15; 4:5; 1Th. 4:11-12; 1Ti. 4:12-15; Tit. 2:6-8; 1Pe. 2:15; 1Pe. 3:13).

Page after page, the Bible is full of appeals to our moral sense. The Holy Scriptures, being His more comprehensive revelation, would be completely unintelligible if God had not first placed His moral witness in us.

Regarding unending punishment, how many believers have allowed their conscience to be seared by this horrific thought? How much biblical truth has been veiled as a result? Who does not struggle with God over such a cruel punishment or simply accepts it without question? How many millions has it kept from coming to Christ because people know a loving God would not do such a thing?

I have always struggled with everlasting punishment. It totally contradicted my understanding of God. It was by far the biggest stumbling block to my faith. I now understand this struggle in my soul was God's moral witness in my heart crying out.

Clark Pinnock, eminent theologian and author of *A Defense of Biblical Infallibility* and the *The Scripture Principle* wrote:

> Everlasting torture is intolerable from a moral point of view because it pictures God acting like a bloodthirsty monster who maintains an everlasting Auschwitz for his enemies whom he does not allow to die. How can one love a God like that? I suppose one might be afraid of him, but could we love and respect him? Would we want to strive to be like him in such mercilessness?[11]

Hans Kung, renowned theologian who won the chair of Fundamental Theology at Tubingen University asked, "What would we think of a human being who satisfied his thirst for revenge so implacably and insatiably?"[12] Philip Yancey, author of *What's So Amazing About Grace*, wrote, "What can be said about God if from eternity he decided to send most people to eternal damnation in order that his grace toward others might appear more laudable?"[13] Randy Klassen, pastor, seminary teacher, and author of *Jesus Word, Jesus Way* wrote:

> An eternal hell poses the problem of a glaring inconsistency in the character of God. There is an affront to an enlightened sense of justice. There is also the matter of what purpose is served by it all. Whose victory is finally won if most people are in hell? Made in the image of God, all humans have a moral sense, a judicial sentiment. Even the unredeemed cringe when the Holocaust is reviewed. Our moral intuition rejects the idea that anyone, human or divine, who endlessly inflicted pain on another, could be called "good." Throughout history we read of religious factions and political parties justifying their cruelty to others. The Nazis justified their anti-Semitic atrocities, the Communists their anti-Christian murders, and the early Americans their slavery. But history has judged such violations of human rights as breaching a universal moral code.[14]

I believe these testimonies find their echo in the hearts of every believer. I urge you to accept the whole counsel of God, especially His moral witness in your heart. Don't let your conscience be seared by the tradition of men, or suppressed when confronted by what seem to be conflicting Scriptures. The moral witness is God's defense system protecting us from error. Truth will not contradict it.

Oh, If Only...

Oh, if only the Christians who participated in and condoned the torture and murder of fellow believers had followed the voice of their conscience instead of their tradition, they would not have committed horrible atrocities. John Calvin, as legal prosecutor, argued the case against a brother over a point of doctrine and asked for his execution. Michael Servetus was burned at the stake on October 27, 1553.[15] Such an act reflects the character of the God Calvin believed in.

Those who blindly accept what they are taught are no different from modern religious terrorists who do the same. How many terrorists have critically examined their traditions to verify if what they have been taught is true? Their traditions have seared their conscience. Are we any different?

What is the most heinous of terrors? Is it being captured by terrorists, tortured, and beheaded? Or is it being cast into a lake of fire to burn forever without any hope of ever being released? Who is truly the world's greatest terrorist if not the Father of our Lord Jesus Christ? What blasphemy!

Are we terrorists? Have we ever sowed the fear of everlasting torment in one of Christ's little ones? It would be better if a millstone were hung around our necks, and we were thrown into the sea, than we should offend one of His little ones (Lu. 17:2).

We are not immune from the same trap as Calvin or Bin Laden. Even Paul was at one time a terrorist! (Ac. 22:4; 26:11). God calls us to judge for ourselves what is right (Lu. 12:57), to test all things and hold fast that which is good (1Th. 5:21). It is not enough to claim Scripture as our authority for so did Paul, the K.K.K., Queen Mary (Bloody Mary), and the Spanish inquisitors. Believers can be just as brutal and cruel in the name *Yahweh* as other religious extremists are in the name of their god. "Keep you heart [conscience] with all diligence, for out of it spring the issues of life." (Pr. 4:23).

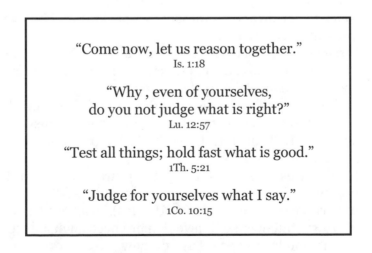

"Come now, let us reason together."
Is. 1:18

"Why , even of yourselves,
do you not judge what is right?"
Lu. 12:57

"Test all things; hold fast what is good."
1Th. 5:21

"Judge for yourselves what I say."
1Co. 10:15

Good Fruit

You will know them by their fruits.
(Mt. 7:16)

Belief in the Blessed Hope...

+ Transforms us into His likeness as we naturally reflect who we admire. Mother Theresa knew an impartial God who loves His enemies, and her life reflected it. John Calvin knew a partial God who hates His enemies and fought to have a fellow believer executed over a point of doctrine.
+ Fosters genuine affection for God enabling us to fulfill the first great command (Mk. 12:30). What can bar us from loving God more than the thought He might send us to eternal suffering? It would be natural to fear such a God, but love Him?
+ Challenges us to be like God in never giving up on difficult-to - love people, thus fulfilling the second great command (Mk. 12:31).
+ Strengthens our trust (faith) in God knowing He will never forsake anyone.
+ Instills a healthy fear of judgment. In contrast, a penalty, which to reason and moral sense is shocking and unbearable, loses all force as a threat.
+ Satisfies our conscience (God's moral witness in our hearts).
+ Comforts all who mourn, especially those grieving for loved ones who have died outside the faith.
+ Empowers us in evangelism for the same reason, and also because it presents God as infinitely loving to all, just, and all-powerful. He is incontestably GOD Almighty, and people are attracted to such a God.
+ Harmonizes the comforting Scriptures with those that frighten.
+ Imparts lasting joy and peace (1Pe. 1:8). In all my years under the Augustinian yoke, I never experienced such a deep, consistent, and lasting peace as I do now.
+ Enriches our worship.
+ Satisfies the heart of Him who died for all.

Bad Fruit

Belief in everlasting punishment...

+ Makes abortion a heroic act of mercy.
+ Makes Adam's sin greater than what the cross of Christ has accomplished. (See Ro. 5:12-21).

> *Makes abortion an heroic act of mercy.*

+ Fosters a boastful attitude. "They deserve what they get!"
+ Coerces love. "Love me or else!"
+ Compromises the Good News of the Gospel.
+ Breeds skepticism and unbelief by maligning God's character before the world.
+ Fosters a spirit of cruelty. Remember Tertullian, the Crusades, De Montfort, the massacre of St. Bartholomew (where 30-40,000 Christians perished), the horrendous Inquisitions, Queen (Bloody) Mary (who set her victims aflame to expedite God's judgment), the K.K.K., etc.. Believers with a hell mindset have committed the most unimaginable atrocities. See www.HopeBeyondHell.net "Religious Cruelty".
+ Makes the devil more powerful than Christ since he ultimately wins most of humanity.
+ Negates the most glorious passages in the Bible. (See Appendix I).
+ Makes it impossible to obey the Word of God. Commands such as "Do not worry," "Rejoice always," and "Love God with all your heart" are impossible to keep when loved ones are in danger of an eternal hell.
+ Is unworthy of God. It strips Him of His glory, unlimited power, and unfailing love. It mars His holy and just character before all, depriving Him of the awesome worship He so deserves.
+ Robs Christ of His victory over evil and dishonors His shed blood by limiting its power to save.
+ Destroys belief in One all-powerful GOD, and replaces Him with a pseudo god who co-rules the earth with SATAN.
+ Is unworthy of man. It denies his infinite value to God, making man worthless and fit only for the dung pile. But the blood of

Christ affirms man's infinite value. He does not annihilate or torment forever what has infinite value in His sight.

♦ Has brought untold anguish the world over. Millions have despaired over it, even to the point of emotional breakdown and suicide. What unimaginable anguish it has caused.

♦ Breeds terrorism. Oh, if terrorists only knew the glad tidings of great joy (Lu. 2:10). There would be no need to commit suicide to escape hell!

♦ Offends Christ's little ones. It would be better to be thrown into the sea (Lu. 17:2).

If we would but examine critically and objectively the fruits of our theologies, we would see which glorifies our heavenly Father. Now wouldn't you agree that the theology which brings Him glory must be the truth?

♦ ♦ ♦ ♦ ♦

You have heard powerful testimony from six key witnesses whose authority is undeniable. What carries more authority than the Old Testament, the Apostles, the early Church, God's moral witness, and the fruits of our faith? Their witness, sufficient in itself, only supplements the evidence presented in other chapters. Let us now consider over twenty additional points of evidence for the Blessed Hope.

CHAPTER NINE

CIRCUMSTANTIAL EVIDENCE

Convince...with all longsuffering and teaching.
(2Ti. 4:2)

*T*hus far, we have evaluated the supporting pillars of infinite tor-ment and have found them invalid (Chapter 1). We then focused on God's glorious nature, His unlimited power, and His essence which "is" love with no "buts" attached (Chapter 2). Such love then found expression in His just and purposeful judgments (Chapter 3). From there we stepped back to see the big picture of His blessed plan for all mankind, a plan that cannot fail (Chapters 4 and 5). From that vantage point, we narrowed in on many precious proclamations supporting powerfully both directly and indirectly the Blessed Hope (Chapters 6 and 7). With such glorious proclamations still resonating in our hearts, we heard six key witnesses give incontestable testi-mony reaffirming this hope (Chapter 8). Now, with hearts filled with anticipation for what still lies ahead, let us examine the circumstan-tial evidence of our case. It is my prayer that as you evaluate this evidence, God will open your eyes and heart to receive a deeper unveiling of His indescribable grace and mercy for all people.

Abortion Is Merciful

If pro-life Christians truly believe what their churches teach about hell, what motivates them to fight abortion? What is the better strategy to get the most people into heaven—evangelism or abortion? Well, most Christians would say abortion has a 100 percent success rate; pretty hard to beat, don't you think? Remember Andrea Yates, who drowned her five children? She was captivated with Michael Woroniecki's preaching that "bad children [go] to hell."[1] Was she really insane? Maybe she was simply a loving mother who wanted to spare her children an unimaginable and horrendous fate.

Beyond Horror

To reflect upon the horror of unending punishment is its own refutation. Whatever the actual torments may be, the horror is its never ending character. It is impossible to conceive suffering forever. It is a horror beyond description and incompatible with a God of mercy and grace.

Calvinism Affirms

J. I. Packer, a Calvinist and one of the most influential theologians of our time, believes that to say Christ died for everyone logically leads to believing that all men will be saved.[2]

Is he right? Think about it. If you believed in God's power like Packer does (that man is powerless to override God's will), you would know God brings to faith all for whom Christ died (for Packer, this is only the elect). Well, his prediction is exactly what has happened in we who embrace the Blessed Hope. Calvinism (because of its global scope, wide acceptance, and influence) gives our hope great credibility, since Calvinism and the Blessed Hope proclaim the same view of God's Sovereignty. In truth, their theologians

> *To say Christ died for everyone logically leads to believing all men will be saved.*[2]

unwittingly offer the strongest arguments in support of the Blessed Hope. In essence, we who hold dear this view of God's sovereignty in the very context of Christ's death for all mankind have confirmed Packer's deduction. Packer is right. You cannot believe in God's absolute Sovereignty and at the same time believe Christ died for all without embracing the Blessed Hope. It is impossible.

Christ, Our Model?

If saving people from an eternal hell is our mission, why did Christ not model this objective? (The same question can be asked of the Apostles—see Chapter 8). If you read through the Gospels, you will not find Jesus hurrying about trying to get people saved. He was content with healing infirmities and teaching people how to live. When He did teach, it was all too frequently in parables, a code language designed specifically to conceal truth from His hearers.

Why would the world's Savior allow people to march right on by into eternal damnation? His life does not line up with our theology. Something is amiss, and I do not think it is Him. Christ was not in a rush because He has the ages in which to operate. "With the Lord a thousand years are as one day" (2Pe. 3:8).

Comforts the Grieving

We all from time to time encounter friends or family members who are deeply hurting in the loss of a loved one. Often, it involves someone who made no outward profession of faith in Christ. How do you comfort them in their grief? Do you tell them they will be re-united in heaven, or tell them they are suffering in hell for all eternity? Do you take advantage of the opportunity, like some, to tell them they can escape such a fate? Not if you are a sensitive human being. All you can do is hold their hand and say nothing except, "I'm praying for you." Not so with the Blessed Hope! The Bible abounds with hope for all who grieve.

Cross of Christ

The cross does not simply give people an "opportunity" for salvation, but assures its ultimate reality. The difference here is paramount. Allin declared:

> The popular creed [Augustinian tradition] dishonors the Cross by limiting its power to save to the brief moments of earthly life. Further, it virtually teaches the Cross is a stupendous failure. This is easily shown. For plainly that which misses its end is a failure. The scriptural evidence is overwhelming, that the object of Christ's death was to save the world. If the world be not in fact saved, the Atonement is so far a failure. Disguise the fact as men may, the dilemma is inevitable. Answer, or evasion, there is none.[3]

In his movie, *The Passion*, Mel Gibson has truly given us a vivid picture of the awful price Christ paid to achieve His objective. It is impossible to imagine all He suffered for every person. It is even harder to think after all that, He failed to achieve His goal. I believe in the power of the cross. There is no greater power in the universe. For in it, we see the extent of God's love. I cannot imagine the cross failing to any degree. However, I can conceive it accomplishing all for which it was meant. Nothing less would satisfy Christ, or His Father.

Cruel World

We live in a cruel world. Every single human being must face innumerable sorrows in this life. We all have to face the death of a loved one eventually, not to mention our own approaching death. We have only old age to look forward to with all its uncertainty, loneliness, grief, pain, and for many, anguish. And after that, what? Millions of people are filled with fear, are lonely, have no way to provide for their family. Life is hard—even cruel. No wonder so many take their own lives, turn to drugs, sex, and all kinds of worldly distractions. They have no purpose in life.

I realize I am painting a gloomy picture here, but it is the truth. Few take the time to reflect today. They are afraid to. They would rather watch TV, go to movies, play sports, work, read books, and do anything except think about life or the future. Worst of all, they worry about their fate in the next world. Then some will drive by a billboard like this one:

> *"You think it's hot here?"*
> *—GOD*

What does this say about God? Christians who promote such turn-or-burn evangelism know not what they do. They think through such fear tactics they will draw souls to Christ. But in reality, they are only turning people further away from God. And what does it do to Christ's "little ones"? It is better to be cast into the sea and drowned than to "offend"[KJV] one of them (Mk. 9:42).

How many people (especially believers) are tormented by the thought of an eternal hell for themselves and for their loved ones? What kind of God would place people in such a cruel world only to send them to something infinitely worse in the hereafter?

There have been times when I felt God to be distant and cruel. One of those times was in the aftermath of the Tsunami catastrophe of January 2005. Soon after the tragedy, I had a dream. In it, I was struggling with the horror of this disaster. One specific thought stuck with me upon awakening: "Faith is to believe God is good even in the midst of all the bad." As I thought of this that morning, I remembered the beatitudes Christ addressed to the multitudes in Lu. 6:19-21. He said the poor will receive the kingdom, the hungry will be filled, and the weeping will laugh! These words brought great light and comfort to my heart. No matter what difficult experiences and sufferings people go through in this life, the bottom line is, God will make it right (Ge. 18:25). His peace returned to my spirit.

What is the heart of God regarding this cruel world? When Christ saw the multitudes, He was moved with compassion for them (Mt. 9:36-38). Oh, how all people need to know they are loved by a compassionate God! The "goodness" and "kindness" (NAS) of God leads to repentance (Ro. 2:4). We do not need clever religious clichés of terror like the aforementioned sign. A cruel world testifies there must be something better, or this life is worse than meaningless. And there is! His name is Jesus Christ, Prince of Peace, Everlasting Father, Savior of the world.

False Hopes Raised

How can hope for the restoration of all be as abundantly set forth in Scripture (see Appendix I), if it were not a legitimate hope? Is God out to taunt us? Does He give us passages which raise our hopes only to shatter them in others? The very existence of such wondrous and hopeful passages affirm their validity and plead their acceptance.

Hell's Purpose

Doug Henderson, author of *Why Inclusion*, asked what he called a "nagging" question, "Sending people to Hell for eternity would serve what purpose for God? Revenge? Entertainment? How would that benefit the people sent there?"[4]

Have you ever asked yourself what purpose hell serves? This is one of the most pertinent and weighty questions anyone could raise. Why? Because an unsatisfactory answer maligns God's character.

Would you not think if an eternal hell were true, the Bible would have thrown light on this solemn question? The fact that God offers no explanation argues against an eternal hell. Such a horrific thought, one that is so incomprehensible to every sincere thinker, demands at least some kind of explanation. Where is it?

Incredible

Regarding everlasting torment, Allin proposed:

> If true, can this strange fact be explained—that nobody acts
> as if he believed it? I say this, for any man who so believed,
> and who possessed but a spark of common humanity—to
> say nothing of charity—could not rest, day or night, so long
> as one sinner remained who might be saved. To this all
> would give place—pleasure, learning, business, art, litera-
> ture; nay, life itself would be too short for the terrible
> warnings, the burning entreaties, the earnest pleadings,
> that would be needed. No society, no individual, can possi-
> bly act, or has in fact acted, on such a creed, in the real
> business of life. It is simply impossible: who would dare so
> much as to smile, if he really believed endless torments
> were certain to be the portion of some member of his
> household—it may be of himself? Marriage would be a
> crime, and each birth the occasion of an awful dread. The
> shadow of a possible hell would darken every home, sad-
> den every family hearth...." The world would be one vast
> madhouse," says the American scholar HALLSTED.[5]

Last Sunday, Rev. Smith preached a powerful message on the
second coming of Christ, and the last judgment. He boldly laid the
grim destiny of humanity before his congregation. After his sermon
and the closing prayer, he announced: "We're all meeting at Kingdom
Park this afternoon at 1pm for our Annual Fellowship Banquet. Men,
don't forget your golf clubs, and the pastries, Ladies!"

The reality that our lives can go on so casually after such a heart
wrenching sermon proves one of three possibilities:

- We are totally oblivious to the horror of everlasting punishment.
- If we are not oblivious, then in our heart of hearts, we really
  do not believe it.
- Or, (and please brace yourself and forgive me for saying so),
  we must be the most despicable, pathetic, detestable, wretch-
  ed, and loathsome creatures in the universe worthy of the severest punishment.

Which is the case for you?

In Love with God

Do you believe the majority of the earth's people will suffer forever in hell because they did not meet God's criteria for heaven? Have you come to grips with the fact that you and those you love might actually fall short of this criteria, and to your ultimate horror and despair find yourself in the company of the majority on the last day? (See Appendix II.) If you answered "yes" to these two questions, can you with a true and genuine affection love this God with "all" your heart?

What would you think of a bride on her wedding day kissing the bridegroom's feet out of fear that he would cast her in the lion's den if she didn't? Would those kisses be real? Any love you think you have for such a being is your survival instinct. Do homage or die! This is no different than Islam where one billion Muslims bow in adoration to Allah five times a day. Are they "in love" with Allah, or "in dread" of him?

Only the God of the Blessed Hope can instill in our hearts true and lasting affection for Him. Why? Because we can depend on Him and know that we and those we love are forever safe in His loving arms. We know that His love for us will never end nor fail (1Co. 13:8), because His unfailing plan encompasses the whole creation, not just a select few (Ps. 66:3-4; Is. 46:10-11; Ro. 8:20-22; Jn. 1:29; 4:42; 12:32; 1Jn. 2:2; 4:14, etc. See Appendix 1) Oh what an awesome God!

Love...As Yourself

The whole law is summed up in one word...love. "You shall love your neighbor as yourself"(Ga. 5:14 NAS). The key word is "as." Can we really love another person as much as we love ourselves? I believe we can because God is at work in us to do all His good pleasure (Ph. 2:13). Now picture the person you love most in the whole world being tormented in an eternal hell. With this horrific thought before you, can you rejoice in your "personal" salvation? Of course not, for as long as a loved one is hurting, you will hurt and find no comfort in any exclusive blessing you might have. See 1Co. 12:26; Ro. 12:5, 15.

I contend that if we truly fulfilled the chief commandment to love our lost neighbors "as " we love ourselves, it would be impossible to rejoice in our "personal" salvation, or know inner peace, so long as any of these beloved neighbors remained lost or in hell. Yet Scripture is clear—love, joy, and peace are integral to true Christian experience. This in itself confirms that the Augustinian tradition of infinite punishment is a grave error since it impedes or bars these precious fruits of the Spirit from our lives.

However, knowing God is a loving Father to all those I love and that His judgments are a necessary expression of His love gives me peace and allows me to maintain my joy in Him. For I know His judgments are right and in faithfulness He afflicts us (Ps. 119:75). "Though he brings grief, he will show compassion. So great is his unfailing love" (La. 3:32 NIV).

Life's Potential

Lorraine Day, M.D. pointed out:

> Methuselah had 969 years to find God and get his life right. Yet a child may be born to a prostitute, drug addict mother and an alcoholic father (Mafia hit man) who beats his wife and kids everyday. The child grows up on the streets in the ghetto, joins a gang, and is murdered in a shootout at the age of 14. According to what we are taught, God says, "Well, kid, you had 14 years to find Me and get your life straight. Sadly, you didn't get it right." In this "parable," the boy responds by saying "But why did you give Methuselah 969 years and me only 14 years?"[6]

Popular tradition says if we do not get it right here, there will never be another opportunity. Is this really so? Are we not God's masterpiece of creation? He spent thousands, perhaps millions of years preparing this planet for our arrival. Is He so impatient as to only allow us but a few short years to develop our full potential? What of those who die as babies, or as young children? Or even the mentally handicapped? Are they a privileged group allowed to circumvent the system, leaving the rest of us to prove ourselves? Is this fair? Oh, that we would all have died as babies if that were true!

All creation, through the world of nature with its seasons and cycles, and the dreams living in our hearts point to a God with everything under control. This life cannot be all there is! It is one

> *God is not defeated by circumstances, war, evil, fate,…for He is GOD!*

age of many (Ep. 2:7). His will for unborn babies and all those whose lives were cut short will be realized! For our God is not defeated by circumstances, war, evil, fate, or anything else, for He is GOD! (Ro. 8:31-39). This planet and age are only part of His creation. They are not the Alpha and Omega; Jesus is!

Natural Instincts

Earlier, I discussed abortion and showed that Christians, in spite of their belief in an eternal hell for most of mankind, are still compelled to combat against it. I did not explain why that is, only that it contradicted their theology. I think Allin explained it well. He wrote;

> Wherever human beings exist, in what form of community it matters not, in what climate or under what conditions of life whatsoever, there is found everywhere a deep spontaneous belief, call it feeling, instinct, what you please, that connects the marriage tie and the birthday with joyful associations, with mirth and gladness. Now why is this—has it no meaning?...Is it possible that our Heavenly Father should bid His creatures everywhere to rejoice with a special joy at the marriage feast, at the natal hour, if these births were in fact destined to add largely to the ranks of hell?...As you think it over, take with you these words of Jesus Christ... "joy that a man is born into the world." Dwell on these words, that you may grasp all they convey. Indeed, it may almost be said that in this lies the whole matter. It is a joy that a man—any man—should be born into the world (John xvi : 21) See how wide the words are. If you tell me that this joy is but a blind instinct of the mother: Yes, I reply, it is this very blindness, as you call it, of the instinct that constitutes its force, for it thus betrays its origin; it is implanted, and by whom? By the Great Parent, for it is spontaneous and betrays His hand. Do you ask me to believe that He has done this without a meaning, without a certain purpose of good? Can I believe that our Father bids any mother's heart to stir with joy at the sight of her infant, while He knows that this infant is destined to be, will be, in fact, shut up into endless torment and sin?[7]

What does it all boil down to? It is a matter of the heart. We can hear of the theologies of men such as Augustine teaching the precepts of men as commandments of God. "Their fear toward Me is taught by the commandment of men" (Is. 29:13). But what is really believed in our heart of hearts is that life is good and the Judge of all the earth will do what is right. We instinctively know we will not be disappointed in that day. The Blessed Hope provides the biblical basis for what our hearts already know to be true.

Parents!

Do you remember the time when you first held your little ones in your arms and the affection that filled your heart and still does? Is God less loving toward His children than you are? Of course not. If you give good gifts to your children, how much more will your Father (Mt. 7:11)?

Picture your daughter (or son) when she was about three years old. You told her many times not to play with the stove. Finally, you had enough. In order to teach little "Rosy" her lesson, you will hold her tiny, delicate finger over a lighted candle for two full seconds. Is this how you would discipline Rosy? Ridiculous. Such a crime would never even cross your mind! Yet believers, claiming belief in a loving Father, maintain He will send His children to everlasting torment! Such a thought has never crossed His mind!

> *They built the high places of Baal, which are in the Valley of the Son of Hinnom [Gehenna], to cause their sons and their daughters to pass through the fire to Molech, which I did not command them, **nor did it come into My mind** that they should do this abomination* (Jer. 32:35)...

What would society do to Rosy's mom? Yet if the Supreme Being does something infinitely worse, it is somehow acceptable. How? How has it come to this? How could we have allowed ourselves to believe this way about God?

Personal Reflection

One day as I was wrestling with the idea of the Blessed Hope, I reflected on my own salvation. I began to realize how unworthy I was of it. I thought, "If God will save me, why will He not save all people, since that is His will? Am I morally superior? No. Is not my very faith His gift?" Yes. Then it hit me—He will! He must!

As I reflected further, I realized something else. Only if we believe that God will ultimately save all people is it possible to experience true and lasting joy, the supposed fruit of Christian experience (1Pe. 1:8). For to believe in a God who accepts some and rejects others forever is unsettling to say the least. I know all too well. For how can we know for sure we, or those we love, will not be included with those eternally rejected in the end? "For if God did not spare the natural branches, he will not spare you either" (Ro. 11:21 NIV). "Therefore let him who thinks he stands take heed lest he fall" (1Co. 10:12).

Thus, the realization that God will ultimately bring all people to Himself, filled my heart with joy—a joy Peter expressed as "joy so glorious that it cannot be described" (1Pe. 1:8 JB).

Prayer and Thanks

Our Lord taught us to pray that the Father's will be done on earth (Lu. 11:2). Is not His will the salvation of all men? Paul writes, "I exhort that...prayers...and giving of thanks be made for all men....For this is good and acceptable in the sight of God our Savior; who will have all men to be saved" (1Ti. 2:1-4 KJV).

Who has not prayed for the salvation of someone dear? Do we not do so because we know He wills it and has the wherewithal to bring it to pass? If we can pray in faith for certain individuals we love, why can we not pray for the whole world like Paul commands? In fact, we are to give thanks for all men. What greater thing can we be thankful for than the salvation of all? For is this not His will? Would God have us pray and give thanks for what He cannot or would not grant? Our Lord's exhortation to pray, "Thy will be done," and Paul's, to thank Him for all men (in the very context of the salvation of all), assures me He will do it.

Scripture Harmonized

All who know the Bible must admit that there are comforting parts, and frightening ones. Consider these:

GROUP A

- *The LORD is my light and my salvation; Whom shall I fear* (Ps. 27:1)?
- *Come to Me, all you who labor and are heavy laden, and I will give you rest. Take My yoke upon you and learn from Me, for I am gentle and lowly in heart, and you will find rest for your souls. For My yoke is easy and My burden is light* (Mt. 11:28-30).
- *Do not fear, little flock, for it is your Father's good pleasure to give you the kingdom* (Lu. 12:32).

GROUP B

- *Unless your righteousness **exceeds...Pharisees**, you will by no means enter the kingdom of heaven* (Mt. 5:20).
- *He who **endures to the end** will be saved* (Mt. 10:22).
- *You are saved, **if you hold fast**...unless you believed in vain* (1Co. 15:1-2).

How are we to reconcile these two groups? Do we have the option to pick and choose? I do not think so. For most of my Christian life I was at a loss. But in the Blessed Hope, I am settled. I can identify with Job: "Though He slay me, yet will I trust Him" (Job 13:15). How could he say this? He knew his God! "Those who know Your name will put their trust in You..." (Ps. 9:10). I now understand that even in His most severe judgments, He has a purpose, and His love is ever present. The above groups are no longer contradictory in my mind.

TRADITION AT BAT

We have been called to trust God with all our heart (Pr. 3:5). It is His command, and to not trust Him is sin (Ro. 14:23). How, may I ask, can we trust a Being who will torment us forever if we mess up? Other believers have fallen, how can we be sure we won't? Are we a cut above the rest? Paul did not warn "take heed lest you fall" for nothing (1Co. 10:12). See Appendix II. Why did Hymenaeus and Alexander (1Ti. 1:19-20) fall? Was it inadequate faith, or works? Or were their hearts too wicked for God to change? How can we judge the adequacy of our faith, our works, or our heart? For our "heart is deceitful above all things, and desperately wicked: who can know it" (Jer. 17:9)? STRIKE ONE!

The Bible exhorts us not to worry about anything, or to let our hearts be troubled and afraid. It even commands us to rejoice at all times (Mt. 6:25; Jn. 14:1, 27; Ph. 4:6; 1Th. 5:16). Please be completely honest with yourself. If you truly believe there is the slightest chance you or any of your loved ones might be tormented forever, how is it even remotely possible not to worry, be troubled, be afraid, or to rejoice at all times? You just cannot. I know. I've tried. STRIKE TWO!

> *I now understand that even in His most severe judgments, He has a purpose, and His love is ever present.*

The Bible tells us God is love (1Jn. 4:8, 16) and love never fails (1Co. 13:8). Yet, our popular theologies say either God does not love everyone (Calvinism), or God in some cases fails, hiding under the pretense of "free" will (Arminianism). This finds itself in the midst of a religious system claiming there are no contradictions in Scripture. Who, with unbiased reflection, does not see contradiction in all the above examples? STRIKE THREE!

GOD AT BAT

Consider this critical point. Of the three theologies discussed in this book (see page 82), which removes the contradictions in Scripture and enables us to really obey the injunctions to trust and not fear? Only the Blessed Hope can. What stronger evidence for truth can there be? This precious hope has restored my faith and confidence in God's Word. It has taught me to view His unsearchable and unfathomable judgments (Ro. 11:33) through the clear light of His character and sure promises to restore all people. It is nothing less than God's GRAND SLAM!

Spirit of the New Testament

The Spirit of grace which radiates throughout the pages of the New Testament is totally out of sync with the spirit of the Augustinian tradition of infinite torment. Grace permeates the whole New Testament. It shines forth with love, mercy, longsuffering, joy, and peace.

Also, we are exhorted to meditate on what is noble, just, pure, lovely, of good report, virtuous, and praiseworthy (Ph. 4:8). In other words, on the Spirit of the New Testament. Upon these I can meditate. I can also meditate on God's infinite power, His infinite love, His righteous judgments. In essence, I can meditate on the Blessed Hope emanating through the Spirit of grace from all parts of this testament.

But one thing I know, I could never meditate on everlasting punishment for there is nothing noble, just, pure, lovely, of good report, virtuous, or praiseworthy about it.

Shouldn't this tell us something when we are evaluating the substance of truth in these two theologies? Which truly fits the Spirit of the New Testament? Which conforms to the character of our Lord?

Status of World Missions

What is the status of Christianity in the world? *U.S. News and World Report* reported in June 2005, "Islam is the world's fastest growing religion, and that if current trends continue in the U.S., there will be more Muslims by mid-century than Protestants or Jews."[8] *Mission Frontiers* claims Christianity is growing fastest. Who is right? Consider these statistics:

Global Missions Statistics 2,000

- 1.1 billion—Muslims
- 1.0 billion—Roman Catholics
- 890 million—Hindus
- 875 million—Non-Religious/Atheists
- 680 million—Evangelicals (11 percent of world's population)
- 340 million—Buddhists
- 340 million—Chinese Folk Religions
- 220 million—Tribal Religions
- 17 million—Judaism[9]

A.W. Tozer and Billy Graham are quoted by Dr. R. L. Hymers Jr. to have said only 10-15 percent (respectively) of church members are saved.[10] If you subtract Tozer and Graham's 15 percent from *Mission Frontier*'s 11 percent global Evangelical Christianity figure, you have over 98 percent of the world's population going to an eternal hell. (To my understanding, these statistics reflect how we Evangelicals regard who are "truly" saved. We do not recognize Catholics and Protestant non–Evangelicals as "saved" unless they have had a "genuine" born again experience as we define it.) For Calvinists this is not new, for they have already accepted that God predestines only a few to salvation. But for the majority of believers, this is very serious indeed since we believe that God wills the salvation of all. But can it really be? Will 98 percent of humanity be forever lost in spite of the precious blood of Christ shed for all—i.e. 100 percent of the earth's men, women, and children?

God must be greater than these statistics show. If He is not, then He is not GOD ALMIGHTY. What a contradiction we are. We make bold claims for God's power, but we do not believe them. We say Satan is defeated, but admit most of mankind is forever lost. When will we own up to our double talk? Ponder the following passages as we truly believe them. "For as in Adam all die, even so in Christ [a miniscule number] shall be made alive." "Where sin abounded, grace abounded [much less]" (1Co. 15:22; Ro. 15:20).

Testimony of Song

Visitors on a typical Sunday morning visiting our church have no idea what we really believe about God. Our positive, upbeat songs offer no hint. How filled they are with words expressive of the Blessed Hope! We are taught to believe one thing with our heads, but deep in our heart of hearts, where songs are birthed, the doctrine is strangely absent. Should not this testimony of the corporate body of Christ in its worship tell us something? Is this not the Spirit's witness to the truth? (See Appendix VIII: Testimony in Song).

Worship Magnified

Worship reflects what we admire about God. We sing of His goodness, faithfulness, love, etc. It is not in us to sing of His judgments as they are commonly understood. Nevertheless, His just and righteous judgments are indeed praiseworthy! By not praising Him here, we are failing to worship Him for all He is. The revelation that even in judgment His love is victorious, draws our hearts into a depth of worship transcending all we have experienced. David rejoiced in God's just judgments. Notice the mood surrounding judgment in the following passages. They are set in the context of singing and rejoicing.

+ *Let the heavens be glad...the earth rejoice...the fields rejoice....Then shall the trees...sing out at the presence of the Lord, because He cometh to judge the earth* (1Ch. 16:31-33 KJV).

- *Sing unto Him a new song....He loveth righteousness and judgment: the earth is full of the goodness of the Lord (Ps. 33:3-5 KJV).*
- *Justice and judgment are the habitation of thy throne: mercy and truth shall go before Thy face. Blessed is the people who know the joyful sound... (Ps. 89:14-15 KJV).*
- *He shall judge the people righteously. Let the heavens rejoice, and let the earth be glad....Let the field be joyful...then shall all the trees of the wood rejoice before the Lord: for He cometh to judge the earth: He shall judge the world with righteousness, and the people with His truth (Ps. 96:10-13 KJV).*
- *Let the floods clap their hands, the hills be joyful together before the Lord; for He cometh to judge the earth: with righteousness shall He judge the world, and the people with equity (Ps. 98:8-9 KJV).*
- *I will sing of mercy and judgment: unto Thee, O Lord, will I sing (Ps. 101:1 KJV).*

> *The revelation that even in judgment He remains loving will draw our hearts into a depth of worship that will transcend all we have yet experienced.*

The Church is not singing the above passages of Scripture. God is not yet receiving all the praise His glorious character deserves. Why? I encourage you to read Psalm 98. I am longing for the day when the Church will worship God for both His mercies and His judgments! For truly, "the judgments of the Lord are true and righteous altogether. More to be desired are they than gold, Yea, than much fine gold; Sweeter also than honey and the honeycomb" (Ps. 19:9-10).

◆ ◆ ◆ ◆ ◆

Please carefully weigh all the evidence—the pillars, God's nature, His purpose-driven judgment, salvation and election's purpose, the fullness of times, the proclamations, the six witnesses, the circumstantial evidence, the conclusions of chapter ten, and finally the supporting evidence of the appendices and my website. May God open His truth to your heart.

CHAPTER TEN

CHRIST TRIUMPHANT

I...accomplished the work You have given me to do.
(Jn. 17:4 NAS)

*I*f Christ is not the Triumphant One, there can be no basis for the Blessed Hope or any hope for that matter. But if He is, that fact alone establishes the validity of our Hope. In this chapter, we will consider God's oath on the matter, consider Christ's title as Savior of the world, establish that He fully accomplished His mission, contemplate the results of His ultimate sacrifice, reflect on God's mercy for all in light of His glorious Being, and make note of encouraging signs on the horizon.

Oath of God

Of what importance is an oath? It is of the utmost importance, for it signifies with immense gravity the seriousness of a given promise. God, the Almighty Creator, possessor of all power, has made an oath that He will bless every family (Ac. 3:25-26) on earth and that every knee shall bow in worship before Him (Is. 45:23; etc). An oath reveals the unchangeableness of His purpose (He. 6:17). Nothing can stop Him, for He is well able even to subdue all things to Himself (Ph. 3:21). In fact, an oath means the end of all dispute (He. 6:16).

- *I will perform the oath I swore...in your seed all the nations [families Ac. 3:25] of the earth shall be blessed* (Ge. 26:3-4; 22:16-18).
- *I have sworn...every knee shall bow* (Is. 45:23).
- *To show...the unchangeable character of his purpose, he interposed with an oath* (He. 6:17 RSV).
- *An oath...is for them an end of all dispute* (He. 6:16).

172 Hope Beyond Hell

We are reflecting on God's oath. When you think of the scant evidence proffered in favor of infinite punishment, and compare it to the massive evidence against it submitted in this book, to then ignore God's very oath on the matter would be very serious indeed.

Indeed the World's Savior

Scripture refers to Christ as the Savior of the World. In fact, "Jesus" means savior (Mt. 1:21). The Father sent Him as such (1Jn. 4:14). Though popular theology gives lip service to this title, it actually denies it. It attests instead that Christ is merely the Savior of "some out" of the world. Or again, He is the "wish to be" Savior of the world. If the mass of humanity is lost forever, call Him what you will, He is not the Savior of the world. It does not matter that few, many, or most of the world is saved. Even if none are saved, He would still be referred to as "Savior of the world." For the reasoning is simple: to offer salvation, makes a savior. That is strange indeed—"The Savior of the world not saved." What would you think of a lifeguard who was hailed as the hero of the day at the funeral of a young child for merely having offered her a life preserver and then threw it to the other end of the pool? Which of the following is the accurate version of John 12:47?

A. "I did not come to judge the world but to offer salvation to the world."
B. "I did not come to judge the world but to save the world."

Either the world is saved or it is not. Part of the world saved does not make Him the "Savior of the world." He can be called "Savior" if He saves some. But He cannot be called "Savior of the world," unless He saves the world. If God knew from the beginning the world could never be saved, He would not have "sent the Son as Savior of the world" (1Jn. 4:14). Nor would the Apostle John have said Christ was "indeed...the Savior of the world" (Jn. 4:42). Being Almighty and all-knowing, the Father sent Christ to do exactly what He knew He would do.

Mission Accomplished

Christ came for the very purpose of destroying the devil's works (1Jn. 3:8), rendering powerless him who has the power of death, and freeing those who through fear of death are subject to slavery all their lives (He. 2:14-15 NAS). Christ is greater than he who is in the world (1Jn. 4:4), and He will cast him out! (Jn. 12:31). If only some of the devil's works are destroyed, it would mean His mission failed; for Christ came to rescue the world, not merely part of it (1Jn. 4:14). Allin claimed:

> If evil be as strong as God, as enduring as God Himself, there is no escape from the conclusion that you proclaim the triumph of the evil one. You are proclaiming, not the true faith, but a dualism. You blot from the faith of Christendom its fundamental article, "I believe in one God the Father Almighty." What are all heresies, all errors, that have stained the Church of God, compared with this supreme heresy, this dualism, which seats evil on the throne of the universe, a power enduring as God Himself?[1]

But evil is not on the throne, Christ is, and these texts testify powerfully to it!

+ *Christ puts an end to all rule, authority, and power....* (1Co. 15:24).
+ *I accomplished the work You have given me to do* (Jn. 17:4 NAS).
+ *The Lord's pleasure has prospered in His hand* (Is. 53:10).
+ *Christ has abolished death...* (2Ti. 1:10; 1Co. 15:26).
+ *It is finished [paid in full]* (Jn.19:30).[2]
+ *He gave Himself a ransom for all to be testified in due time* (1Ti. 2:6).
+ *He shall see the travail of His soul, and be satisfied* (Is. 53:11 KJV).
+ *He is the propitiation for our sins, and not for ours only but also for the whole world* (1Jn. 2:2).
+ *O Death, where is your sting? O Hades, where is your victory* (1Co. 15:55)?
+ *The sting of death is sin....But God gives us the victory through Jesus Christ* (1Co. 15:56-57).

> *He is the propitiation for our sins, and not for ours only but also for the whole world.*
> *(1Jn. 2:2)*

Allin continued:

> It is wholly inconceivable that the definite plan of an Al-
> mighty Being should end in failure—that this should be the
> result of the agony of the eternal Son. God has, in the face
> of angels and of men, before the universe and its gaze of
> wonder, entered Himself into the arena, become Himself a
> combatant, has wrestled with the foe, and has been de-
> feated. I can bring myself to imagine those, who reject the
> Deity of Christ, as believing in His defeat; but it is passing
> strange that those who believe Him to be "very God Al-
> mighty," are loudest in asserting His failure.[3]

I have good news for you. Christ will not be defeated! Satan is
not on the throne of the universe, the great "I AM" is! Truly God's
plan for man is unfailing.

Ultimate Price

He paid the ultimate price for all our sins, not a few, not some,
not even many, but for all. The ransom has been paid in full for every
person that has ever walked this earth. There is no way anyone will
ever have to pay again for what Christ has already paid for. For that
would mean Christ suffered for that person in vain. That is not
possible! He bought us all at a price, and we belong to Him.

The sufferings we, both believers and unbelievers, incur as a result of God's righteous judgments are remedial and retributive, not
redemptive. They come to all men in the same spirit of fatherly love
as is exemplified in He. 12:5-11. Why? Does not God love all men
impartially and will the salvation of all? Though He chastises, His
chastisement could never take the place of the blood of Christ as a
propitiation and ransom. Without His perfect sacrifice for the world,
there would be no hope for anyone.

It is inconceivable God would have created the world without
first anticipating the atonement. Even if all were to incur the second
death described in Revelation, all men are still redeemed by the
blood of the lamb slain before the foundation of the world! (1Pe.
1:20; 2Ti. 1:9; Re. 13:8). He purchased all men on the cross (Jn.
19:30). He died for the whole world! (1Jn. 2:2). Christ's blood was
not shed in vain for anyone! It will achieve all the glorious purpose
for which God has ordained it. It cannot miss its mark!

"It pleased the Father to reconcile to Himself all things on earth and in heaven, having made peace through the *blood* of His cross" (Col. 1:19-20). The restoration of all cost our Lord a most horrendous price, as anyone who has viewed "The Passion" can testify. "Through the blood" entails all the suffering Christ endured throughout His life, even from His boyhood. Think of...

- How He emptied Himself to take on the form of a bond servant.
- His battle in the wilderness for 40 days and nights.
- His agony in the garden.
- His abandonment by His friends.
- His torture over the span of 24 hours.
- The crown of thorns.
- The crucifixion with all its excruciating pains (who can imagine it?).
- Hanging for hours (like an eternity) on the cross with every nerve writhing in pain.
- Finally...His last struggling breath.

What horror He suffered for every single human being! For each one of us has infinite value in His sight. That is why He yielded Himself to all this. Oh, how He loves us all! What love He expressed while hanging on the cross—"Father, forgive them." What a redeemer! What a Savior! How could we have ever thought all this fell short of its intended aim?

Mercy on All

*God has shut up all in disobedience so that He may show mercy to all. Oh, the depth of the riches both of the wisdom and knowledge of God! How **unsearchable** are His judgments and **unfathomable** His ways!...For from Him and through Him and to Him are all things....*
(Ro. 11:32-33, 36 NAS)

All Paul's exposition through chapters nine, ten, and eleven lead up to this final summary exclamation—"that He may show mercy to all." God's mercy is for every single human being on the planet. Such mercy is beyond our comprehension. Notice in the very context of such measureless mercy are His unsearchable judgments and unfathomable ways. How is this? Why are His judgments so vitally linked to His mercy for all? Could it be that His mercy finds expression through unsearchable judgments of which we can only know in part (1Co. 13:9-12)?

How is it Augustine has figured out for the Church what Christ said was hidden from the wise and prudent and only revealed to babes (Mt. 11:25-26)? What is supposed to be past finding out (Ro. 11:33), Augustine has found, searched out, and made complete. See *Enchiridion* and *The City of God*. What a depressing theology of partial love, limited mercy, and injustice for the mass of humanity. "And their fear toward Me is taught by the commandment of men" (Is. 29:13). If you would really like to discover where the fruit of such a theology leads, read the Muslim holy book, the Koran, for Mohammed picked up where Augustine left off. If you want to know the fruits of that, watch the news. Thousands of devoted Muslims are waiting in line to give their lives as suicide bombers so they can be guaranteed an escape from Augustine's hell.

Glorious God

What is God like? Is He kind? Is He cruel? Is He loving? Is He evil? Is He fair? These are the questions that matter, the questions all people want answered. This is no peripheral issue for it affects our very concept of God. And that, affects everything—absolutely everything!

Any human or demon can destroy lives. So could God, of course. But only God can create, transform, and restore. What do you think would give God greater pleasure and glory, destruction or restoration? Shall we restrict His possibilities by placing limits on His power and purpose? What would you expect from an all-powerful and all-loving God? I would expect the unexpected, the impossible, and that alone which reaches the highest and most noblest of thoughts!

+ *To Him who is **able** to do **exceedingly abundantly above all** that we can ask or **think**."* (Ep. 3:20). Wow!!!
+ *He will swallow up death forever and will wipe away tears from **all** faces* (Is. 25:8).

How will He wipe all tears in heaven? By a lobotomy of the memory of our lost loved ones in hell, or by His great power and wisdom in winning the hearts of the rebellious? Between the conflicting theologies of a fifth century theologian (Augustine) and the early Church, is it not clear which is most worthy of our glorious God?

Here is a God who does not destroy His enemies by annihilating or eternally tormenting them. He destroys them by making them His friends!

The Blessed Hope and the Augustinian Tradition present two opposing views of God. Of these two ancient theologies, only the first does justice to the character of our glorious God as He is revealed in Christ. It is what the prophets, the apostles, and the early Church embraced. The second, on the other hand, is shackled by a theology of terror which I contend is the primary reason the Gospel has not yet taken the world by storm. Is it by coincidence that once it dominated the western church the medieval world plunged into the "dark ages"?[4] The following are the key reasons why I believe the Blessed Hope, above all theologies, most honors God: It...

- satisfies the heart of Him who died for all.
- transforms us into His likeness as we naturally reflect what we admire.
- fosters genuine and lasting affection for God.
- empowers us to fulfill the two great love commands.
- strengthens our faith and trust in Him.
- instills in us a healthy fear of His judgments.
- satisfies our issues of conscience.
- comforts all who mourn.
- empowers us in evangelism and missions.
- harmonizes the Scriptures.
- imparts lasting joy and peace.
- gives rise to higher heights and deeper depths in worship.

> *Of these two ancient theologies, only the Blessed Hope does justice to the character of our glorious God.*

Change on the Horizon

I have good news for you. Positive signs indicating Christianity is already well on its way out of the dark ages of terror are beginning to emerge. Among those are that books and papers presenting a glorious view of God's judgments are being written by Christians from a wide spectrum of denominational backgrounds.

(For example, in the 18th-19th centuries, among the key writers were Charles Chauncy, Hosea Ballou, Elhanan Winchester, Thomas Whittemore,

Thomas Allin, Thomas Thayer, Andrew Jukes, J. W. Hanson, Erasmus Manford, J.H. Paton, Samuel Cox, A.P. Adams. In the 20th-21st centuries: John Robinson, A. E. Knoch, Adlai Loudy, Charles Pridgeon, Bert Bauman, Ray Prinzing, Preston Eby, L. Abbott, Joseph Kirk, V. Gelesnoff, John Essex, Dean Hough, James Coram, A. Thomson, G. H. Todd, Michael Clute, Loyal Hurley, George Hawtin, Harold Lovelace, John Gavazzoni, Larry/Betty Hodges, Jack Jacobsen, S. Jones, E. R. Capt, David Watson, Jan Bonda, Randy Klassen, M. Phillips, Thomas Talbott, Kalen Fristad, Charles Slagle, Gary Amirault, Mercy Aiken, Ken Eckerty, Mark Chamberlain, Carlton Pearson, Doug Henderson, Leslie Weatherhead, Robert Short, Brian McLaren, Lorraine Day, Bob Evely, Ravi Holy, Ken Vincent, G. MacDonald (pseudonym), Grady Brown, Thomas Kissenger, etc. Please forgive me if I left one of your favorite writers out.

Other positive signs include:

+ The average believer has access to study tools which facilitate the study of Scripture based on Greek and Hebrew (unprecedented in church history).
+ Very few, in their heart of hearts, truly believe in everlasting punishment.
+ Such a punishment is not reflected in our worship songs.
+ Nor is it hardly preached from our pulpits anymore.
+ Whole denominations are making official declarations against it (see below).

R. Albert Mohler Jr. in *Modern Theology: The Disappearance of Hell*, pointed out:

> In 1995, the Church of England Doctrine Commission released *The Mystery of Salvation*, an official report commended by the House of Bishops. The report embraced a hope of universal salvation, arguing that it is "incompatible with the essential Christian affirmation that God is love to say that God brings millions into the world to damn them."[5]

In this same report it said: "Over the last two centuries the decline in the churches of the western world of a belief in everlasting punishment has been one of the most notable transformations of

Christian belief."[6] And relative to the Protestant Evangelical world, he also wrote:

> "The Nature of Hell," (2000) a report of the *Evangelical Alliance Commissions on Unity and Truth Among Evangelicals (ACUTE)*, affirmed hell as an evangelical belief but concluded "specific details of hell's duration, quality, finality, and purpose which are at issue in the current evangelical debate are comparatively less essential."[7]

Did you know the specific details of hell's duration, finality, and purpose were at issue in the current evangelical debate? Even the Catholic church, the largest branch of the Christian world, after 1,500 years of teaching Augustine's hell redefined it. Mohler continues:

> Pope John Paul II redefined hell in a 1999 General Audience at the Vatican. The traditional doctrine of hell was redefined to remove virtually all threat of eternal torment and any sense of place. "Hell is not a punishment imposed externally by God, but the condition resulting from attitudes and actions which people adopt in this life" declared the Pope. With this single sentence, the Pope denied that God imposes hell as a punishment, and insisted that hell is now merely a "condition." He continued by explaining that "more than a physical place, hell is the state of those who freely and definitely separate themselves from God, the source of all life and joy. So eternal judgment is not God's work but is actually our own doing."[8]

Again, he wrote:

> A fixture of Christian theology for over sixteen centuries [notice the writer did not say 20 centuries], hell went away in a hurry. Historian Martin Mary reduced the situation down to this: "Hell disappeared. No one noticed."...The sudden disappearance of hell amounts to a theological mystery of sorts. How did a doctrine so centrally enshrined in the system of theology suffer such a wholesale abandonment? What can explain this radical reordering of Christian theology?[9]

My answer: God. God is bringing light to the Church in the Spirit, which is making it harder and harder to maintain this cruel anti-Christ dogma. He is removing this odious stain on His character, and the whole Christian world is being affected. Who can say God is not at work in all these signs? His very name is at stake!

"The night is far spent, the day is at hand. Therefore let us cast off the works of darkness, and let us put on the armor of light" (Ro. 13:12). The Church on a broad scale is being readied for the truth that God is really GOD, and His love for all will not fail! And when it enters into this in fullness and in unity (Jn. 17:21, 23), in His due time, God's power will be released through it such that the Gospel, even with signs following (Ac. 4:30), will take the world by storm! This is God's unfailing plan for man. This is the Blessed Hope.

Come To Jesus and Find Joy, Peace, and Purpose in Life

I am the door. If **anyone** *enters by Me, he will be saved, and will go in and out and find pasture. I have come that you may have life and that you may have it more abundantly. I am the good shepherd...who gives His life for the sheep.* [10] **Come** *to me,* **all** *you who labor and are heavy laden, and I will give you rest. Take my yoke upon you and learn from me, for I am gentle....For My yoke is easy and My burden in light.* [11]

If you are reading this book and do not know Jesus Christ as your Lord and Savior, I invite you to come to Him. As the Son of God[12] and our very Creator,[13] He became a man[14] and died on the cross over 2,000 years ago for the sins of the whole world.[15] Our sins have separated us from God[16] and Christ is the only one[17] who can cleanse[18] us from them. He, the sinless one,[19] paid the penalty for all our sins[20] by dying in our place.[21] He redeemed us, restoring us to God.[22]

The Apostle Paul, in response to someone asking what he must do to be saved, replied, "Believe on the Lord Jesus Christ."[23] What more can we do? Christ paid our debt in full![24] We being dead in trespasses, He has made alive together with Him, having forgiven us all trespasses.[25] "For by grace you have been saved through faith[26] and that not of yourselves; it is the gift of God, not of works, lest anyone should boast. For we are His workmanship, created in Christ Jesus for good works...that we should walk in them."[27]

Salvation in one sense is an accomplished fact,[28] due to Christ's work on the cross—a gift.[29] Yet in another sense, it is a process involving good works,[30] not completed "until we all reach unity ...attaining the full measure of perfection found in Christ."[31]

In knowing Christ, we become a new person[32] and experience a genuine, personal relationship with God.[33] Won't you come to Him? Most people come in the way of a simple prayer, something like this:

> Thank you Lord for dying on the cross for the sins of the whole world, including mine. Thank you for forgiving all my sins. I come to you now and welcome your yoke. I want to know and love you more, and fulfill the purposes and good works you have for my life.

If you will contact me, I'll send you a booklet that will help you grow in your relationship with God. Please don't let the truth of God's unfailing love[34] become an issue between you and other believers. We are all one in Him,[35] though we may differ on some points.[36] What unites us all is the precious blood of Christ.[37] Let your light shine[38] before a hurting world. We have a message of hope, of life, of joy hurting people are longing to hear.[39]

To My Fellow Believers

If after considering the evidence in these pages you do not share my hope, please do not be too quick to judge or condemn those who do. I pray you would share the same attitude as Billy Graham as seen in a recent interview with Jon Meacham of Newsweek:

> In Graham's view, the core message of the Gospel, and the love of God "for all people" should take priority....But more recent years have given him something he had little of in his decades of global evangelism: time to think both more deeply and more broadly....He...refuses to be judgmental...thinks God's ways and means are veiled from human eyes and wrapped in mystery. "There are many things that I don't understand," he says. He does not believe that Christians need to take every verse of the Bible literally; "sincere Christians," he says, "can disagree about the details of Scripture and theology—absolutely"....he is arguing that the Bible is open to interpretation, and fair-minded Christians may disagree or come to different conclusions

about specific points. Like Saint Paul, he believes human beings on this side of paradise can grasp only so much. "Now we see but a poor reflection as in a mirror," Paul wrote, "then we shall see face to face."...."As time went on, I began to realize the love of God for everybody, all over the world," he says. "And in his death on the cross, some mysterious thing happened between God and the Son that we don't understand. But there he was, alone, taking on the sins of the world....I spend more time on the love of God than I used to.".... When asked whether he believes heaven will be closed to good Jews, Muslims, Buddhists, Hindus or secular people, though, Graham says: "Those are decisions only the Lord will make...I believe the love of God is absolute. He said he gave his son for the whole world, and I think he loves everybody regardless of what label they have." [40]

Let us follow Rev. Graham's lead and refuse to be judgmental, believe the love of God is absolute, acknowledge His ways are veiled from human eyes and wrapped in mystery, and spend more time contemplating the love of God. Dare we condemn our fellow believers for believing God's power, love, and mercy are greater than we are willing to accept?

There is no hope of any kind without Christ's death on the cross! How many are those who throughout history have trodden under foot the Son of God and counted the blood of the covenant an unholy thing, in persecuting His redeemed walking in grace and love. Remember, we only know in part. Now abide faith, hope, and love...but the greatest is love (1Co. 13:13).

If this Hope has found a place in your heart, please proceed humbly. Knowledge puffs up, but love edifies. Do not distance yourself from those who do not yet embrace it. Continue in your community of faith, being a beacon of peace, joy, and love. Realize this hope will be foreign to most engrained in the Augustinian tradition. Pray about and think through the Scriptures for yourself. Be ready to give your own defense for the hope that is in you with meekness and fear and in God's timing (1Pe. 3:15; Is. 50:4).

Let this understanding do its work in your heart, that you may truly love Him with your whole being, and your neighbor as yourself. Be thankful He has opened your heart to see Him in such splendor. Be ready to lay your life down for the One who gave His all for you.

Persecution will come if you confront tradition head on just as it has with the prophets, apostles, and saints throughout the ages. May you bear abundant fruit to His glory counting it all joy to suffer for his name.

Most of all, pray God will impart this Blessed Hope into the hearts of His people so it will impact the world for His glory. How many are tormented by the thought of an eternal hell? I wish someone had shared with me these precious truths in my youth! I believe the Gospel of Jesus Christ, unshackled by the terror of man's tradition, is the only hope we have against the rising tide of radicalism in the world. It powerfully sets Christianity apart from all other religions—being the Gospel in its pristine glory and power.

"Now may the God of **hope** fill you with all joy and peace in believing, that you may **abound in hope** by the power of the Holy Spirit" (Ro. 15:13).

> If this book has brought you peace and hope, I would love to hear from you. Gerry@hopebeyondhell.net

♦ ♦ ♦ ♦ ♦

Has this book drawn you closer to God? Then join me in proclaiming God's all conquering love into the highways and hedges...i.e. far and wide! (Lu. 14:23). "What you hear in the ear, preach on the housetops!" (Mt. 10:27). Let's fill the Church and the world with this word of hope! A hurting world needs Good News!

Who does not enjoy receiving a gift in the mail, especially a good book? People trash junk mail, but rarely a book. They recognize its inherent value, even if for no other reason than to pass it along. There is power in the written word, and books travel from hand to hand. You never know where they might end up. Think of the impact this book could make if every reader gave ten or more copies away! Books are free when ordered directly from the author! See page 247.

I invite you to my website (HopeBeyondHell.net) for more supporting documentation. **See "Book Updates"** for updated notes on this book. I hope to do a bi-monthly newsletter. Let me know if you would like to receive it.

Partner with Us!

Would you prayerfully consider partnering with us in helping to widely distribute this book? If we all pray and work together, we will have an impact! There are a number of tasks we all can do. We welcome whatever the Lord would have you do. Contact me. Let's talk, share ideas, and work together. I look forward to hearing from you. We need you!

Free Books

To facilitate and encourage the sharing of books, we offer them free while supplies last. Just pay for shipping. Also, donations are welcome and appreciated! Please don't let books collect dust. Let's get them out there where they will bring joy, comfort, and peace. To order, see page 247.

Get Connected

May I introduce you to my friend Rick Spencer, of *Action Ministry (A-C-T-I-O-N - A Church That's In Our Neighborhood)*. Rick has a vision to unite and connect believers across North America regarding the all-inclusive love of God. He is being used of the Lord organizing state conferences, round table leadership discussions, and home meetings. Rick wants to help you get connected, both in your region and nationally. His big event takes place every summer on Father's Day hosting a National Conference in various parts of the country. Visit www. restoration-nation.us Call Rick at (979) 540-9900 or email actionministry@hotmail.com.

WWW.HOPEBEYONDHELL.NET

TO ORDER BOOKS: SEE PAGE 247

APPENDIX I:
Over 180 Encouraging Passages

A passage which for me supports the Blessed Hope may not for you and vice versa. The Holy Spirit opens our minds and hearts to His truth. This list is not nor could ever be comprehensive. I submit it only to show that my hope is solidly anchored in Scripture.

Genesis
* 1:31 God [Who declares the end from the beginning - Is. 46:10.] saw everything He had made as indeed very good!
* 12:3 "All the families of the earth shall be blessed."
* 18:25 "Shall not the Judge of all the earth do right?"
* 26:3-4 He makes an oath to bless all nations.

1Samuel
* 2:6 "The Lord kills and makes alive; He brings down to the grave [*Sheol*, rendered "hell" 31 times in the KJV] and brings up."

2Samuel
* 14:14 "God does not take away life; instead, He devises ways so that a banished person may not remain estranged from Him."

1Chronicles
* 16:34 "He is good! For His mercy endures forever."
* 16:41 "His mercy endures forever." Repeated 41 times in the O.T.

Job
* 5:17-18 "Do not despise the chastening of the Almighty. For He bruises, but He binds up; He wounds, but His hands make whole."
* 23:13 "Whatever His soul desires, that He does."
* 42:2 "You can do all things; no plan of yours can be thwarted." NIV

Psalms
* 2:8 He receives the nations for an inheritance.
* 16:9-10 "My heart is glad...my flesh also will rest in hope. For You will not leave my soul in Sheol [rendered "hell" 31 times in KJV]."
* 22:27 "All the ends of the world shall...turn to the Lord. And all the families of the nations shall worship before You."
* 22:29 "All those who go down to the dust shall bow before Him...who cannot keep himself alive."
* 30:5 "His anger is but for a moment, His favor is for life; weeping may endure for a night, but joy comes in the morning."
* 33:5 "He loves righteousness and justice ["judgment"—KJV]; the earth is full of the goodness of the Lord."

- 49:15 "God will redeem my soul from the power of [*Sheol*] the grave for He shall receive me."
- 62:12 "To You, O Lord, belongs mercy; for You render to each one <u>according to his work</u>."
- 65:2-3 "To You <u>all</u> flesh <u>will come</u>...You will provide <u>atonement</u>."
- 66:3-4 "Through the <u>greatness of Your power</u> <u>Your enemies shall submit themselves</u> to You. <u>All</u> the earth shall <u>worship</u> You and sing praises to You."
- 66:11-12 "You laid affliction on our backs...We went through <u>fire</u>...but You brought us out to <u>rich fulfillment</u>."
- 67:1-4 "God...cause His face to shine upon us, that Your way may be known on earth, Your salvation among <u>all</u> nations...let <u>all</u> the peoples praise You. Oh, let the nations be <u>glad</u> and <u>sing for joy! For You shall judge</u> the people righteously."
- 72:11 "<u>All</u> kings shall fall down before Him; <u>all</u> nations shall serve Him."
- 72:17 "<u>All</u> nations shall call Him blessed."
- 82:8 "O God, judge the earth; for You shall inherit all nations."
- 86:9 <u>All</u> nations shall come, worship, and glorify Him.
- 86:10 "You are great, and do <u>wondrous</u> things."
- 86:13 "<u>Great</u> is Your <u>mercy</u>...You have delivered my soul from the depths of <u>Sheol</u>."
- 89:30-34 God will visit His son's transgressions with the rod and stripes. "Nevertheless, My lovingkindness I will not utterly take from him, nor allow My faithfulness to fail. My covenant I will not break, nor alter the word that has gone out of My lips."
- 90:3 "You turn man to destruction, and say, "return..."
- 98:6-9 "Shout <u>joyfully</u>...for He is coming to <u>judge</u> the earth. With righteousness He shall judge the world...the peoples with equity."
- 103:8-9 He is merciful and gracious, slow to anger, <u>abounding in mercy</u>. He will not always strive with us, nor keep his anger forever.
- 107:1 "He is good! For His mercy endures forever."
- 135:6 "Whatever the Lord pleases He does, in heaven and in earth."
- 136:1-26 "His mercy endures forever." Repeated in each verse!
- 138:4 "<u>All</u> the kings of the earth shall praise You, O Lord, when they hear the words of Your mouth."
- 145:7-10 "They shall utter the memory of Your <u>great goodness</u>, and shall sing of Your righteousness. The Lord is gracious and <u>full of compassion</u>, slow to anger and <u>great in mercy</u>. The Lord is <u>good to all</u>, and His <u>tender mercies are over all His works</u>. <u>All</u> Your works shall praise You, O Lord."
- 145:14-16 "The Lord upholds <u>all</u> who fall, and raises up <u>all</u> who are bowed down. The eyes of <u>all</u> look expectantly to You... You open Your hand and satisfy the desire of <u>every</u> living thing."

Proverbs

- 16:9 "A man's heart plans his way, but the Lord directs his steps."
- 19:21 "There are many plans in a man's heart, nevertheless the Lord's counsel- ["purpose"—RSV, "will"—Douay] that will stand."
- 20:24 "A man's steps are ordained by the Lord, how then can man understand his way?" NAS

Isaiah

- 2:2 In the last days His house shall be established and all nations shall flow into it.
- 14:24 "The Lord... has sworn, saying, 'surely, as I have thought, so it shall come to pass, and as I have purposed, so it shall stand.'"
- 14:27 "The Lord of hosts has purposed, and who will annul it? His hand is stretched out, and who will turn it back?"
- 25:6-8 He will make a feast for all people and destroy the covering cast over all people, and the veil that is spread over all nations. He will swallow up death ["in victory"—KJV] forever, and will wipe away tears from all faces.
- 26:9 "When Your judgments are in the earth, the inhabitants of the world will learn righteousness."
- 26:10 "Let grace be shown to the wicked, yet he will not learn righteousness."
- 40:5 His glory shall be revealed and all flesh shall see it.
- 45:21-25 "There is no other God beside Me, a just God and a Savior...Look to Me, and be saved, all you ends of the earth!...I have sworn by Myself; the word has gone out of My mouth in righteousness, and shall not return, that to Me every knee shall bow, every tongue shall take an oath. 'Surely in the Lord I have righteousness and strength. To Him men shall come, and all shall be ashamed who are incensed against Him. In the Lord all the descendants of Israel shall be justified, and shall glory."
- 46:10-11 "Declaring the end from the beginning, and from ancient times things that are not yet done, saying, 'My counsel shall stand, and I will do all my pleasure'... Indeed I have spoken it; I will also bring it to pass. I have purposed it; I will also do it."
- 48:10 "Behold, I have refined you...tested you in the furnace of affliction."
- 49:6 "I will also give You as a light to the Gentiles, that You should be My salvation to the ends of the earth."
- 50: 2 "Is My hand shortened at all that it cannot redeem? Or have I no power to deliver?"
- 52:10 "All the ends of the earth shall see the salvation of our God."
- 53:10-11 "The pleasure of the LORD shall prosper in His hand. He shall see of the labor ["travail"—KJV] of his soul, and be satisfied."
- 54:8 "With a little wrath I hid My face from you for a moment; but with everlasting kindness I will have mercy on you, says the Lord, your Redeemer."

- 55:7b-8 He will "abundantly pardon. For" His thoughts are not our thoughts, nor are His ways our ways.
- 55:11 "So shall My word be that goes forth from My mouth; it shall not return to Me void, but it shall accomplish what I please, and it shall prosper in the thing for which I sent it."
- 57:16 "I will not contend forever, nor will I always be angry; for the spirit would fail before Me, and the souls which I have made."

Jeremiah
- 3:17 "At that time Jerusalem shall be called The Throne of the Lord, and all the nations shall be gathered to it... No more shall they follow the dictates of their evil hearts."
- 10:23 "I know the way of man is not in himself; it is not in man who walks to direct his own steps."
- 23:20 "The anger of the LORD will not turn back until he fully accomplishes the purposes of his heart. In days to come you will understand it clearly. " NIV
- 31:33-34 "I will put My law in their minds, and write it on their hearts.... They all shall know Me....For I will forgive their iniquity, and their sin I will remember no more."
- 32:17 "There is nothing too hard for You."
- 32:40 "I will put My fear in their hearts so that they will not depart from Me."

Lamentations
- 3:31-33 "The Lord will not cast off forever. Though He causes grief, yet He will show compassion according to the multitude of His mercies. For He does not afflict willingly, nor grieve...men."

Ezekiel
- 36:23 "The nations shall know that I am the Lord...when I am hallowed in you before their eyes."
- 36:26 "I will give you a new heart and put a new spirit within you; I will take the heart of stone...and give you a heart of flesh."
- 36:27 "I will put My Spirit within you and cause you to walk in My statutes, and you will keep My judgments and do them."
- 36:36 "Then the nations which are left all around you shall know that I...will do it."
- 16:55 "When your sisters, Sodom and her daughters, return to their former state, and Samaria and her daughters return to their former state, then you and your daughters will return to your former state."
- 18:4 "All souls are Mine." Thus, will not God provide for all His creation? See 1Ti. 5:8. Absolutely!

Daniel
- 4:35 "He does according to His will...No one can restrain His hand."

+ 7:14 "To Him was given dominion...that <u>all</u> peoples, nations, and languages should <u>serve</u> Him."
+ 9:24 "Seventy weeks are determined...to make an end of sins, to make reconciliation for iniquity, to bring in everlasting righteousness." All in due time!

Hosea
+ 13:14 "I will ransom them from the power of the grave [*Sheol*]...O death, I will be your plagues! O grave [*Sheol*], I will be your destruction!" *Sheol* is rendered "hell" in the KJV 31 times!

Joel
+ 2:28 "I will pour out My Spirit on <u>all</u> flesh."

Jonah
+ 4:2 "You are a gracious and merciful God, slow to anger and abundant in lovingkindness, One who relents from doing harm."

Micah
+ 7:18-19 "He does not retain His anger forever, <u>because He delights in mercy</u>.... and <u>will subdue our iniquities</u>."

Habakkuk
+ 2:14 "The <u>earth</u> will be <u>filled</u> with the knowledge of the glory of the LORD, as the waters cover the sea."

Malachi
+ 2:10 "Have we not <u>all one Father</u>? Has not one God created us?"
+ 3:6 "I am the Lord, <u>I do not change</u>; therefore you are not consumed, O sons of Jacob."

Matthew
+ 5:26 "<u>Assuredly</u>....you will by no means get out of there [*Gehenna* prison] <u>till</u> you have paid the last penny." Mt. 18: 34-35; Lu. 12: 59
+ 5:44 "Love your enemies...that you may be sons of your Father." Will God do less?
+ 7:2 "With what judgment you judge, you will be judged; and with the measure you use, <u>it will be measured</u> back to you."
+ 9:36-38 "When He <u>saw the multitudes</u>, He was <u>moved with compassion</u> for them, because they were <u>weary and scattered</u> ["<u>distressed and dispirited</u>"—NAS], like sheep having no shepherd. Then He said... 'The harvest truly is plentiful, but the laborers are few. Therefore pray the Lord...to send out laborers into His harvest.'"
+ 12:20-21 "Till He send forth <u>judgment unto victory</u>. And in His name shall the Gentiles trust." KJV
+ 18:11 "The Son of Man has come to save <u>that</u> which was lost." How many of the lost are included in the word "that"?

- 18:14 "It is not the will of your Father...that one of these little ones should perish."
- 23:1, 9 "Jesus spoke to the <u>multitudes</u> and to His disciples....One is your <u>Father</u>."

Mark

- 9:49 "<u>Everyone</u> will be seasoned ["salted"—NIV] with <u>fire</u>." Everyone?
- 10:26-27 "Who then can be saved?...With men it is impossible, but not with God; for with God <u>all</u> things are possible."

Luke

- 2:10 "I bring you good tidings of <u>great joy</u> which will be to <u>all</u> people."
- 3:6 "<u>All</u> flesh shall see the salvation of God."
- 3:38 "Adam, the <u>son</u> of God." Is not God the Father of humanity?
- 4:18 "He has anointed Me to preach the gospel to the <u>poor</u>...sent Me to heal the <u>brokenhearted</u>, to proclaim liberty to the <u>captives</u> and recovery of sight to the <u>blind</u>, to set at liberty those who are <u>oppressed</u>." Also, " To comfort all who <u>mourn</u>... give them beauty for ashes...oil of joy for mourning, the garment of praise for the <u>spirit of heaviness</u>." Is. 61:2-3. See also Mt. 9:36-38.
- 4:22 All <u>marveled</u> at His <u>gracious words</u>.
- 9:56 "The Son of Man did not come to destroy men's lives but to <u>save them</u>."
- 12:57 "Why do you not <u>even on your own</u> initiative judge what is right?" NAS "<u>Test all</u> things; hold fast what is <u>good</u>." 1 Th. 5:21.
- 15:4 "What man of you, having a hundred sheep, if he loses one of them, does not leave the ninety-nine...and go after the one which is lost <u>until</u> he finds it?" Would the Good Shepherd do differently?
- 23:34 "Father, <u>forgive them</u>, for they do not know what they do."

John

- 1:7-9 "This man came...to bear witness of the Light, that <u>all</u> through him might believe...the true Light which gives light to <u>every</u> man coming into the world."
- 1:13 "Born, <u>not</u>...of the <u>will</u> of man, but of God."
- 1:29 "Behold! The Lamb ...who takes away the <u>sin of the world</u>!"
- 3:17 "God did not send His Son into the world to condemn the world, but <u>that the world</u> through Him might <u>be saved</u>."
- 4:42 "We <u>know</u> that this is <u>indeed</u> the ...<u>Savior of the world</u>."
- 6:33 "He...comes down from heaven and gives <u>life</u> to the <u>world</u>."
- 6:51 "I shall give My flesh...for the <u>life</u> of the <u>world</u>."
- 8:12 "I am the light of the <u>world</u>."
- 8:56 "Abraham rejoiced to see My day...and was <u>glad</u>." Only a triumphant Savior would bring him joy.
- 12:32 "I...will draw [<u>drag</u>] <u>all</u> peoples to Myself."
- 12:47 "I did <u>not come to judge</u> the world but to <u>save the world</u>."
- 17:4 "I have <u>finished</u> the work which You have given Me to do."

Acts

♦ 3:21 "Heaven must receive [Jesus Christ] <u>until the times</u> of restoration of <u>all</u> things, which God has spoken by the mouth of all His holy prophets since the world began."

♦ 3:25-26 "In your seed <u>all</u> the families of the earth shall be blessed. To you <u>first</u>, God...sent Him to bless you, in turning away <u>every one</u> of you from your iniquities."

♦ 10:34 "God shows <u>no</u> partiality." See page 56.

♦ 17: 28-29 "As even some of your own poets have said, 'For <u>we also are His children</u>.' Being then the <u>children</u> of God..." NAS

Romans

♦ 2:4 "Do you despise the riches of His goodness, forbearance, and <u>longsuffering</u>, not knowing that the <u>goodness</u> of God leads you to repentance?" (Not the terror of God).

♦ 3:3-4 "Will their unbelief make the faithfulness of God without effect? Certainly not!"

♦ 4:21 "What He had promised He was also <u>able</u> to perform."

♦ 5:8 "<u>While</u> we were still sinners, Christ died for us."

♦ 5:17 "For if by the one man's offense death reigned through the one, <u>much more</u> those who receive abundance of grace and of the gift of righteousness will reign in life through the One, Jesus Christ." "Receive" is passive, not active. See pages 118-120.

♦ 5:18 "Therefore, as through one man's offense judgment came to <u>all men</u>, resulting in condemnation, even so through one Man's righteous act the free gift came to <u>all men</u>, resulting in justification of life." Read the whole context from verses 12-21.

♦ 5:20 "Where sin abounded, grace abounded <u>much more</u>."

♦ 8:21 "The creation [includes all people] itself also will be delivered from the bondage of corruption into the glorious liberty of the children of God."

♦ 11:15-16 "If their [Jews] being cast away is the reconciling of the <u>world</u>, what will their acceptance be but <u>life from the dead</u>? For if the firstfruit is holy, the <u>lump</u> [of mankind] <u>is also holy</u>."

♦ 11:26 "<u>All</u> Israel will be saved...He will turn away ungodliness from Jacob."

♦ 11:29 "The gifts and the calling of God are irrevocable."

♦ 11:32 "God has committed them <u>all</u> to disobedience, that He might have <u>mercy on all</u>."

♦ 11:33 "Oh, the depth of the riches both of the wisdom and knowledge of God! How <u>unsearchable</u> are His judgments and His ways past finding out!"

♦ 11:36 "Of Him and through Him and to Him are <u>all</u> things."

♦ 12:21 "Overcome evil with good." God is our model.

♦ 14:11 "<u>Every</u> knee shall bow to Me, and <u>every</u> tongue shall confess to God." See page 114.

1Corinthians
- 3:15 "If anyone's work is burned, he will suffer loss; but he himself will be saved, yet so as <u>through fire</u>."
- 13:8 "Love <u>never</u> fails ["<u>ends</u>" RSV]." "God is love." 1Jn. 4:8,16.
- 15:22 "<u>For as</u> in Adam all die, <u>even so</u> in Christ all shall be made alive."
- 15:23 "But each one [Christ, elect, all men] in his own <u>order</u>." In God's appointed time. See pages 103–106.
- 15:26 "The <u>last</u> enemy that will be destroyed is death [2nd death]."
- 15:28 "<u>When</u> all "things" are made subject to Him, <u>then</u>...that God may be all in all." In God's due time!
- 15:54 "Death is swallowed up in <u>victory</u>."
- 15:55 Where is death's sting or Hades' [hell's] victory?

2 Corinthians
- 5:14 "If One died for <u>all</u>, then <u>all</u> died." All die to sin in Christ!
- 5:19 "God was in Christ <u>reconciling the world</u> to Himself."

Galatians
- 3:8 "The Scripture, foreseeing that God would <u>justify</u> the Gentiles <u>by faith</u>, preached the <u>gospel</u> to Abraham beforehand, saying, 'In you <u>all</u> the nations <u>shall be blessed</u>.'"

Ephesians
- 1:9-11 "Having made known to us the mystery of <u>His will</u>, according to His <u>good pleasure</u> which <u>He purposed</u> in Himself, that in the dispensation of the <u>fullness of the times</u> He might <u>gather together in one all</u> things in Christ, both which are in heaven and which are on earth—in Him...<u>who works all things according to the counsel of His will</u>." Wow!
- 2:7 "In <u>the ages to come</u> He might <u>show</u> the <u>exceeding riches of His grace</u> in His kindness toward us in Christ Jesus." Show to whom, and for what purpose?
- 3:6 The Gentiles are <u>fellow heirs</u> with Israel. What a glorious truth knowing all Israel will be saved - Ro. 11:26! See also Ep. 2:14.
- 4:8-10 "When He ascended on high, He <u>led captivity captive</u>, and gave gifts to men. Now this, 'He ascended' – what does it mean but that He also <u>first descended into the lower parts of the earth</u>? He who descended is also the One who ascended far above all the heavens, that He might fill <u>all</u> things." See 1 Pe. 3:19 below.

Philippians
- 2:10-11 "At the name of Jesus <u>every knee will bow</u>, of those who are in heaven, and on earth and under the earth, and that <u>every tongue will confess</u> that <u>Jesus Christ is Lord</u>, <u>to the glory of God</u> the Father."
  3:21 "He is able <u>even to</u> subdue all "things" to Himself."

Colossians

♦ 1:19-20 "It <u>pleased</u> the Father...by Him to <u>reconcile all</u> "things" to Himself, by Him, whether things on earth or things in heaven, <u>having made peace through the blood</u> of His cross."

1 Timothy

♦ 1:19-20 "Concerning the faith have <u>suffered shipwreck</u>, of whom are Hymenaeus and Alexander, whom I <u>delivered to Satan</u> that they may <u>learn</u> not to blaspheme."

♦ 2:3-4, 6 "This is good and acceptable in the sight of God our Savior; Who <u>will have all men to be saved</u>, and to come unto the knowledge of the truth...Who <u>gave Himself a ransom for all</u>, <u>to be testified in due time</u>." KJV

♦ 4:9-11 "This is a faithful saying and worthy of <u>all acceptance</u>. For to this end we both labor and suffer reproach, because we trust in the living God, <u>who is the Savior of all men</u>, <u>especially</u> [not exclusively] of <u>those who believe</u>. These things command and teach."

♦ 5:8 "If anyone [God included?]does not provide for his own [All souls are His.—Eze 18:4], and especially for those of his household, he has denied the faith and is <u>worse</u> than an unbeliever." Can God be worse than we are? Will He violate His own principles?

2 Timothy

♦ 1:9 "God...<u>saved us</u> and called us...not according to our works, but according to His own purpose and grace which was given to us in Christ Jesus <u>before</u> time began."

♦ 1:10 "Our Savior Jesus Christ...has <u>abolished death</u> and brought life and immortality to light through the gospel."

Titus

♦ 2:11 "The grace of God has appeared, <u>bringing salvation to all</u> men." NAS

Hebrews

♦ 2:2 "<u>Every</u> transgression and disobedience received a <u>just</u> reward."

♦ 2:9 "Jesus...tasting death for... <u>everyone</u>." CLT

♦ 2:14-15 "Through death He might destroy him who had the power of death, that is, the devil, and <u>release those</u> [all people] who through fear of death were all their lifetime subject to bondage."

♦ 7:25 "He is...<u>able</u> to save to the uttermost."

♦ 8:10-11 "I will put My laws in their mind and write them on their hearts...and they shall be My people...for <u>all</u> shall know Me, from the <u>least</u> of them to the greatest."

♦ 13:8 "Jesus Christ is the <u>same</u> yesterday, today, and forever."
Always a Savior!

James
- 1:18 "Of His own <u>will</u> He brought us forth...that we might be a kind of <u>firstfruits</u> of His <u>creatures</u>." See Ro. 8:20-23.
- 2:13 "Mercy triumphs over judgment." Does this not apply to God?
- 5:11 "You have heard of the perseverance of Job and seen <u>the end intended</u> by the Lord—that the Lord is very compassionate and merciful." When is God not in full control?

1Peter
- 1:8 "You <u>greatly rejoice</u> with <u>joy inexpressible</u> and full of glory." NAS
- 2:12 The Gentiles <u>will glorify God</u> in the <u>day of visitation</u> because they observed our good works.
- 3:19-20; 4:6 "He...went and <u>preached to the spirits in prison</u>, who formerly were disobedient....the <u>gospel</u> was preached also <u>to those who are dead</u>, that they might be judged according to men in the flesh, but live according to God in the spirit."

2Peter
- 3:8 "With the Lord...a thousand years [is] as <u>one</u> day."
- 3:9 "The Lord is not slack concerning His promise...but is <u>longsuffering</u> toward us, <u>not willing</u> that <u>any</u> should perish but that <u>all</u> should come to repentance."
- 3:15 "The <u>longsuffering</u> of our Lord <u>is</u> salvation." Since a 1000 years are as a day to God, when does His longsuffering for the lost end? Will He seek His lost sheep "until" He finds them? Lu. 15:4.

1John
- 2:2 "He...is the propitiation for our sins, and <u>not for ours only</u> but also for the <u>whole world</u>."
- 3:8 "The Son of God appeared for <u>this purpose</u>, to destroy the works of the devil." NAS Did He really succeed?
- 4:8, 16 "God <u>is</u> love." There are no "buts" about it.
- 4:14 "The Father has sent the Son as <u>Savior of the world</u>." Fact or fiction?

Revelation
- 1:17-18 "<u>Fear not</u>; I...have the <u>keys</u> of hell and of death." KJV
- 5:13 "<u>Every creature</u> which is in heaven and on the earth and under the earth...I heard saying: "Blessing and honor and glory and power be to Him who sits on the throne."
- 15:4 "<u>Who shall not</u> fear You, O Lord, and <u>glorify</u> Your name?...For <u>all</u> nations <u>shall come</u> and <u>worship</u> before You, <u>for Your judgments have been manifested</u>." Wow!
- 20:13 "Death and <u>Hades delivered up the dead</u> who were in them. And they were <u>judged</u>, each one <u>according to his works</u>."
- 21:5 "Behold, I make <u>all</u> things new....these words are true and faithful."
- 22:3 "There shall be <u>no more curse</u>."

APPENDIX II:
Warnings to Believers

*For the time has come for judgment to begin
at the house of God....*
(1Pe. 4:17)

Many Christians assume believers have nothing to fear because they are "saved." Let me advise you that if you seriously reflect on the following list of passages, it will unsettle you in that confidence. The Blessed Hope has enabled me to face such passages with an optimism I never had before. I can say like Job, "Though He slay me, yet will I trust Him..." (Job 13:15). Why? Because I know His name—His character. "Those who know Your name will put their trust in You" (Ps. 9:10). He chastens...for our profit, that we may be partakers of His holiness...afterward it yields the peaceable fruit of righteousness to those who have been trained by it" (He. 12:6-11).

I do not wish by this list to put fear in your heart or rob you of your peace in God. I want to merely show that we, as believers, will be held accountable for how we live. Too many of us seem to reject this reality. God's *aionion* judgment, though severe, is nevertheless the discipline of a loving Father towards His children. Though not infinite and an expression of His love, it is nonetheless a solemn reality to contend with. I do not minimize that. However, let me inform you that these verses are not in context. They are not compiled like this anywhere in Scripture, and in such a format will overwhelm us. Such a list is but the "letter" of the law and can only bring death. Only when God's Spirit quickens His word (including warnings), in its proper context, does it produce life. God uses warnings to help us see our sinfulness, and drive us to seek His limitless mercy, grace, and strength. Please do not dwell on this list. Meditate instead on what is noble, lovely, of good report, and praiseworthy (Ph. 4:8). Meditate on His "life giving" promises found in Appendix I.

- Your righteousness must surpass that of the Scribes...to enter the kingdom (Mt. 5:19).
- Endure to the end and you will be saved (Mt. 10:22).
- Confess Him before men and He will confess you before His Father (Mt. 10:32).
- Forgive from the heart and thus not be delivered to the torturers (Mt. 18:34).

- Be faithful and thus not be cut in two and receive your portion with the unbelievers (Lu. 12 :43-46).
- Be counted worthy to attain that age, and the resurrection from the dead (Lu. 20:35).
- Abide in Him and thus not be cast out as a branch, thrown into the fire, and burned (Jn. 15 :6).
- Put to death the deeds of the body for if you live according to the flesh you will die (Ro. 8:12).
- Continue in His goodness or otherwise you will be cut off (Ro. 11:20-22).
- Do not judge for you shall all stand before the judgment seat of Christ (Ro. 14:10; 1Co. 11:31).
- Discipline your body lest when you have preached to others, you are disqualified (1Co. 9:27).
- Do not think you stand lest you fall (1Co. 10 :12, see 1-12).
- Hold fast the word by which you are saved unless you believed in vain (1Co. 15:1, 2).
- [Do good] for you will receive according to what you have done, whether good or bad (2Co. 5:10).
- Do not do wrong or you will be repaid...there is no partiality (Col. 3:25).
- Provide for your family, or you have denied the faith and are worse than an unbeliever (1Ti. 5:8).
- Do not want riches and be snared into desires which drown men into ruin and destruction (1Ti. 6:9 NAS).
- Guard yourself and avoid idle talk like some that have strayed concerning the faith (1Ti. 6:21).
- Die with Him if you want to live with Him (2Ti. 2:11).
- Do not deny Him, or He will deny you (2Ti. 2:12).
- Give earnest heed to the things you have heard lest you drift away (He. 2:1).
- Do not neglect salvation or you shall not escape the just penalty for every transgression (He. 2:2, 3).
- Beware, lest there be in you an evil heart of unbelief in departing from the living God (He. 3:12).
- Hold your confidence steadfast to the end, to show you are a partaker of Christ (He. 3:14).
- Be diligent to enter that rest lest you fall according to the same example of disobedience (He. 4:11).
- Do not bear thorns and briars, or you will be rejected and end up being burned (He. 6:8).
- Show diligence until the end that through faith and patience you inherit the promises (He. 6:11, 12).

- Do not trample the Son of God underfoot....Do not count the blood of the covenant by which you were sanctified a common thing....Do not insult the Spirit of grace, for these punishments merit worse than those of Moses (He. 10:28-29).
- It is a fearful thing to fall into the hands of the living God (He. 10:31).
- Endure so that after you have done the will of God, you may receive the promise (He. 10:36).
- Do not refuse Him who speaks from heaven, or you shall not escape (He. 12:25).
- [Be merciful] for judgment is without mercy to the one who has shown no mercy (Ja. 2:13).
- Do not grumble...lest you be condemned...the Judge is standing at the door! (Ja. 5:9).
- Beware lest you fall from your own steadfastness (2Pe. 3:17).
- Abide in Him, that...you may have confidence and not be ashamed...at His coming (1Jn. 2:28).
- Ask life for the sinning brother who does not sin unto death (1Jn. 5:16).
- Abide in Christ and do not transgress or you do not have God (2Jn. 9).
- Overcome and you will eat from the tree of life (Re. 2:7).
- Overcome and you shall not be hurt by the second death (Re. 2:11).
- Know that He will give to everyone according to his work (Re. 22:12).

IMPORTANT! The above passages are not meant to be meditated upon. They are not compiled like this in Scripture. Such a list is but the "letter" of the law. Only when God's Spirit quickens His warnings in context can they produce life. God uses them to help us see our sin and drive us to seek His limitless mercy, grace, and strength. Meditate instead on what is noble, lovely, of good report, and praiseworthy.

APPENDIX III:
Objections

Always be ready to give a defense to everyone
who asks you a reason for the hope that is in you,
with meekness and fear.
(1Pe. 3:15)

What we believe to be God's truth, can and will be challenged by others. The Lord, for His own good purpose, has not chosen to reveal truth so it can be undeniably acknowledged by all men. The myriads of denominations in Christendom attest to this. I cannot possibly answer to everyone's satisfaction every possible objection possibly raised against the Blessed Hope. Like Paul, I only know in part (1Co. 13:9-11). Furthermore, God's judgments are unsearchable and past finding out (Ro. 11:33), and this, after all, is a treatise on judgment. However, though I cannot show you the smoking gun and make my case incontestable before any possible jury, I need only create a measure of reasonable doubt regarding the contested doctrine. Once I have achieved this, the ball is in your court to seek the truth for yourself. Only God, can reveal it to you. "You have *hidden* these things from the wise and prudent and have *revealed* them to babes" (Mt. 11:25). Please note the very context (vs. 20-24) of this passage pertains to judgment!

Below are 18 objections I have had and wrestled with over these last years. Thanks to other fellow believers who have attempted to answer them, I have been able to glean from what they have found and draw my own conclusions. I have virtually come to a peace with all of them:

1. Appointed Once to Die
2. "All" not all
3. "Things" not people
4. Undermines missions
5. Let's party!
6. Unrighteous & Kingdom
7. Rich man and Lazarus
8. Losing the soul
9. Undermines faith
10. Unpardonable sin
11. Esau hated
12. Judas
13. While He may be found
14. Fear of the Lord
15. Everlasting destruction
16. Gnashing teeth
17. Cruel God
18. Why hidden?

1. Appointed Once to Die, After Judgment (He. 9:27)

Yes, judgment will come; all Christians know this. However, the issue in question is the nature and duration of that judgment, not its incontestable fact. Is there a remedial or restorative element to it, or is it solely retributive? This passage does not address this.

2. "All" Does Not Mean All.

Some claim the "all" in the context of the Blessed Hope promises does not mean every single person, that is not all without exception, but merely all without distinction. However, Dr. Keith DeRose, Yale Philosophy professor (areas of Spec. Philosophy of Language), also a believer, wrote:

> Quantifier phrases...are to be understood...relative to a contextually determined domain....When the domain is limited, there has to be some fairly clear clue about what the limited domain is. When "all" is used in the NT, as in "All have sinned [Ro. 3:23] and fallen short of the glory of God," the "all" I take it, refers to all people. It could possibly refer to some restricted class of people, but that suggestion is to be rejected, because (a) there is no such restricted class that clearly presents itself, (b) it's incumbent on a speaker to make clear what the class is if he means it to be restricted, and (c) the N.T. does not specify any such restricted class. So, "All have sinned" means that all people have sinned, as almost all would agree.[1]

DeRose goes on to say as "all" have sinned is not restricted, so are the passages supporting our theme (as found in Appendix I). He continues,

> What restricted class of people could be meant? [Ro. 5:18 and 1 Co. 15:22 for example] Surely not all the saved; that would turn the statements into useless tautologies: all the saved are saved? The Biblical writers aren't so incompetent as to mean some specially restricted class that doesn't clearly present itself without making it clear.[2]

Were it not for the prevailing view's agenda, the "all," in such passages as 1Co. 15:22 would never have been questioned in the first place. Consider a text shedding light on this. "You have put all things in subjection under His feet" (He. 2:8). Is there a restricted sense to "all" in this passage?

A "You have put all things in subjection under his feet.
B For in that He put all things in subjection under Him,
C He left nothing that is not put under Him.
D **But now** we do **not yet** see all things put under Him."

This is a unique passage, as it provides its own built in commentary. What if this passage only contained clause A, like most Blessed Hope passages? Then some could argue "all" only means all without distinction, because "all things" are not presently in subjection. However, those additional clauses give us a biblical model for other Blessed Hope promises.

The passage reveals two very important truths. "All" in this promise means all without exception and not distinction. It will find its fulfillment in God's appointed time. Note the words "but now" and "not yet." Clause C shows "all" is without exception. No one would contest this. Clause D specifies God's promises will find their fulfillment in due time though at present, it is not so. If there is any question about the compatibility of this passage with other Blessed Hope texts, it is refuted by the following statement directly linked by a second "but." "But we see Jesus...by the grace of God...taste death for everyone" (He. 2:9). We can wholeheartedly trust God when He says "all" in His Blessed Hope promises; "all" is not a mysterious code word for "some."

3. "Things" Do Not Mean "People"?

See "Restoration of All Things," Chapter 7.

4. Undermines Missions

When He saw the multitudes, He was moved with compassion, because they were weary and scattered, ["distressed and dispirited"—NAS] like sheep having no shepherd. Then He said, "The harvest truly is plentiful, but the laborers are few. Therefore pray the Lord to send out laborers into His harvest."
(Mt. 9:36-38)

The world is full of hurting people. They are weary, scattered, distressed, and dispirited, longing for some good news about life. Christ was moved with compassion as He contemplated that reality. He responded by urging prayer for workers in the harvest! People need to know the loving Creator who wants to bring joy, hope, and peace to their lives. "He has anointed Me to preach the gospel [good tidings] to the poor...heal the brokenhearted, proclaim liberty to the captives, recovery of sight to the blind, set at liberty...oppressed" (Lu. 4:18).

Dare we deprive the hurting, brokenhearted, captives, blind, and oppressed of the abundant life Christ paid so dearly to give them? Think back a moment to what your life was like without knowing God. Did your life have meaning and purpose? How did you handle the idea of your approaching death or that of your loved ones? Do you want to go back to that? What a depressing thought to think this life may be all there is. It is anchored in the heart of man the desire to live forever. Everyone needs hope, peace, joy, and a future to look forward to. Christ exhorts us to not let our hearts be troubled because He goes to prepare a place for us! We need to reach out to all around us with troubled hearts! "Blessed be the Father of mercies and God of all comfort, who comforts us in all our tribulation that we may be able to comfort those who are in any trouble, with the comfort with which we ourselves are comforted by God" (2Co. 1:3, 5).

The fear of death is the greatest curse this world has ever known. No person born is spared this lifelong bondage (He. 2:15). How can we be fulfilled in our daily walk with Christ if we do not embody His compassion for the multitudes hurting all around us? They may not show it outwardly, but deep down in their heart of hearts, the dreaded fear lurks…it waits…waits for an opportune moment to remind them once again of their fate. What a curse! Let us proclaim the Good News to the poor, heal the brokenhearted, and proclaim liberty to the oppressed.

In summary, why evangelize? People are hurting; Christ commands us (Mt. 28:18-20; Mk. 16:15); and woe to us if we do not (1Co. 9:16; Lu. 12:47; Ro. 14:10). Why should we need Christ's command or warnings to motivate us? Should not His compassion in us be sufficient? At times the Holy Spirit will lead us to refer to God's just and righteous judgments when presenting the Good News as we sometimes see in Acts. We must be careful in so doing that we do not compromise the "Good News." It must always remain "glad tidings of great joy" (Lu. 2:10). "How beautiful are the feet of those who preach the gospel of peace, who bring glad tidings of good things" (Ro. 10:15)!

5. If God Accepts Everyone in the End, Let's Party!

Be warned, "it is a fearful thing to fall into the hands of the living God" (He. 10:31). "Do not be deceived, He will not be mocked; for whatever we sow, we reap" (Ga. 6:7). "To whom much is given much is required" (Lu. 12:48. 10:29). Of how much worse punishment will one deserve who has trampled the Son of God underfoot, counted the blood of the covenant (by which he was sanctified) a common thing, and insulted the Spirit of grace (He. 10:29)? To take God's just and righteous judgments lightly, does injustice to the blood of the covenant and will not go unaccounted. If you are of this mindset, see Appendix II.

6. The Unrighteous Shall Not Inherit The Kingdom (1Co. 6:9, Ep. 5:5)

The unrighteous, while in that state, cannot inherit God's Kingdom. But they will not always be such. God will make them righteous. We too were in their company, remember? (Ro 5:6, 10) Throughout the ages, God will continue His transforming work in His creation until such a time as all are transformed into the likeness of Christ. The key lies in the mystery of the ages. God's plan for mankind will not fail.

7. What About the Rich Man and Lazarus? (Lu. 16:19-31)

Between us and you there is a great gulf fixed, so that those who want to pass from here to you cannot, nor can those from there pass to us.
(Lu. 16:26)

This passage is saying that while the chastisement is taking place, one cannot up and leave at will. It does not say that once the last penny is paid, there will be no release. For Christ says, "You will by no means get out of there till you have paid the last penny" (Mt. 5:26). Rightly dividing the Word of truth requires we compare Scripture with Scripture, line upon line, to arrive at truth. We must not read and interpret passages in isolation from others, especially the symbolic portions, like this parable. This leads to error, for one part provides light on another. If you have a flawed concept of a key word (*Hades* in this case) or theme (judgment), you will naturally read that idea into the passage, and your understanding of the whole passage will be flawed.

The "fixed gulf" refers to a situation relative to a given period of time. If a road has been covered with deep snowdrifts, we well might tell someone who wants to drive through it, "You cannot cross over from there to us." However, once the snow trucks plow the road, or the sun melts the snow, the road is clear once again.

This parable does not contradict that Christ has the keys of Hades, which signify He has the authority over it to lock or unlock it at will. "I have the keys of Hades and of Death" (Re. 1:18). "He who has the key of David, He who opens and no one shuts, and shuts and no one opens" (Re. 3:7).

Neither does it contradict that Christ went and preached to the spirits in prison who formerly were disobedient in the days of Noah (1Pe. 3:19-20), and preached the gospel to the dead that they might be judged according to men in the flesh, but live according to God in the spirit (1Pe. 4:6). "He ascended on high and led captivity captive, giving gifts to men. Now this ascending means that He first descended into the lower parts of the earth [Hades]. He who descended is also the One who ascended far above all the heavens, that He might fill all things" (Ep. 4:8-9).

Christ, having all authority and power, who holds the keys of Hades, has Himself crossed the gulf, as Peter and Paul stated. Besides, even if He had not already demonstrated this, is anything too hard for the Lord (Ge. 18:14; Jer. 32:17; Mt. 19:26; Mk. 10:26-27; Lu. 1:37; 18:27)?

With all confidence, the Psalmist could say, "God will redeem my soul from the power of the grave [*Sheol*, Strongs #7585]" (Ps. 49:15). "You brought my soul up from the grave [*Sheol*]" (Ps. 30:3). "I will ransom them from the power of the grave [*Sheol*]; I will redeem them from death. O Death, I will be your plagues! O Grave [*Sheol*], I will be your destruction" (Hos. 13:14)!

Even if Christ lacked the power or will to cross the "gulf," (which is inconceivable) it will be destroyed in the lake of fire, also called the second death (Re. 20:14). Once Hades and Death are destroyed (1Co. 15:26), all will be subjected to Christ that God may be all in all (1Co. 15:28). "O Death, where is your sting? O Hades, where is your victory" (1Co. 15:55)? But, if most of humanity were locked in hell forever, Hades would be victorious.

8. Losing the Soul?

For what will it profit a man, if he gains the whole world and forfeits his life? Or what shall a man give in return for his life?
(Mt. 16:26 RSV)

The word "soul" in some translations is misleading because it conjures up the idea of the "eternal spirit" thought to be forever lost in hell. A close study of the Greek word, *psuchē*, will show that it is commonly translated "life." The Jerusalem Bible translates this passage, "What, then will a man gain if he wins the whole world and ruins his life? Or what has a man to offer in exchange for his life?"

I think the idea of "ruining" one's life is more in tune with Christ's own amplification of this passage in the following verse. "And then He will reward each according to his works" (Mt. 16:27). To "reward each according to his works" is a confirmation of the Blessed Hope, which acknowledges that God renders to each person according to what they deserve, no more, no less. The spirit of the passage is the same as Mt. 19:21: "If you want to be perfect, go, sell what you have and give to the poor, and you will have treasure in heaven...." Here Christ is speaking of perfection.

With this in mind, I would say to lose one's life, means one is losing the opportunity of living a perfect life, one that is fruitful. It is a great loss because only through sacrificing oneself for God and others, do we find joy and meaning in life. It is a great deception to seek after that which is only worthless in the end. Jesus taught us to lay up treasures in heaven, and not on earth (Mt. 6:19). These treasures consist of good works that bless others (Mt. 25:44-45; Ja. 1:27; 1Jn. 3:17-18). This is the true wealth.

Bottom line: "I have come that they may have life, and that they may have it more abundantly" (Jn. 10:10). If you seek to gain life's pleasures for yourself, you are missing out on the abundant life Christ came to give you. You are losing, or wasting your life. Does that mean God is going to throw you out like a piece of trash? No! He will chastise you (according to your works) like the loving Father He is. He, in His own way and time, will cause you to learn the lessons you are destined to learn about life. It may not be easy, but it will be fruitful. Read He. 12:5-11. Whatever else it might mean to lose one's life, it does not mean God cannot or will not restore it in His own "due time," in keeping with all His Blessed Hope promises, so abundantly attested to throughout His Word.

9. He That Believes Not the Son Shall Not See Life (Jn. 3:36)

Here is a more accurate translation of this passage as presented in the Concordant Literal Translation. "He who is believing in the Son has life *eonian*, yet he who is stubborn as to the Son shall not be seeing life, but the indignation of God is remaining on him" (Jn. 3:36 CLT). No one, while in unbelief, is seeing life, but the indignation of God is remaining on him. This indignation, does not mean God is not loving that person, but the contrary, it is an expression of His love working in that life to effect change. For if this passage presented a hopeless scenario, then none of us could have ever received salvation, for we all at one time were in unbelief. "God hath concluded them all in unbelief, that He might have mercy upon all"(Ro. 11:32 KJV).

10. Unpardonable Sin (Mk. 3:29-30)?

This is discussed on page 67, fourth text. The word "never" is not in the Greek! Consider how the literal translations read:

- ♦ *'Whoever should be blaspheming against the Holy Spirit is having no pardon for the eon, but is liable to the eonian penalty for the sin'—for they said, 'An unclean spirit has he'* (Mk. 3:28-30 CLT).
- ♦ *'Whoever may speak evil in regard to the Holy Spirit hath not forgiveness—to the age, but is in danger of age-during judgment;' because they said, 'He hath an unclean spirit'* (Mk. 3:28-30 YLT).
- ♦ *'Whosoever shall revile against the Holy Spirit, hath no forgiveness, unto times age-abiding,—but is guilty of an age-abiding sin': because they were saying—'An impure spirit, he hath!'* (Mk. 3:28-30 ROTH).

206 Hope Beyond Hell

11. Esau Hated (Mal. 9:13)?

This is a play on words similar to Christ's command to hate our family (Lu. 14:26). Of course Jesus wants us to love our families, but in our heart of hearts, our deepest love should be for God. This is hyperbole, something very common in ancient biblical writings. God's hate regarding Esau relates to something about Esau that is disliked in a greater way than what God dislikes about Jacob the "deceiver." When God elects one over another, it does not mean He loves them more, but rather He is delegating to them a greater responsibility in His service.

12. Better Had Judas Not Been Born?

The Son of Man indeed goes just as it is written of Him, but woe to that man by whom the Son of Man is betrayed! It would have been good for that man if he had not been born.
(Mt. 26:24)

This passage posed a real obstacle for me as I contemplated the Blessed Hope. It did not take long to resolve however, once I dug deeper and found that this is a mistranslation. Observe closely the difference in how the following literal translations read. The Wycliff and Tyndale translations read the same. The Revised Version of 1881 and the American Standard Version of 1901 put in the margin "Good for him if that man."

- *The Son of Man doth indeed go, as it hath been written concerning him, but woe to that man through whom the Son of Man is delivered up! Good it were for him if that man had not been born* (Mt. 26:24 YLT).
- *The Son of Mankind is indeed going away, according as it is written concerning Him, yet woe to that man through whom the Son of Mankind is being given up! Ideal were it for Him if that man were not born* (Mt. 26:24 CLT)!
- *The Son of man indeed goeth, as it is written of him. But woe to that man by whom the Son of man shall be betrayed. It were better for him, if that man had not been born* (Mt. 26:24 Douay).
- *The Son of Man, indeed, goeth his way, according as it is written concerning him,—But alas! for that man, through whom the Son of Man, is being delivered up: Well, had it been for him, if, that man, had not been born* (Mt. 26:24 ROTH)!

Consider how the Greek Interlinear presents it:

o <3588> {**THE**} *men* <3303> {**INDEED**} *uiov* <5207> *tou* <3588> {**SON**} *anyrwpou* <444> {**OF MAN**} *upagei* <5217> (5719) {**GOES,**} *kaywv* <2531> {**AS**} *gegraptai* <1125> (5769) {**IT HAS BEEN WRITTEN**} *peri* <4012> {**CONCERNING**} *autou* <846> {**HIM,**} [Christ] *ouai* <3759> *de* <1161> *tw* <3588> {**BUT WOE**} *anyrwpw* <444> *ekeinw* <1565> {**TO THAT MAN**} [Judas] *di* <1223> {**BY**} *ou* <3739> {**WHOM**} *o* <3588> {**THE**} *uiov* <5207> *tou* <3588> {**SON**} *anyrwpou* <444> {**OF MAN**} *paradidotai* <3860> (5743) {**IS DELIVERED UP;**} *kalon* <2570> {**GOOD**} *hn* <2258> (5713) {**WERE IT**} *autw* <846> {**FOR HIM**} [Christ] *ei* <1487> *ouk* <3756> {**IF**} *egennhyh* <1080> (5681) *o* <3588> {**HAD NOT BEEN BORN**} *anyrwpov* <444> *ekeinov* <1565> {**THAT MAN.**} [Judas] (Mt. 26:24).

German Bible Scholar and translator, A.E. Knoch wrote:

Dr. Leander van Ess, in his German version, renders it "for him were it better, such a human were never born." In the context immediately preceding, the identity of those referred to is fixed beyond question. It may be set forth as follows: Him = The Son of Mankind; That man = Judas

The (Son of Mankind) is indeed going away, according as it is written concerning (Him). Yet woe to "that man" through whom the (Son of Mankind) is being betrayed! Ideal were it for (Him) if "that man" were not born!

If it had read "Ideal were it for "that man" if "he" had not been born (as usually mistranslated) then both would refer to Judas. But no unprejudiced reader of the English or the Greek can possibly refer the Him to anyone but our Lord, Who is so termed in the preceding sentence. But if all the translations ever made rendered the passage incorrectly, that would not prove anything except human fallibility. The original speaks of the Son of Mankind as "Him" and of Judas as "that man," and makes it clear that it were ideal for Him if that man were not born.

The real cause of this mistranslation is the hardness of the human heart. On the one hand, who has been concerned with the feelings of our Lord and His distress at having the traitor in His company? Even His saints seem utterly unable to sympathize with Him in this trial. On the other hand, they have allowed a just indignation at Judas" dreadful deed to degenerate into vindictiveness, and attribute to our Lord the harshness of their own hearts. In judging Judas they have condemned themselves.

The Scriptures show the utter helplessness of Judas. How could he flee from his fate? Not only were the powers of evil against him, but the powers of good were just as determined to make him play his part. God Himself had determined the role he should have. What can a mortal do when Satan, Christ, and God all force him to commit a deed so awful in his own eyes it drives him to desperation and death?

It may help if I confess I once feared to face this issue. I tried to find a way for God to get out of this dilemma. The idea that He could make vessels for dishonor (Ro. 9:21), and then punish them eternally was incredible. And I was right. God could not do such a thing. My mistake was to disbelieve God's plain statement and all the evidence which sustains it in the Scriptures, because I had accepted a false theology in regard to His future dealings with these vessels which He fits for destruction. Because I now know God will not only deal justly with them, but lovingly, I am able to believe God, and glorify God, and exult in the God Who remains Love, even when He hardens and hates.[3]

13. Seek...While He May Be Found (Is. 55:6)?

I think this is calling people to take God seriously now, and that they need Him now. There is a sense of urgency about the present. It could also be inferring that God deals with us for a season through grace, but if we persist in resisting Him, a time will come when we will be judged during which He is beyond our reach until this judgment has run its course. It does not say a time will come when people will never be able to find God or that He will not find them. We must guard from reading into the text what is not there.

14. Knowing the Fear of the Lord, We Persuade Men. (2Co. 5:11 NAS)

A friend quoted to me this passage in support of the idea that the motivation for proclaiming the gospel should be the terror of everlasting torment for those who reject the gospel. I asked him to examine closely the context:

> Paul...and Timothy...To the church of God which is at Corinth, with all the saints who are in the whole of Achaia....
> For we must all appear before the judgment seat of Christ, so that each one may receive good or evil, according to what he has done in the body. Therefore, knowing the fear of the Lord, we persuade men...(2Co. 1:1, 5:10-11 RSV).

Paul said "we must all" appear before the judgment seat of Christ, so that each one may receive good or evil, according to what he has done in the body. The "we must all" consists of believers. In his first letter, Paul said, Woe is me if I do not preach the gospel! (1Co. 9:16). This "fear" relates to what they as believers would receive if they failed to preach the gospel.

15. Punished with Everlasting Destruction. (2Th. 1:9)

Marvin Vincent, in *Word Studies in the New Testament* regarding *olethron aionion* in 2Th. 1:9 explained:

> If *olethros* is extinction, then the passage teaches the annihilation of the wicked, in which case the adjective *aionios* is superfluous, because extinction is final, and excludes the idea of duration....In this passage, the word destruction is qualified. It is "destruction from the presence of the Lord and from the glory of his power," at his second coming, in the new *aeon*. In other words, it is the severance, at a given point of time, of those who obey not the gospel from the presence and the glory of Christ. *Aionios* may therefore describe this severance as continuing during the millenial *aeon* between Christ's coming and the final judgment; as being for the wicked prolonged throughout that *aeon* and characteristic of it, or it may describe the severance as characterising or enduring through a period or *aeon* succeeding the final judgment, the extent of which period is not defined. In neither case is *aionios*, to be interpreted as everlasting...[4] (See "Eternity" on my website for full quote.)

If we cross reference *olethros* with 1Co. 5:5, and its derivative *olothrūo* in He. 11:28, we will see that utter annihilation does not fit. For example, take the extermination of the "first-born" of Egypt (He. 11:28). Were all these innocent babies utterly annihilated before God? What do you think? Also, though Satan destroys the flesh of the saved, we all know God will restore it in the resurrection (1Co. 5:5). Even were God to utterly annihilate someone, has He not the power to restore (De. 32:39; 1Sa. 2:6; Mt. 3:9)? (See also *Inescapable Love of God* by Thomas Talbot page 104. See bibliography).

16. Weeping and Gnashing of Teeth.

Barclay wrote, "It was the eastern custom to use language in the most vivid possible way. Eastern language is always as vivid as the human mind can make it."5 (See also Allin's quote on page 33).

The following scene depicts a very serious disappointment for God's unfaithful children, called "sons of the kingdom" in Mt. 8:12 and "unprofitable servants" in Mt. 25:30. In no case, is it proven to be an eternal state. In fact, the context indicates the contrary:

> *In that place there will be weeping and gnashing of teeth when you see Abraham and Isaac and Jacob and all the prophets in the kingdom of God, but yourselves being thrown out. And they shall come from the east, and from the west, and from the north, and from the south, and shall sit down in the kingdom of God. And, behold, there are last which shall be first, and there are first which shall be last* (Lu. 13:28-30).

It is likely the ones thrown out are the very ones who came first but were not ready. Perhaps they came without their wedding garment (Mt. 22:11-12)? Once their judgment outside runs its course, they will return as the "first which shall be last." Note the compassionate heart of Christ in what He says just a few verses further:

> *O Jerusalem, Jerusalem, the one who kills the prophets and stones those who are sent to her! How often I wanted to gather your children together, as a hen gathers her brood under her wings, but you were not willing! See! Your house is left to you desolate [with weeping and gnashing of teeth?]; and assuredly, I say to you, you shall not see Me **until the time** comes when you say, "Blessed is He who comes in the name of the LORD"* (Lu. 13:34, 35)!

The Lord said they would not see Him "until" the time comes when they say, "Blessed is He...." This is separation for a season, not eternity. These who are left desolate are the "first" who are thrown out (Lu. 13:30). Though thrown out for a time, the "first" will return as "last" (Lu. 13:30) after they have paid the last cent and washed their robes (Mt. 5:26; 18:34-35; Lu. 12:59; Re. 22:14). "Blessed are those who wash their robes, so that they may have the right to the tree of life, and may enter by the gates into the city" (Re. 22:14). "Thou hast delivered my soul from the lowest hell" (Ps. 86:13 KJV).

17. Cruel God

How do you reconcile the cruel God of the Old Testament with the Blessed Hope? I believe Jesus Christ is the exact representation of the One true God (He. 1:3). If the Father is seen as cruel in the Old Testament, it is precisely because we do not know the Blessed Hope. Though God is seen wiping out entire groups of people from the earth, that does not mean He won't resurrect them again and see His ultimate purposes fulfilled in them in the fullness of the times. Dr. Norman Geisler, president of Southern Evangelical Seminary, has written, co-authored, or edited more than 50 books, including *When Skeptics Ask* and *Inerrancy*. He wrote regarding the Canaanite and Amalekite cultures:

> This was a thoroughly evil culture, so much so that the Bible says it nauseated God. They were into brutality, cruelty, incest, bestiality, cultic prostitution, even child sacrifice by fire. They were an aggressive culture that wanted to annihilate the Israelites. God took action not only for the sake of the Israelites but, ultimately, for the sake of everyone through history whose salvation would be provided by the Messiah who was to be born among them.

> God's purpose in these instances was to destroy the corrupt nation because the national structure was inherently evil....Many verses indicate that God's primary desire was to drive these evil people out of the land they already knew had been promised for a long time to Israel. That way, Israel could come in and be relatively free from the outside corruption that could have destroyed it like a cancer. He wanted to create an environment where the Messiah could come for the benefit of millions of people through history.

> Besides, under the rules of conduct God had given the Israelites, whenever they went into an enemy city they were to

first make the people an offer of peace. The people had a choice: they could accept that offer, in which case they wouldn't be killed, or they could reject the offer at their own peril. That's appropriate and fair. Most of the women and children would have fled in advance before the actual fighting began, leaving behind the warriors to face the Is-raelites. The fighters who remained would have been the most hardened, the ones who stubbornly refused to leave, the carriers of the corrupt culture....God is not capricious, he's not arbitrary, he's not cruel...he is undeniably just.[6]

Is this not the way we would expect a just God to act to protect His world? He had to establish a certain degree of righteousness on earth to allow for His purposes to be fulfilled.

18. Why Would God Allow This to Be Hidden?

It has not always been so. It was well known and accepted during the first 500 years of Church history when believers read the Scriptures in Greek. Yet, it is true God veils truth from certain groups of people for specific times and purposes. The Church was blinded to salvation by faith for over a millennium until Luther. The adherents of the major religions of the world have been blinded for centuries upon centuries. The Lord blinded the hearts and minds of His audience from understanding His parables. In the words of Andrew Jukes:

When have God's people as a body ever seen or received any truth beyond their own dispensation? Take as an instance Israel of old, whose ways, "ensamples of us," prefigure the Church of this age. Did they ever receive the call of the Gen-tiles, or see God's purpose outside their own election? A few all through that age spoke of blessings to the world, and were without exception judged for such a testimony:— "Which of the prophets have not your fathers slain?" Was God's purpose to the Gentiles therefore a false doctrine: or, because His people did not receive it, was it not to be found in their own Scriptures? The doctrine of the "restitution of all things" is to the Church what "the call of the Gentiles" was to Israel. Is Israel's path to teach us nothing? Are men's traditions about God's purpose to be preferred to His own unerring Word? But the path is not a new one for the sons of God. All the prophets perished in Jerusalem. And, above all, the Lord was judged as a Deceiver, by those whom God had

called to be His witnesses. The Church's judgment, therefore, cannot decide a point like this, if that judgment be in
opposition to the Word of God.[7]

Mercy Aiken, author of *If Hell Is Real*, writes:

In the time of Christ most of Israel completely missed the
Word of God when He was in their midst. They were too
busy with their nose in the book, to perceive the Word
Himself as He came and dwelt among them! Certainly the
masses must have thought...."But none of the teachers,
Pharisees, or priests believe that Jesus is the Messiah! And
they know the scripture better than me!" That fact alone
kept many Jews from daring to believe in Jesus. To do so
was heresy and to admit faith in Him was basically asking
for scorn and rejection. We have been quick to point the
finger at the Pharisees, and not realize that we as the
church follow the same pattern today. Are we going to play
it safe and side with the majority, who are clinging to their
traditions and what their teachers have taught them, or will
we risk it all and step out and follow Him?[8]

Are we to reject the truth of the Blessed Hope on the grounds that it
has not yet been revealed to the Church in fullness? I trust God has His
reasons why He has allowed this to be hidden (Pr. 25:2). Strong evidence
reveals God is beginning to roll away this dark cloud from His Church in
earnest in our time. (See page 177, "Change on the horizon").

CONCLUSION

I do not have all the answers, but God does. Hopefully my answers will
be helpful, and in the very least, provide a model demonstrating how
perplexing passages can be approached.

It's amazing how critical one's prevailing paradigm is. If your paradigm
is the Augustinian view of eternal judgment, then all Bible passages will be
filtered through that mindset. It is not easy to make a transition in paradigm. What has dominated our thinking all our lives is ingrained in us, and
the grooves run deep. We are not even aware how powerfully it governs our
whole thinking. Only through a committed and determined effort are we
enabled to overcome it. This can only come with God's help. I pray He works
it out in your life as He is doing it in mine.

Here's some food for thought. Craig Nolin of "Student of the Word Ministries" writes:

> A new article written by Dr. Drew Westen of Emory University has concluded a long researched subject on human perception and decision making...Dr. Westen's research concludes that when people draw conclusions about particular events, they're not just weighing the facts. "Without knowing it, they're also weighing what they would feel if they came to one conclusion or another, and they often come to the conclusion that would make them feel better, no matter what the facts are." Dr. Westen found that knowing an individual's predisposition proved to be a perfect predictor of their ultimate decision 84 percent of the time, which suggests that no amount of facts would change their original position. His findings also suggest why, regardless of whether we're talking about our diets, exercise routines, political disposition, religious indoctrination or strategies to compete in business, most of us refuse to change until a full-blown crisis hits. Our need to process information in a way that provides maximum emotional comfort convinced Dr. Westen that the facts made virtually no difference in predicting what the vast majority of individuals will decide to do or think. This characteristic is the inspiration of the old line, "Don't confuse me with the facts. My mind is made up!"[9]

Our Augustinian paradigm, as unsettling as it is when meditated upon, has nevertheless brought us a certain degree of selfish security. When confronted with new information that threatens this security, we are shaken. "Better the lost suffer forever than I suffer at all." It is grievous to say some think this way. The thought that we as believers could suffer under God's judgments is not a welcomed idea.

Keith Morrison, of NBC News wrote: "Hell is for other people! Fully three-quarters of survey participants [Americans] felt pretty sure they will be going to heaven when they die, while just 2 percent expected they would wind up in hell."[10] This is very enlightening since we have bought into a theological system that implies that only 2% of humanity will be saved. The only way God will reveal His truth to us is if we are willing to embrace it at any price. Are you willing to pay the price?

For further treatment of objections in the future, see my website "Book Updates" page 199.

APPENDIX IV:
Gehenna / Lake of Fire

Gehenna,... Hebrew Ge-Hinnom, or Valley of Hinnom... to the south of Jerusalem, where, after the introduction of the worship of the fire-gods by Ahaz, the idolatrous Jews sacrificed their children to Molech...(2 K. 23.10). After this it became the common refuse-place of the city, into which the bodies of criminals, carcasses of animals, and all sorts of filth were cast. From its depth and narrowness, and its fires and ascending smoke, it became the symbol of the place of the future punishment of the wicked... As fire was the characteristic of the place, it was called the Gehenna of fire. It should be carefully distinguished from Hades, which is never used for the place of punishment, but for the place of departed spirits, without reference to their moral condition. This distinction, ignored by the A.V., is made in the Rev. 1

The Second Time "*Gehenna*" Is Used by Christ

(Mt. 10:28, Lu. 12:5 parallel passage)
[Please read Mt. 10:17, 24-31.]
Here, our Lord in one breath says to fear God and not to fear Him. Unless the Spirit opens our understanding, we will see much contradiction in the Bible. So, which is it? Do we fear, or do we not?

God uses adversity, persecution, sickness, and suffering in all its forms to refine and mold us into the image of Christ (Ja. 1:2-4; 1Pe. 4:1-2, 12-14). Here God is urging us to accept the cross of suffering (in this case, persecution) for our spiritual development. To cower from our ordained trials only impedes God's refining work in us. Those whom He is not allowed to refine and mold now, must yet be refined in the *Gehenna* fire of purification in a more encompassing way—body and soul. The *Gehenna* destruction must break down the resisting strongholds of self-will in the soul. This apparently is a more painful process warranting a greater degree of fear than that which is experienced merely in the physical body.

We consist of more than just soul and body, but also of spirit. Even if our soul and body were to be annihilated (if God were to do that), our spirit is not mentioned. The apostle Paul identified three parts of our being. "May your spirit, soul, and body be kept sound and blameless at the coming of our Lord Jesus Christ" (1Th. 5:23 RSV). And why are we commanded to love God with all our heart, soul, mind if there are no distinctions (Mt. 22:37)? What is meant by the Word of God piercing even to the division of soul and spirit (He. 4:12)? What is the difference between these two terms? In defining soul, W. E. Vine, in his *An Expository Dictionary of Biblical Words* provides 11 separate definitions![2] This is a challenging word! Regardless of the specific meaning of "soul," it is the end purpose of God's judgments that is the issue. For light here, we must search the whole revelation of God. Our study of the word "destruction" in Chapter 1 demonstrated that "destruction" does not necessitate eternal ruin, or annihilation, but on the contrary, can be shown to result in a glorious and constructive purpose.

Those of the Calvinist and Reformed traditions do not see this as a real threat to the elect or firstfruits. He is merely "able" to destroy. They support this with Mt. 3:9: "God is able to raise up children to Abraham from these stones." They reason that because He does not really raise children from stones, though He could, neither does He annihilate or eternally torment His children, though He could.

It was important to Christ that His disciples understood the *Gehenna* judgment was from their "Father." As a father of three, this speaks volumes to me. A loving father always has the welfare of his children at heart in all his disciplines. That our Lord links it with such an endearing term is strong evidence against the prevalent view.

So, are we to fear our Father or not? He clearly did not intend that His hearers should continue in fear as He immediately completes His thought by exhorting them not to fear. Now, consider the outcome had the disciples understood His threat as everlasting torment. Would they have cared if they were of more value than birds if everlasting torment hung over their heads? Such apparent words of comfort would be a mockery. Why even express such a trifle? It is certainly not the "fear not" they would remember, but the "fear Him" who can torment forever. Since our Lord immediately followed His threat with such comforting words, it is very hard for me to believe everlasting torment could have possibly been in anyone's mind that day.

The Third Time "*Gehenna*" Is Used by Christ

[Please read Mt. 23:15.]

If *Gehenna* is everlasting (beyond measure), how can one deserve it twice as much as another? Only a measurable penalty can be merited twice as much.

[Please read Mt. 23:33, 36-39.]

We must not make too much of the words, "serpents" and "vipers," for even Peter, whom He loved, He called "Satan." In asking, "How will you escape the sentence of *Gehenna*?" (vs. 33), the Lord is asserting that they will not escape; verse 36 confirms this. Then He says, "Jerusalem, Jerusalem...how often I wanted to gather your children together, the way a hen gathers her chicks under her wings, and you were unwilling." Do you not sense God's broken heart, His true heart for His wayward children? "**Truly I say to you, all** these things [the sentence of Gehenna (vs. 33) and the guilt of all the righteous blood (vs. 35)] **will come upon** this genera-tion....Behold, your house is being left to you desolate! For I say to you, from now on you will not see Me **until** you say, 'Blessed is He who comes in the name of the Lord!" Here is that word "until" again (vs. 39). The sentence of *Gehenna* endures only "until" they say, "Blessed is He...." These in *Gehenna* will once again see the Lord and call Him Blessed. Furthermore, would the eternally lost call Him "Blessed," an expression of worship (Ps. 66:4-8; Re. 5:12-13)?

THE LAST OCCASION *"GEHENNA"* IS USED BY CHRIST
[Please read Mt. 18:9 and Mk. 9:43-50.]

This passage is similar to what was said on the first occasion except it in-troduces two new concepts—a fire that is not quenched, and the undying worm. A few translations have translated "unquenchable fire" as "fire that never goes out" (vs. 43). This is unjustified, as "never" is not in the Greek. The literal translations do not use it (YLT, CLT, ROTH, ESV 2001), and most of the others do not use it either, such as RSV, NAS, JB, NEB, DBY, Douay, etc.

"...the fire is not quenched. **For** everyone will be salted with fire" (Mk. 9:48-9). The word "for" links *Gehenna* fire to fire that salts everyone. What is the relationship between these two? Are they one and the same? If not, why are they linked together? This link is strong evidence that in some way, they both (the *Gehenna* and salt fires) must carry a constructive purpose.

Fire Not Quenched

Thomas Allin, D.D., historian, author, and clergyman of the English Episcopal Church North London (late 19th and early 20th centuries), observed in *Christ Triumphant*:

> Any good lexicon will show us how little the term trans-lated "unquenchable" really conveys that idea. Homer of-ten applies it to "glory," "laughter," "shouting," to the brief fire that consumed the Grecian Fleet. Eusebius twice says that martyrs were consumed in "unquenchable" fire. Church Hist. Vi.41. Cyril calls the fire, that consumed the burnt offering, unquenchable.–De ador.lib.x. It is terrible to think of the agony caused to loving hearts by misleading translations; perhaps, most of all by that disgraceful ren-dering, "never shall be quenched." Mk. 9:43-45 (now re-moved after it has worked such evil.)[3]

To understand what Mark meant by "unquenchable," we must go to the Old Testament. "The *fire* on the altar is *burning* on it, it is *not quenched*, and the priest hath burned on it wood morning by morning...*fire* is *continually burning* on the altar, it is *not quenched*" (Le. 6:12-3).

Here we have a fire kept continually burning by the constant efforts of the priests each day. It is a fire with a purpose. Once it accomplished its purpose in the Aaronic priesthood, it was allowed to go out. Who believes the fires burning on those Old Testament altars are still burning today?

[Please read 2K. 22:17; Is. 34:8-10; Jer. 21:12.]

Generation to generation is not forever. God's "unquenching" fury against Israel in these passages do come to an end. "Circumcise...your hearts...lest My fury comes forth like fire, and burn so that no one can quench it, because of the evil of your doings....Take Refuge!...For I will bring disaster from the north, and great destruction" (Jer. 4:4-7). The words, "no one can quench it," mean no one can extinguish it while it runs its course. It is another way of saying "unquenchable." The terminology here points to some form of remedial judgment. It is important to note that He brings chastisement because of the evil "of" their doings and not because they "are" evil beings beyond recovery. The prevalent theology is built on the latter.

"Its cities were broken down,...by His *fierce anger*....'The whole land shall be desolate; yet I will *not make a full end* ["destroy completely"—NIV; see also Jer. 5:10, 18]. For this shall the earth mourn,...because I have spoken. I have *purposed* and will *not relent*, nor will I turn back from it'" (Jer. 4:26-28).

"*You have stricken them*, but they have not grieved; *You have consumed* [burned] *them, but they have refused to receive correction;...They have refused to return...for they do not know* the way of the LORD, the *judgment of their God*" (Jer. 5:1-4).

Why does the fire of His fury burn so no one can quench it? Is there a purpose? Absolutely! (Jer. 4:28). It is a refiner's fire (Mal. 3:2, 3). He consumes to correct (Jer. 5:3; 30:11). If they continue to refuse, He continues to consume for He is relentless (Jer. 4:28). "Unquenchable" means "unstoppable." He will not cease until His purpose is achieved. "Behold, My anger and fury will be poured out on this place—on man and beast, the trees of the field, the fruit of the ground. And it will burn and not be quenched" (Jer. 7:20). If unquenchable is not forever for beasts, trees, and fruits, why must it be so for people?

> *The words, "no one can quench it," means no one can extinguish it while it runs its course.*

"Behold, My anger and My fury will be poured out...and it will burn and not be quenched....This is a nation that does not obey the voice of the LORD their God nor *receive correction*....For the children of Judah have done evil in My sight" (Jer. 7:20, 28, 30). The purpose of God's judgments are correction for "having done" evil, not annihilation or eternal torment for "being hopelessly evil." An infinite difference lies between these two ideas.

"If you will not heed Me...then I will *kindle a fire* in its gates, and it shall devour *the palaces of Jerusalem*, and it *shall not be quenched*" (Jer. 17:27). Have the palaces stopped burning yet?

> *I will kindle a **fire in you**, and it shall devour every green tree and every dry tree **in you**; the **blazing flame shall not be quenched**, and **all faces** from the south to the north shall be **scorched** by it. All flesh shall see that I, the LORD, have kindled it; **it shall not be quenched**. Then I said, "Ah, Lord GOD! They say of me, "Does He not speak parables?"* (Ez. 20:47-49).

Yes, He does speak in parables, and the meaning of "shall not be quenched" is not the same as "shall not ever be quenched." Note that they are not to be tormented forever, but scorched! Those who received our Lord's words understood that "unquenchable" did not last forever, but went on relentlessly until its objective was attained (see also Is. 1:31; Amo. 5:6).

Refining Fire

We all will be salted with His refining and purifying fires. "For everyone will be seasoned with fire" (Mk. 9:49). "Everyone." That includes you and me. What can this mean? I believe "seasoned with fire" signifies the testing and trials God must bring us through to develop us. They are the means by which we are transformed into the image of Christ—the purpose of our salvation. If we resist His purifying fires in this age, we will need to go through them in the next age, for our God is relentless (unstoppable—Jer. 4:28) as we saw above. He will not give up on us until His purposes for us are accomplished! Consider the following texts:

- *You **tested us; refined us** as silver, brought us into the net; **laid affliction on our backs**, caused men to ride over our heads; We went through fire....But You brought us out **to rich fulfillment*** (Ps. 66:10-12).
- *He is like a **refiner's fire** and like launderer's soap. He will sit as a **refiner and a purifier** of silver; He will **purify** the sons of Levi, and **purge** them as gold and silver, that they may offer to the LORD an offering in righteousness* (Mal. 3:2, 3).
- *He will baptize you with the Holy Spirit and with **fire*** (Mt. 3:11; Lu. 3:16).
- *I came to cast **fire** upon the earth; and would that it were already **kindled*** (Lu. 12:47-49 RSV)!

+ *Each man's work will become manifest...it will be revealed with **fire**, and the **fire will test** what sort of work each one has done. If any man's work is **burned up**, he will suffer loss, though he himself will be saved, but only as **through fire*** (1Co. 3:13-15).
+ *Your faith...is **tested by fire**...* (1Pe. 1:7).

God refines, purifies, and purges us to richly fulfill us, that we may offer a righteous offering! Our works can only be evaluated through the testing of what is called "fire." Even our faith must be so tested. Fire is always a good thing. It is for our fulfillment regardless of its pain. No fire. No pain. No gain.

Undying Worm

"And they shall go forth and look upon the corpses of the men who have transgressed against Me. For their *worm does not die*, and their fire is not quenched" (Is. 66:24). "The corpses of this people will be food for the birds of the heaven and for the beasts of the earth. And no one will frighten them away" (Jer. 7:33). The undying worm concept, in my view, has been greatly misunderstood. The term is not a symbolic way for saying people cannot die and thus must live on in perpetual torment. William Barclay pointed out:

> The Valley of Hinnom [*Gehenna*] became the place where the refuse of Jerusalem was cast out and destroyed. It was a kind of public incinerator. Always the fire smoldered in it, and a pall of thick smoke lay over it, and bred a loathsome kind of worm which was hard to kill (Mark 9:44-48). So *Gehenna*, the Valley of Hinnom, became identified in people's minds with all that was accursed and filthy, the place where useless and evil things were destroyed.[4]

Fire and worms reflect the repugnant conditions taking place in the Jerusalem dump. These agents acted as purifying agents by destroying disease carrying organisms. They represented the purifying aspect of the *Gehenna* judgment. These were relentless until all the dross and decayed matter was consumed. Therefore, God's purifying purpose of removing all impurity in those judged will be fully accomplished. This offers no support for the idea that judgment must be endless.

> *God's purifying purpose of removing all that is impure in those judged will be fully accomplished.*

Lake of Fire—An Everlasting Torture Chamber?

I see no reason to think that the "lake of fire" refers to something other than the "*Gehenna*" of which Jesus spoke. If so, how could we explain His silence concerning it, or John's silence regarding "*Gehenna*"? It involves torment (not torture), and is defined as the second death (Re. 20:14; 21:8). Death, as the "last enemy" will be destroyed (1Co. 15:26). And what is the result of death destroyed? Life! This conforms with what Jesus said regarding coming out of the "prison" of *Gehenna* (Mt. 5:26).

Torture or torment?

The word for torture is *tumpanizō* (Strongs #5178). It is used once in the New Testament "others were tortured, not accepting their release, so that they might obtain a better resurrection" (He. 11:35). However, the Greek word associated with "torment" in the fiery lake is not *tumpanizō*, but *basanizo* (Strong's # 928). "Torment" (*basanizo*) is used of one sick of the palsy, of a ship "tossed" with waves; "toiling" in rowing; "vexed" regarding Lot; birth—"pains" (Mt. 8:6; 14:24; Mk. 6:48; 2Pe. 2:8; Re. 12:2). This is a far cry from what is understood by the term "torture."

Charles Pridgeon, president and founder of the Pittsburgh Bible Institute, wrote regarding *basanizo*:

> The original idea of the verb is "to put to the test by rubbing on a touchstone," to test some metal that looked like gold to find whether it was real or not. The meaning and usage harmonizes with the idea of divine purification and the torment which is the test to find whether there has been any change in the sufferer....Sulphur [brimstone] was sacred to the deity among the ancient Greeks; and was used to fumigate, to purify, to cleanse and consecrate to the deity; for this purpose they burned it in their incense. In Homer's Iliad (16:228), one is spoken of as purifying a goblet with fire and brimstone. The verb derived from *THEION* is *THEIOO*, which means to hallow, to make divine, or to dedicate to a god (see Liddell and Scott Greek-English Lexicon, 1897 Edition). To any Greek, or any trained in the Greek language, a "lake of fire and brimstone" would mean a "lake of divine purification."[5]

The *Concordant Greek-English Keyword Concordance* lists both "brimstone" and "divine" as *theion*. It goes on to say regarding sulfur (brimstone) that it is "so called because it was used in the lustrations of false worship."[5] In *The Word Study Concordance*, "brimstone" is listed as Strong's #2303 *thīon* with *thīos*. [Divine] #2304 is listed as the root of the word.[6] Vine says *theion* (brimstone) originally denoted "fire from heaven," and goes on to say "sulfur was used in pagan purifications."[7]

Take a moment with me to consider the biblical references to this "lake of fire," also called the "second death," to see what is said regarding it. "He who overcomes shall not be *hurt* ["injured"—CLT] by the second death" (Re. 2:11). "Blessed and holy is he who has part in the *first* resurrection. Over such the *second death has no power* [jurisdiction], but they shall be priests of God and of Christ, and shall reign with Him a thousand years" (Re. 20:6).

Being "hurt" by something is a far cry from being tormented everlastingly. Also, did those having part in the first resurrection not already die the "second" death when they died to sin during their life on earth (See Romans six)? In addition, on what Scriptural grounds can it be established that the second death as "death" is not included in the "last enemy" (1Co. 15:26) that will be destroyed?

"The dead were judged *according to their works*....Death and Hades delivered up the dead who were in them. And they were judged, each one *according to his works*. Then Death and Hades were cast into the lake of fire. This is the second death" (Re. 20:12-14). Would you not agree that "according to their works" is in direct conflict with a mass generic sentence never-ending for all?

"The cowardly, unbelieving, abominable, murderers, sexually immoral, sorcerers, idolaters, and all liars shall have *their part* in the lake which burns with fire and brimstone, which is the second death" (Re. 21:8). The recipients of the second death receive "their part" which harmonizes perfectly with "according to works," but is logically inconsistent with infinity. For how can what is infinite be "part" of something greater? The closer we look at the language of judgment used in the Scriptures, the more it contradicts the prevalent view.

"They are having no rest day and night, those worshiping the wild beast and its image" (Re. 14:11b CLT). This refers to the time prior to their judgment as it is unthinkable they would continue to worship the beast while being chastised for doing so. Even if they did, it indicates nothing about the duration of their judgment. In addition, as we said concerning "in part," and "according to works," the concept of "day and night" pertains to the time realm, and is inconsistent with eternity.

APPENDIX V:
Disturbing Facts

Young's Literal translation always translates *aion* as "age." Rotherham Literal translation translates it as "age, age-abiding." The Concordant Literal translation translates it "eon." The King James translation however, translates *aion* by nine different words! They are: "age," "course," "end," "eternal," "everlasting," "evermore," (for) "ever," "never," and "world."

How can this be? Unless we use a reference work, such as *The Word Study New Testament*, we have no way of knowing when and where our translators have taken such liberties with the inspired Word. In just the first three chapters of Ephesians, (a key book regarding God's plan for man relative to the fullness of the times) *aion* is used seven times. And out of those seven, the KJV has chosen five different English words ("ages," "course," "end," "eternal," and "world") to translate this one word. And to add to this confusion, it translates the Greek word *genea* (generation), a totally different word, twice as "ages." Talk about confusion compounded! Is it any wonder the Church has been blinded from God's truth about His judgments and the Blessed Hope? To clarify, I have submitted below the KJV and YLT of the first three chapters of Ephesians so you can see how they compare where the word *aion* is used. All underlined words are translations of *aion*.

King James Version

1:21	Not only in this <u>world</u>, but also in that which is to come
2:2	According to the <u>course</u> of this world
2:7	In the <u>ages</u> to come
3:9	From the beginning of the <u>world</u> hath been hid
3:11	According to the <u>eternal</u> purpose
3:5	Which in other ages [*genea*]
3:21	Throughout all ages [*genea*], <u>world</u> without <u>end</u>. Amen.

Young's Literal Translation

1:21	Not only in this <u>age</u>, but also in the coming one
2:2	According to the <u>age</u> of this world
2:7	In the <u>ages</u> that are coming
3:9	Hid from the <u>ages</u>
3:11	According to a purpose of the <u>ages</u>
3:5	Which in other generations [*genea*]
3:21	To all the generations [*genea*], of the <u>age</u> of the <u>ages</u>. Amen.

Would you prefer to study a literal word for word translation and trust the Holy Spirit to give you understanding, or would you rather trust fallible humans to interpret the original words for you based on their underlying theological paradigms? What is to protect you?

Ep. 3:21 is saying something to us about Christ's glory in the church, the *ekklesia*, that Vine defines as "the whole company of the redeemed throughout the present era."[1] This "whole company," are God's "first" fruits. Now, if you wanted to do a study on Ep. 1:9-12, which talks about a mystery, the gathering together of all in Christ, predestination, God's purpose, the counsel of His will, those who "first" trusted in Christ, and the dispensation or administration of the "fullness of times," which one of the these two versions would more likely lead you to the truth? Compare again Ep. 3:21. Are they both saying the same thing? Which is most accurate to the original language? "Unto Him be glory in the church by Christ Jesus throughout all ages, world without end." (KJV) Or "To Him is the glory in the assembly in Christ Jesus, to all the generations of the age of the ages?" (YLT)

The "age of the ages" and "world without end" do not mean the same thing! Why should "age of the ages" be a mystery and require interpretation? Is it not a biblical expression like many others like it? Consider the following: "King of kings and Lord of lords" (Ti. 6:15). "Holy and most Holy" (Ex. 26:33). "Song of songs" (So. 1:1). "Vanity of vanities" (Ec. 12:8). "Servant of servants" (Ge. 9:25). "God of gods and Lord of lords" (De.10:17). "Prince of princes" (Da. 8:25). "Hebrew of Hebrews" (Ph. 3:5). Do you have any problem understanding these expressions? Then why should Ephesians 3:21 be an enigma? It must refer to the final and greatest of all ages.

I realize words often carry different meanings according to context, and thus require different words to translate accurately. The problem comes when fallible humans attempt to translate the "inspired" words of God. The safest and most accurate way to determine their meaning is to study how they are used in all contexts. Here we need a Greek/Hebrew-based concordance, such as *The Word Study Concordance* referred to on page 20. Otherwise, we are at the mercy of human translators who cannot help but interpret everything based on their personal views.

If we want to determine if the Bible teaches everlasting punishment, can we wholeheartedly trust the work of biased translators steeped in that conviction? There is no substitute to doing our own digging (2Ti. 2:15). See Winter's quote on page 20.

Above all, unless the Spirit of God opens our eyes and ears to His truth, all our efforts in Bible study will be of little help.

Appendix VI:
Every Knee Shall Bow

*God also has highly exalted Him and given Him the name which is
above every name, that at the name of Jesus every knee should bow, of
those in heaven, and of those on earth, and of those under the earth, and
that every tongue should confess that Jesus Christ is Lord, to the glory
of God the Father (Ph. 2:9-11).*

Is this a forced worship, or one offered genuinely from the heart? Below are 18 points that together, I believe, unmistakably affirm true worship.

- The phrase "confess that Jesus Christ is Lord" was used in early baptismal services by which those being baptized expressed their commitment to Christ or declared they had been saved through Christ.[1] Now, since "under the earth" refers to the abode of the dead (or hell), then even in death an opportunity remains to confess Christ unto salvation.

- "No one can say that Jesus is Lord except by the Holy Spirit" (1Co. 12:3). This is strong evidence it refers to a sincere worship since fear alone could bring about a forced worship without the need of the Holy Spirit moving the heart.

- Paul links mouth confession with salvation. "If you confess with your mouth the Lord Jesus...you will be saved...with the mouth confession is made unto salvation" (Ro. 10:9).

- This worship brings Him glory. A forced worship would not glorify or satisfy a loving God. "This people honors me with their lips, but their heart is far from me" (Mt. 15:8).

- That this is true worship is confirmed in Re. 5:13 and by the entire context (Re. 5: 11-14). "Every creature in heaven and earth and under the earth...I heard saying: 'Blessing, honor, glory, power be to Him who sits on the throne, and to the Lamb'..." (Re. 5:13). Who believes this passage reflects insincere or forced worship?

- The word "confess" in this passage is the same Greek word *exomologeomai* Christ used in praising His Father in Mt. 11:25 and Lu. 10:21. It is used 11 times: Mt. 3:6; 11:25; Mk. 1:5; Lu. 10:21; 22:6; Ac. 19:18; Ro. 14:11; 15:9; Ph. 2:11; Ja. 5:16; and Re. 3:5. None of these can be seen as "forced" praise. They relate to what flows naturally from the heart. For example, Jesus exclaimed, "I heartily praise Thee, Father...that Thou hast hidden these things..." (Mt. 11:25 Wey). The NIV and the NAS read, "I praise you Father." "I will praise thee among the Gentiles, and sing to thy name" (Ro. 15:9 RSV. See the NIV, NAS, TEV, Phillips, Jerusalem Bible, RSV, NEB, WEY, and so forth). *The Englishman's Hebrew and Chaldee Concordance of the Old Testament* says *exomologeomai* is the word used in Psalms for "praise" (*yadah*) and "give thanks" (*hoday*) in the Septuagint used in Christ's time. Simply reading Psalms confirms the genuine worship of Ph. 2:11.[2]

♦ Ken Eckerty in an article titled, "The Work of the Cross," said:

> I think it's significant that the bowing of every knee and the confessing of every tongue is done "in" the name of Jesus, not "at" as translated by the KJV. Scholars such as Vincent, Robertson, Young, Rotherham, and Bullinger (just to name a few) all say that it is best translated "in." "For where two or three are gathered in my name, there am I...." Mt.18:20 "In" Christ's name implies an "entering into" or an intimacy with His name. Confession "in" His name cannot mean anything but intimacy.[3]

To accurately understand Ph. 2:9-11, we must go to the Old Testament from where it is quoted. Let us look closely at Is. 45:21-25.

> ***21.****There is no other God beside Me, a just God and a Savior; there is none beside me.* ***22.*** *Look to Me and be saved, all you ends of the earth! For I am God, and there is no other.* ***23.*** *I have **sworn** by Myself; the word has gone out of My mouth in righteousness, and shall not return, that to Me every knee shall bow, every tongue shall take an oath.* ***24.*** *He shall say, '**Surely in the LORD I have righteousness** and strength. To Him men shall come, and all shall be **ashamed** who are incensed against Him.* ***25.*** *In the LORD **all** the descendents of Israel shall be **justified**, and shall **glory**.'*

♦ "Surely in the LORD I have righteousness" (vs. 24). Only a genuine believer could say this. Note also it is stated as an oath (vs. 23), making it especially pertinent.
♦ Those who are incensed against Him shall be ashamed (vs. 24). Being ashamed is a sign of genuine repentance, as the following passages will confirm: 2Ch. 30:15; Ezr. 9:6; Jer. 8:12; Ez. 16:62-63; 36:31-33; 2Th. 3:14-15.

◆ "All the descendants of Israel shall be justified and shall glory" (vs. 25). Justification and glory are undeniable evidences of genuine repentance.

◆ "How **awesome** are Your works! Through the greatness of Your power Your **enemies shall submit themselves** to You. All the earth shall worship You and sing praises to You; they shall sing praises to Your name. Selah. Come and see the works of God; He is **awesome** in His doing toward the sons of men (Ps. 66:3-5)."

◆ "Because He delights in mercy. He will again have compassion on us, and **will subdue** our iniquities. You will cast all our sins into the depths of the sea (Mic. 7:18-19)."

◆ "He is **able** even **to subdue** all "things" to Himself (Ph. 3:21)." "Things" is not in the Greek. See pages 132-134

In Ps. 66:3-5, God is described twice as "awesome" in the very context of "enemies submitting themselves" through His "great" power. And this mind you, is all in the context of "all the earth" worshiping and singing praises to God! David then invites us to come and see how awesome is His doing toward humanity! Where is "forced" worship here? As well, they are "submitting themselves," not "being" submitted. Relative to Mic. 7:18-19, how can a "compassionate subduing" from a God "delighting in mercy" (in the very context of sins cast away) possibly coincide with a forced worship of those eternally being tormented in hell? Now Ph. 3: 21 originates in the very same letter as our key text, making it particularly pertinent. It affirms that God's power is "even able" to do something. "Even able" implies something extraordinarily impressive. A compelled submission by brute force is not particularly impressive. But a God winning the hearts of His enemies through His sacrificial love on the cross—that is impressive! That's what makes Him truly a most "awesome" and all powerful God!

◆ "He humbled Himself...even the death of the *cross. Therefore* God also has highly exalted Him...that at the name of Jesus every knee will bow" (Ph. 2:8-9). Every knee bows because of the cross. The word "therefore" links the cross with worship. To deny genuine worship at the foot of the cross is to strip this passage of all its meaning. Worse, it strips the cross of its power to save and insults the Spirit of grace (He. 10:29). Talbott asks:

> Now just what is the power of the Cross, according to Paul? Is it the power of a conquering hero to compel His enemies to obey Him against their will? If that had been Paul's doctrine, it would have been strange indeed, for God had no need of a crucifixion to compel obedience. He was quite capable of doing that all along. God sent His Son into the world, not as a con-

quering hero, but as a suffering servant; and the power that Jesus unleashed as He bled on the Cross was precisely the power of self-giving love, the power to overcome evil by transforming the wills and renewing the minds of the evil ones themselves.[4]

The cross of Christ is the greatest power in the universe because it alone can melt the hearts of God's enemies, and make them His friends. As John Milton, the famous 17th century English author wrote, "Who overcomes by force hath overcome but half his foe."[5]

• Salvation is involved in this confession. "Every tongue will confess that Jesus Christ is Lord, to the glory of God the Father. Therefore...work out your own salvation...for God works in you both to will and to do for His good pleasure" (Ph. 2:11-13). Again the word "therefore" is very significant, for it links the confession that Jesus is Lord directly with salvation.

• God Himself works in them "to will." Does God working in the hearts of His children to will to do His good pleasure mean only a forced submission? The question is its own refutation.

• "When all things are made subject to Him, then the Son Himself will also be subject to Him who put all things under Him that God may be all in all" (1Co. 15:28). The Greek word for "subject" is the same used for Christ. Can it be questioned that Christ's submission is not freely given? Moreover, would God be all in subjects forcefully subjugated?

• Some will say, "Of course they'll confess then, it will all be too obvious. There will be no merit to confessing then." But are we saved by merit? Where is boasting? It is excluded (Ro. 3:27). We, as the Church, have stripped this passage of its full glory. The bottom line is the love of God will do what His power alone could never do: conquer the hearts of His enemies and make them His friends.

I think any honest reflection of the above exposition, must conclude with the evidence presented, that Ph. 2:9-11 affirms sincere and heartfelt worship.

Appendix VII:
Early Church Leaders Testify

Irenaeus: 130 to about 200 A.D. "Bishop of Lyons. His nearness to the apostles makes his testimony most interesting. Irenaeus did not believe evil would last forever. In his treatise *Against Heretics*, he wrote in Book III, chap. 23, §6:"[1]

> Wherefore also He drove him (Adam) out of Paradise, and removed him far from the tree of life, not because He envied him the tree of life, as some dare to assert, but because He pitied him and desired that he should not continue always a sinner, and that the sin which surrounded him should not be immortal, and the evil interminable and irremediable.—Irenaeus.[2]

Theophilus, 160-181 A.D. "Bishop of Antioch (3)."

> And God showed great kindness to man in this, that He did not suffer him to continue being in sin forever; but, as it were by a kind of banishment, cast him out of Paradise, in order that, having by punishment expiated within an appointed time the sin, and having been disciplined, he should afterward be recalled.—Theophilus. *To Autolycus*, Book 2, chap. 26.[4]

Clement of Alexandria, 190 A.D. "Head of the catechetical school there. He speaks of having learned from a disciple of the Apostles.—Strom. lib. ii. His wide and various learning, and his sympathetic spirit combine to give special weight to his teaching."[5]

> All men are Christ's, some by knowing Him, the rest not yet. He is the Savior, not of some (only) and of the rest not (i.e., He is actually Savior of all) for how is He Lord and Savior if He is not Lord and Savior of all? But He is indeed Savior of those who believe...while of those who do not believe He is Lord, until having become able to confess Him, they obtain through Him the benefit appropriate and suitable (to their case). He by the Father's will directs the salvation of all for all things have been ordered, both universally and in part, by the Lord of the universe; with a view to the salvation of the universe....But needful correc-

tion, by the goodness of the great overseeing Judge, through (by means of) the attendant angels, through various prior judgments, through the final (pantelous) judgment, compels even those who have become still more callous to repent.—Clement. Strom. lib. vii. pp. 702-6, Cologne, 1688.[6]

Origen, 185-254 A.D. "Pupil and successor of Clement of Alexandria, founded a school at Caesarea...the greatest theologian and exegete of the Eastern Church."[7]

But he that despises the purification of the word of God and the doctrine of the Gospel only keeps himself for dreadful and penal purifications afterward; that so the fire of hell may purge him in torments whom neither apostolical doctrine nor gospel preaching has cleansed, according to that which is written of being "purified by fire." But how long this purification which is wrought out by penal fire shall endure, or for how many periods or ages it shall torment sinners, He only knows to whom all judgment is committed by the Father.—Origen. *Commentary on Rom.*, Book 8, Chap. 11.[8]

Eusebius of Caesarea, 265-340 A.D. "Bishop of Caesarea in Palestine; friend of Constantine; the greatest of the early Church historians, wrote on Ps. 2:"[9] "The Son's 'breaking in pieces' His enemies is for the sake of remolding them, as a potter his own work; as Jer. xviii. 6, says: i.e., to restore them once more to their former state."–Eusebius. De eccles. theol. iii. 16.[10]

Athanasius, 296-373 A.D. "Called 'the Great,' 'Father of Orthodoxy,' 'Pillar of Orthodoxy;' Bishop of Alexandria and writer of many works; especially noted for defending the deity of our Lord."[11] "While the devil thought to kill one he is deprived of all cast out of Hades, and sitting by the gates, sees all the fettered beings led forth by the courage of the Savior."—Athanasius. De pass. et cruce Darn.[12]

Gregory Nazianzen, 330-390 A.D. "President of the second great Ecumenical Council, was considered the most learned bishop in one of the most learned ages of the Church."[13]

"Until He loosed by His blood all who groan under Tartarean chains."—Carm. xxxv. (ed. Lyons, 1840.) "Today salvation has been brought to the universe to whatsoever is visible and whatsoever is invisible...(today) the gates of Hades are thrown open."—Or. xlii. "Adam receives death as a gain, and (thereby) the cutting off of sin; that evil should not be immortal: and so the vengeance turns out a kindness, for thus I am of opinion it is that God punishes."— Nazianzen. Orat. xlii.[14]

Ambrose, 340-397 A.D. "Bishop of Milan; converted Augustine by his preaching; the Father of Latin hymnology; reproduced many of the writings of the Greek Fathers."[15]

> The mystery of the Incarnation is the salvation of the entire creation...as it is elsewhere said, "the whole creation shall be set free from the bondage of corruption"....So the Son of Man came to save that which was lost, i.e., all, for as in Adam all die, so, too, in Christ shall all be made alive. The subjection of Christ consists not in few, but in all (becoming obedient)...Christ will be subject to God in us by means of the obedience of all...(then) when vices having been cast away, and sin reduced to submission, one spirit of all people, in one sentiment, shall with one accord begin to cleave to God, then God will be All in All.—Ambrose. De fide lib. v. 7.[16]

Didymus, 380 A.D. "The last distinguished head of the school of Alexandria, Didymus, surpassed all of his day in knowledge of the Scriptures." says S. Jerome. He argues, "divine correction (even vengeance), and promise, have the same object in view."—Adv. Man. ch. xviii.[17] Also "God 'destroys liars, so far as they are liars.'—In Ps. v. 6. [Christ] 'descends to Hades and brings back the souls, there detained on account of their sins."'— Didymus. In Ps. lxxi. 20. See, too, De Trin. lib. iii 21, &c.[18]

Gregory of Nyssa, 332-398 A.D. "A leading theologian of the Eastern Church and one of the most prominent figures in the second great Church Council which practically established the orthodoxy of the Nicene Creed."[19]

> The Divine judgment does not as its chief object cause pain to those who have sinned, but works good alone by separating from evil, and drawing to a share in blessedness. But this severance of good from evil causes the pain (of the judgment). In other words, the penalty is the cure; it is merely the unavoidable pain attending the removal of the intruding element of sin.—Gregory. *Dialogue of the Soul and Resurrection.*[20]

Jerome, 340-420 A.D. "Devoted to Scripture study; revised the old Latin translations and translated the Old Testament from Hebrew into Latin of the New Testament. Allin stated he found nearly 100 passages in his works indicating Jerome sympathized with the 'larger hope.'"[21] "When the Psalmist says, 'Your enemies, O God, shall perish,'...every man who has been Your enemy shall hereafter be made Your friend; the man shall not perish, the enemy shall perish."—Jerome. In Ps. xcii. 9.[22]

Hillary, 354 A.D. "Hillary, Bishop of Poictiers, is considered one of the champions of orthodoxy."[23] "The whole human race, who are one, are the one lost sheep, which is destined to be found by the Good Shepherd."—Hillary.[24]

Titus, 364 A.D. "Bishop of Bostra. Caillou, describes as 'the most learned among the learned bishops of his age, and a most famous champion of the truth.' S. Jerome reckons him as one of those, in whom you are at a loss whether to admire most, their learning or their knowledge of Holy Scripture."[25]

> The very pit itself is a place of torments and of chastisement, but is not eternal. It was made that it might be a medicine and help to those who sin. Sacred are the stripes which are medicine to those who have sinned. "Therefore we do not complain of the pits (of hell)—abyssis—but rather know that they are places of torment, and chastisement, being for the correction (amendment of those who have sinned."—Titus Adv. Man. lib. i. 32.[26]

Diodorus, 378 A.D. "Bishop of Tarsus...noted for untiring zeal in defense of the Nicene Faith."[27] "For the wicked there are punishments not perpetual...according to the amount of malice in their works....The Resurrection, therefore, is regarded as a blessing not only to the good but also to the evil."—Diodorus. ASSEM. Bibl. Or. iii. p. 324.[28]

Theodore of Mopsuestia, 407 A.D. "The crown and climax of the school of Antioch...called the 'Master of the East' from his theological eminence." Dorner. (Pers. of Christ, i. 50).[29]

> "Who is so great a fool as to think, that so great a blessing can be to those that arise, the occasion of endless torment?"—Frag. Ex. lib. cont. pecc. orig. "All have the hope of rising with Christ, so that the body having obtained immortality, thenceforward the proclivity to evil should be removed." [God] "recapitulated all things in Christ...as though making a compendious renewal, and restoration of the whole creation, through Him....Now this will take place

in a future age, when all mankind and all powers (virtutes) possessed of reason, look up to Him, as is right, and obtain mutual concord and firm peace."—Theodore. In Eph. i. 10.[30]

Cyril of Alexandria, 412 A.D. "He (Cyril) describes Christ as having spoiled Hades, and 'left the devil there solitary and deserted.'—Hom. Pasch. vii. And again, 'Christ, wandering down even to Hades, has emptied the dark, hidden, unseen treasuries.'"—Glaphy in Gen. lib ii.[31] "For when death devoured Him who was the Lamb on behalf of all, it vomited forth all men in Him and with Him....Now when sin has been destroyed, how should it be but that death, too, should wholly perish?"—Cyril. In S. Jno. i. 29.[32]

Maximus of Turin, 422 A.D. "Christ carried off to heaven man (mankind) whose cause He undertook, snatched from the jaws of Hades."—Maximus. In Pent. Horn. ii.[33]

Theodoret, 423 A.D. "Bishop of Cyrus...perhaps the most famous, and certainly the most learned teacher of his age; uniting to a noble intellect a character and accomplishments equally noble."[34] "After His anger, God will bring to an end His judgment; for He will not be angry unto the end, nor keep His wrath to eternity."—Theodoret. In Is. xiii.[35] "He shews here the reason for punishment, for the Lord, the lover of men, torments us only to cure us, that He may put a stop to the course of our iniquity."—Theodoret. Hom in Ezech. cap. Vi. vers 6.[36]

Peter Chrysologus, 433 A.D. "Bishop of Ravenna."[37] On the parable of the hundred sheep he said, "That the one lost sheep represents 'the whole human race lost in Adam,' and so the Good Shepherd 'follows the one, seeks the one, in order that in the one He may find all, in the one He may restore all.'"—Chrysologus. Ser. clxviii.[38]

Appendix VIII:
Testimony of Song

WHEN WILL WE START BELIEVING WHAT WE SING?

♫ ♫ ♫

The love of God is far greater
Than tongue or pen can ever tell.
It goes beyond the highest star
And reaches to the lowest hell....

Could we with ink the ocean fill
And were the skies of parchment made,
Were every stalk on earth a quill
And every man a scribe by trade,

To write the love of God above
Would drain the ocean dry,
Nor could the scroll contain the whole
Tho stretched from sky to sky.

Refrain:
O love of God, how rich and pure!
How measureless and strong!
It shall forever more endure—
The saints and angels' song.[1]

♫ ♫ ♫

Ah Lord God, Thou hast made the heavens
And the earth by Thy great power....
Nothing is too difficult for Thee
Nothing is too difficult for Thee
Great and mighty God...mighty in deed
Nothing, nothing, absolutely nothing
Nothing is too difficult for Thee[2]

♫ ♫ ♫

All of my days I will sing of Your greatness
All of my days I will speak of Your grace
All of my days I will tell of Your wondrous
love[3]

♫ ♫ ♫

Hark! the herald angels sing,
"Glory to the new-born King;
Peace on earth, and mercy mild,
God and sinners reconciled!"

Joyful, all ye nations rise,
Join the triumph of the skies;
With th'angelic host proclaim,
"Christ is born in Bethlehem!"

Hail the heav'n-born Prince of Peace!
Hail the Sun of Righteousness!
Light and life to all He brings,
Ris'n with healing in His wings.[4]

♫ ♫ ♫

Joy to the world, the Lord is come
Let earth receive her King.
Let every heart prepare Him room....
He comes to make His blessings flow
Far as the curse is found.[5]

♫ ♫ ♫

Where is the threat of an eternal hell in these words? Are they not filled with hope, comfort, and peace? Do they not impart life? The love of God goes beyond the highest star and reaches to the lowest hell. Absolutely nothing is too difficult for Him! All of my days I will sing of Your greatness—speak of Your grace—tell of Your wondrous love. Joyful, all ye nations rise, join the triumph of the skies! Light and life to all He brings! He comes to make His blessings flow far as the curse is found!

BIBLIOGRAPHY

THE PROBLEM
[1] Though a fictional account, it accurately and vividly illustrates the plight Christians face when proclaiming what is supposed to be "Good News." It is set in the backdrop of an actual historical event. How many Muslim parents and spouses suffered horrendous grief that fateful September day? Of the several hundred missionaries in Senegal at that time, who among them could offer these sufferers true and genuine comfort? What a tragedy.

PRELIMINARY NOTE
[1] Warren, Rick. *What on earth am I here for?* Grand Rapids, MI: Zondervan, 2004. 63.

INTRODUCTION
[1] Johnson, William J. *Abraham Lincoln the Christian*. Milford, MI: Mott Media, 1976. 62-62.
[2] Klassen, Randy. *What Does the Bible Really Say About Hell*. Scottsdale, PA: Pandora, 2001. 69.
[3] Bonda, Jan. *The One Purpose of God*. Grand Rapids, MI: Publishing Co, 1998. 11-40.
[4] Block, Daniel I. *Hell Under Fire*. Grand Rapids, MI; Zondervan, 2004. 16
[5] (See http://www.k-k-k.com and follow their link to http://www.kingidentity.com where you will find overwhelming Scriptural documentation for their beliefs (though faulty and misguided)).
[6] Barclay, William. *The Gospel of Luke*. The Daily Study Bible Series. Philadelphia: Westminster, 1978. 196.
[7] Wigram, George, and Ralph Winter. *The Word Study Concordance*. Wheaton, IL: Tyndale House, 1978. x, xiii-xiv, xvii.

CHAPTER 1: PILLARS
[1] Hurley, Loyal F. *The Outcome of Infinite Grace*. Santa Clarita, CA: Concordant Publishing Concern, n.d. 19.
[2] Beecher, Edward. *History of Opinions on the Scriptural Doctrine of Retribution*. New York: Appleton, 1887. chapter 17. Put into Electronic Format by Naomi Durkin, 2000.
[3] Morgan, G. Campbell. *God's Methods with Man*. New York: Revell, 1898.
[4] Vincent, Marvin. *Word Studies in the New Testament*. 1887. Grand Rapids, MI: Eerdmans, 1973. 58-59.
[5] Bonda, Jan. *The One Purpose of God*. Grand Rapids, MI: Publishing Co, 1998. 18.
[6] Barclay, William. *William Barclay: A Spiritual Autobiography*. Grand Rapids, MI: Eerdmans, 1977. 65-67.
[7] Talbott, Thomas. "A Pauline Interpretation of Divine Judgment" in Robin Parry and Christopher Partridge (eds.) *Universal Salvation? The Current Debate*. Grand Rapids. MI: Eerdmans, 2003. 47. Note 27; In Rhetoric 1369b,13; Note 28; In Gorgias 477a.
[8] Ibid. 51. Note 28; In Protagoras 324.
[9] Talbott, Thomas. "Eternal Punishment." Online posting. 2005. 2 May 2006. http://www.willamette.edu/~ttalbott/aionios.htm.
[10] Talbott, Thomas. *The Inescapable Love of God*. Salem, Oregon: Universal, 2002. 87-88.
[11] Barclay. Ibid.
[12] Talbott. Ibid. 89-90
[13] Beecher, Edward. *History of Opinions on the Scriptural Doctrine of Retribution*. New York: Appleton, 1887. chapter 19. Put into Electronic Format by Naomi Durkin, 2000.
[14] Barclay, William. *The Gospel of Matthew*. Vol.1. The Daily Study Bible Series. Philadelphia: Westminster, 1978. 141.

15 Strong, James. *New Strong's Concise Dictionary of the Words in the Hebrew Bible*. Nashville, TN: Thomas Nelson,1995. 135.

16 Allin, Thomas. *Christ Triumphant*. 1878. Rpt. 9th ed. Canyon Country, CA: Concordant, n.d. 279-280.

17 Barclay, William. *The Gospel of Luke*. The Daily Study Bible Series. Philadelphia: Westminster, 1978. 196.

18 Vine, W. E. *An Expository Dictionary of Biblical Words*. Nashville, TN: Nelson, 1985. 164.

19 Jukes, Andrew. *The Restitution of All Things*. Santa Clarita, CA: Concordant Publishing Concern, 1867. 170-172.

20 Vanderpool, Charles, Terri Neimann, and Scott L. Adams, eds. *Greek/English Interlinear Septuagint*. Apostolic Bible Polyglot ©. 2 May 2006. ISBN 0-9632301-1-5; http://septuagint-interlinear-greek-bible.com/downbook.htm

21 Strong. Ibid. 12. #684.

22 *Greek/English InterlinearSeptuagint*. Ibid.

23 *Greek/English InterlinearSeptuagint*. Ibid.

24 Jukes. Ibid. 70.

25 Morey, Robert. *Exploring The Attributes of God*. Iowa Falls, IA: World Bible, 1989. 125-129.

26 Eckerty, Ken. "The Work of the Cross." http://www.savior-of-all.com/cross.html.

27 Zodhiates, Spiros. *The Complete Word Study Dictionary New Testament*. Iowa Falls: World Bible, 1992. 727-728.

28 Quillen Hamilton Shinn; Reference unavailable at this time.

29 Hurley, Loyal F. *The Outcome of Infinite Grace*. Santa Clarita, CA : Concordant. 40-41.

30 Dillenberger, John Ed. *Martin Luther: Selections From His Writings*. New York: Garden City, 1961. 199.

31 Outler, Albert C. Ed. *The Works of John Wesley*. Vol. 2. Sermons 34-70. Nashville: Abingdon, 1985. 490.

32 Keizer, Heleen M. *Life, Time, Entirety* - A Study of "AIŌN" in Greek Literature and Philosophy, the Septuagint and Philo; Doctoral dissertation University of Amsterdam. 1999. Slightly amended version 2005. Chapter VI, Sec. I. 241. Personal note from Dr. Keizer : "Dear Mr. Beauchemin...please use this electronic document as you would a paper copy in your possession or borrowed from a library." Contact Gerry Beauchemin for more information.

33 Keizer. Ibid. 244.

34 Keizer. Ibid. Sec. II. 246.

35 Keizer. Ibid. 247.

CHAPTER 2: GOD'S NATURE

1 Allin, Thomas. *Christ Triumphant*. 1878. Rpt. 9th ed. Canyon Country, CA: Concordant, n.d. 19.

2 Allin. Ibid. 173.

3 Allin. Ibid. 70.

4 Allin. Ibid. 76-77.

5 Manford, Erasmus. *One Hundred and Fifty Reasons For Believing In The Final Salvation Of All Mankind*. Cincinnati: Manford and Torrey, 1849. point #68.

CHAPTER 3 : PURPOSE-DRIVEN JUDGMENT

1 Barclay, William. *The Letters of James and Peter*. The Daily Study Bible Series. Philadelphia: Westminster, 1978. 242-243.

2 Jacobsen, Jack. "The Church Fathers Testify to the Ultimate Triumph Of Jesus Christ." 2000. *God's Truth for Today*. Comp. Richard Charles Condon. St. Paul, MN: Redeeming Love. 2 May 2006. From Luther's letter to Hanseu Von Rechenberg in 1522. http://www.godstruthfortoday.org/Library/miscellaneous/ChurchFathers.htm

3 *Oxford American Desk Dictionary and Thesaurus*. Second Ed. New York: Berkley, 2001. 28.

4 Fristad, Kalen. *Destined For Salvation*. Kearney, NE: Morris, 2003. 24-25.

CHAPTER 4 : THE BLESSED HOPE PART ONE
1 Wilkin, Robert. "Repentance and Salvation, Part 2: The Doctrine of Repentance in the Old Testament." *The Journal of the Grace Evangelical Society*. 2 (Spring 1989): 14.
2 Dillow, Joseph. *The Reign of the Servant Kings*. Hayesville, NC: Schoettle, 1992. 132-133.
3 Mclaren, Brian. *A Generous Orthodoxy*. Grand Rapids: Zondervan, 2004. 101.
4 Lewis, C.S. *Mere Christianity*. New York: Simon & Schuster, 1980. 153-154.
5 Pridgeon, Charles H. *Is Hell Eternal or Will God's Plan Fail?*" Third Ed. n.p. 1931; Chapter 14.
6 Outler, Albert C. Ed. *The Works of John Wesley*. Vol. 2. Sermons 34-70. Nashville: Abingdon, 1985. 490.
7 *The Bible Knowledge Commentary*. 1983. 340.

CHAPTER 5: THE BLESSED HOPE PART TWO
1 Bonda, Jan. *The One Purpose of God*. Grand Rapids, MI: Publishing Co, 1998. 11-16.
2 Pink, A. W. *The Sovereignty of God*. 4th ed. Grand Rapids, MI: Baker Book House, 1984. Introduction to chapter four.
3 Jukes, Andrew. *The Restitution of All Things*. Santa Clarita, CA: Concordant, 1867. 44-45.
4 Jukes. Ibid. 28.
5 Strong, James. *New Strong's Concise Dictionary of the Words in the Greek Testament*. Nashville, TN: Thomas Nelson, 1995. 94.

CHAPTER 6: PROCLAMATIONS PART ONE
1 Knoch, Adolph E. "The Last Enemy Destroyed." Details not available.
2 Strong, James. *New Strong's Concise Dictionary of the Words in the Hebrew Bible*. Nashville, TN: Thomas Nelson, 1995. 94. #1670.
3 Vine, W.E. *An Expository Dictionary of Biblical Words*. New York: Nelson, 1985. 368.
4 Kirk, Joseph E. "The Salvation of All—When Should It Be Taught?" 1999. *God's Truth for Today*. Comp. Richard Charles Condon. Concordant Publishing. 2 May 2006. http://www.godstruthfortoday.org/Library/kirk/WhenShouldTheSalvationOfAllBeTaught.htm
5 Bell, Richard H. "Rom 5.18–19 and Universal Salvation" New Testament Studies, Vol. 48, Issue 03, Jul 2002, pp 417-432 http://journals.cambridge.org/action/quickSearch; Online by Cambridge University Press 16 Jul 2002

CHAPTER 7: PROCLAMATIONS PART TWO
1 Barclay, William. *William Barclay: A Spiritual Autobiography*. Grand Rapids: W. B. Eerdmans, 1977. 65-67.
2 Barnes, Albert. *Barnes' Practical Sermons*. Biblical Repository for July, 1840. 123-125.
3 http://www.studylight.org/isb/bible.cgi?query=Acts+3%3A21&section=2&it=kjv&ot=bhs&nt=na&Enter=Perform+Search Aug. 10, 2006
4 http://bible.crosswalk.com/Lexicons/Greek/grk.cgi?number=3956&version=kjv) Aug. 10, 2006
5 Allin, Thomas. *Christ Triumphant*. 1878. Rpt. 9th ed. Canyon Country, CA: Concordant, n.d. 75.
6 Keil, C.F. and F. Delitzsch. *Biblical Commentary on the Pentateuch*. 3 Volumes. n.d. Trans. James Martin. Grand Rapids: Eerdmans, 1968. Sec. 3:467.
7 Morey, Robert. *Exploring The Attributes of God*. Iowa Falls, IA: World Bible, 1989. 93.
8 Aiken, Mercy. *If Hell Is Real*. www.tentmaker.org/articles/ifhellisrealprintable.htm

CHAPTER 8: THE WITNESSES
1 Block, Daniel I. *Hell Under Fire*. Grand Rapids, MI: Zondervan, 2004. 44, 59, 61.
2 Zodhiates, Spiros. *The Complete Word Study Dictionary New Testament*. Iowa Falls: World Bible, 1992. 605.

3 Beecher, Edward. *History of Opinions on the Scriptural Doctrine of Retribution*. New York: Appleton, 1887. Chapter 28. Justinian's letters. Put into Electronic Format by Naomi Durkin, 2000.
4 Pridgeon, Charles H. *Is Hell Eternal or Will God's Plan Fail?"* Third Ed. n.p. 1931; Chapter xxvii.
5 Phillips, Michael. *Universal Reconciliation*. Eureka, CA: Sunrise Books, 1998. 44.
6 Pridgeon. Ibid.
7 Pridgeon. Ibid.
8 Pridgeon. Ibid.
9 Pridgeon. Ibid.
10 Beecher. Ibid. Chapter 35.
11 Pinnock, Clark. "The Conditional View." *Four Views on Hell*. Ed. W. V. Crockett. n.p. n.d. 149.
12 Kung, Hans. *Eternal Life: Life After Death as a Medical, Philosophical, and Theological Problem*. New York: Double Day, 1984. 136.
13 Yancey, Philip. *What's So Amazing About Grace*. Grand Rapids: Zondervan, 1997. n.pag.
14 Klassen, Randy. *What Does the Bible Really Say About Hell*. Scottsdale, PA: Pandora, 2001. 84.
15 Parker, T. H. L. *Portrait of Calvin*. n.p. SCM Publishers, n.d. 102. Quoted in "The Devine Majesty of the Word. John Calvin: The Man and His Preaching." 1997. *Desiring God*. Comp. John Piper. 2 May 2006. http://www.desiringgod.org/library/biographies/97calvin.html

CHAPTER 9: CIRCUMSTANCIAL EVIDENCE
1 Montaldo, Charles. "Profile of Andrea Yates." *About*. 27 July 2006. http://crime.about.com/od/current/p/andreayates.htm
2 Meithe, Terry. "The Universal Power of the Atonement." *The Grace of God, the Will of Man*. Ed. Clark Pinnock. Grand Rapids, MI: Zondervan, 1989. 75.
3 Allin, Thomas. *Christ Triumphant*. 1878. Rpt. 9th ed. Canyon Country, CA: Concordant, n.d. 14.
4 Henderson, Doug. "Why Inclusion;" Owasso, OK: Douglas Henderson, 2004. 39 #3. 2 May 2006. http://www.inclusion.ws/Inclusion_why2.pdf.
5 Allin; Ibid; p. 56-57
6 Day, Lorraine. *What Happens at the Judgment*. Palm Desert, CA: Spencer, 2000. 17.
7 Allin. Ibid. 59.
8 "Secrets of Islam." *U.S. News & World Report*. Collector's Edition. (Summer 2005). 4.
9 Johnstone, Patrick. "World Evangelism: How Are We Doing?" *Mission Frontiers*. 2001. 2 May 2006. www.missionfrontiers.org/newslinks/statewe.htm.
10 Hymers, Dr. R. L., Jr. "A Warning To Those Who Think They Are Saved." From sermon preached at "Fundamentalist Baptist Tabernacle" of Los Angeles, CA, March 25, 2001. 2 May 2006. http://www.rlhymersjr.com/Online_Sermons/03-24-01_A_Warning_to_Those_Who_Think_They_Are_Saved.htm

CHAPTER 10: CHRIST TRIUMPHANT
1 Allin, Thomas. *Christ Triumphant*. 1878. Rpt. 9th ed. Canyon Country, CA: Concordant, n.d. 287, 35-36.
2 *The Bible Knowledge Commentary*. 1983. 340.
3 Allin. Ibid. 53-54.
4 Beecher, Edward. *History of Opinions on the Scriptural Doctrine of Retribution*. New York: Appleton, 1887. Chapter 32. "The Effects of False Belief." Put into Electronic Format by Naomi Durkin, 2000.
5 Mohler, R.Albert Jr. "Modern Theology: The Disappearance of Hell." in *Hell Under Fire*. Grand Rapids, MI: Zondervan, 2004. 32. Taken from: "The Mystery of Salvation, The

Story of God's Gift: A Report by the Doctrine Commission of the General Synod of the Church of England." London: Church House Publishing, 1995. 180.

[6] Ibid. p.33. Original source: p.199

[7] Ibid. p.33. Original source: "The Nature of Hell, A report of the Evangelical Alliance Commissions on Unity and Truth Among Evangelicals." Carlisle, UK: ACUTE/Paternoster, 2000. 128.

[8] Ibid. p.27. Original source: Paul, Pope John II. "General Audience." *Vatican News Service.* Wednesday, July 28, 1999.

[9] Ibid. p.16. Original source: Marty, Martin E. *Hell Disappeared. No One Noticed. A Civic Argument.* HTR 78 (1985):381-98

[10] Jn. 10:9-11

[11] Mt. 11:28-30

[12] Mk. 1:1

[13] Jn. 1:3

[14] Jn. 1:14

[15] 1Jn. 2:2

[16] Is. 59:2

[17] Ac. 4:12

[18] 1Jn. 1:7

[19] 2Co. 5:21; He. 4:15

[20] Is. 53:4-6

[21] Is. 53:4-6; 2Co. 5:21; 1Jn. 2:2

[22] Col. 1:14; 1Pe. 1:18; 3:18

[23] Ac. 16:31

[24] See p. 93

[25] Col. 1:14, 19-20; 2:12-14; Ro. 5. 5:6-8

[26] Faith is a gift and work of God in us: He. 12:2; Ro. 12:3; (These passages will lend support to this. Mt. 11:27; 16:16-17; Jn.1:13; 6:44; 15:16; 1Co. 4:7; Ep. 2:8-9; 3:16-17; Ph. 1:6; 1:29; 2:13; Col. 1:12; 1Ti. 1:14; Ez. 36: 26-27; Jer. 24:7; 31:33-34; 32:39-40) Faith is to rely upon what Christ has done. See Vine, W.E. *An Expository Dictionary of New Testament Words.* New York: Nelson, 1985. 61. Faith is rest from our works. He. 4:3,10.

[27] Ep. 2:8-10

[28] 2Ti. 1:9; Tit. 3:5

[29] Jn. 4:10; Ac. 8:20; Ro. 3:24; 6:23; Ep. 2:8-9

[30] Ph. 2:12; 1Ti. 4:16; Col. 1:28

[31] Ep. 4:13 NIV; Ga.4:19

[32] Jn. 1:13; 3:3; 2Co. 5:17

[33] Is.1:18; Ja. 2:23 with Ro. 4:22-24; Jn. 15:15; 1Jn 1:3; Re. 3:20

[34] 1Co. 13:8

[35] Ep. 4:1-6

[36] Ph. 3:15

[37] 1Pe. 1:19; Re. 5:9-10

[38] Mt. 5:16; 28:19-20

[39] Jn. 14:27; 16:33; Lu. 2:10; Ro. 10:15; 14:17; 2Co. 1:3-5; He. 6:19

[40] Meacham, Jon. *Newsweek Magazine.* 14 August 2006. Excerpt from interview with Billy Graham. http://www.msnbc.msn.com/id/14204483/.

APPENDIX III

[1] DeRose, Keith. "Universalism and the Bible: The Really Good News." 2 May 2006. http://pantheon.yale.edu/%7Ekd47/univ.htm#3.

[2] DeRose. Ibid.

3 Knoch, Adolph E. "The God of Judas Iscariot." 1999. *God's Truth for Today*. Comp. Richard Charles Condon. Concordant Publishing. 2 May 2006. http://www.godstruthfortoday.org/Library/knoch/judasgod.htm

4 Vincent, Marvin. *Word Studies in the New Testament*. 1887. Grand Rapids, MI: Eerdmans, 1973. 61-62.

5 Barclay, William. "The Gospel of Luke." *Daily Study Bible Series*. Philadelphia: Westminster, 1978. 196.

6 Geisler, Norman. Quoted in *The Case For Faith*. Lee Strobel. Grand Rapids, MI; Zondervan, 2000. 121-122.

7 Jukes, Andrew. *The Restitution of All Things*. Santa Clarita, CA: Concordant, 1867. 97-101.

8 Aiken, Mercy. *If Hell Is Real*. www.tentmaker.org/articles/ifhellisrealprintable.htm.

9 Nolin, Craig. "Student of the Word Ministries." http://studentoftheword.com/ConfusinFacts.html

10 Morrison, Keith. From an email received Aug. 2006 quoting Keith Morrison of NBC News giving a preview description of an interview with Bishop Carlton Pearson to be aired on NBC's Dateline Sunday, Aug. 13, 2006.

APPENDIX IV

1 Vincent, Marvin. *Word Studies in the New Testament*- 2nd Ed. Mclean, VA: Mcdonald Publishing. 1888. Vol. I 40.

2 Vine, W.E. *An Expository Dictionary of Biblical Words*. New York: Nelson, 1985. 588.

3 Allin, Thomas. *Christ Triumphant*. 1878. Rpt. 9th ed. Canyon Country, CA: Concordant, n.d. 265-266.

4 Barclay, William. "The Gospel of Luke." *Daily Study Bible Series*. Philadelphia: Westminster, 1978. 141.

5 Pridgeon, Charles H. *Is Hell Eternal or Will God's Plan Fail?* Third Ed. n.p. 1931. Chapter 11

6 Knoch, A.E. *Concordant Greek-English Keyword Concordance*. Canyon Country, CA: Concordant, 1947. 80, 293.

7 Wigram, George, and Ralph Winter. *The Word Study Concordance*. Wheaton, IL: Tyndale House, 1978. 2307.

8 Vine, W.E. *An Expository Dictionary of Biblical Words*. New York: Nelson, 1985. 80.

APPENDIX V

1 Vine, W.E. *An Expository Dictionary of Biblical Words*. New York: Nelson, 1985. 42.

APPENDIX VI

1 Fristad, Kalen. *Destined for Salvation*. Kearney, NE: Morris, 1997. 14-15. Original source: *The Interpreter's Bible: A commentary in Twelve Volumes*. Vol. 11. Nashville: Abingdon, 1955. 51.

2 Wigram, George W. *The Englishman's Hebrew and Chaldee Concordance of the Old Testament*. n.p. n.p. n.d. 499-500.

3 Eckerty, Ken. "The Work of the Cross." http://www.savior-of-all.com/cross.html.

4 Talbott, Thomas. *The Inescapable Love of God*. Salem, Oregon: Universal, 1999. 65.

5 Milton, John. Quoted by Ken Eckerty in "The Work of the Cross." http://www.savior-of-all.com/cross.html.

APPENDIX VII

1 Pridgeon, Charles H. *Is Hell Eternal or Will God's Plan Fail?* Third Ed. n.p. 1931. Chapter 27.

2 Pridgeon. Ibid.

3 Pridgeon. Ibid.

4 Pridgeon. Ibid.

5 Allin, Thomas. *Christ Triumphant*. 1878. Rpt. 9th ed. Canyon Country, CA: Concordant, n.d. 107.

6 Allin. Ibid.

[7] Pridgeon. Ibid.
[8] Pridgeon. Ibid.
[9] Pridgeon. Ibid.
[10] Allin. Ibid. 112.
[11] Pridgeon. Ibid.
[12] Allin. Ibid. 99.
[13] Allin. Ibid. 117.
[14] Allin. Ibid. 117.
[15] Pridgeon. Ibid.
[16] Allin . Ibid. 131-132.
[17] Allin. Ibid. 126.
[18] Allin. Ibid. 126.
[19] Pridgeon. Ibid.
[20] Pridgeon. Ibid.
[21] Allin. Ibid. 136.
[22] Allin. Ibid. 136.
[23] Allin. Ibid. 114.
[24] Allin. Ibid. 114.
[25] Allin. Ibid. 116.
[26] Allin. Ibid. 116.
[27] Allin. Ibid. 137.
[28] Allin. Ibid. 137.
[29] Allin. Ibid. 142-143.
[30] Allin. Ibid. 142-143.
[31] Allin. Ibid. 102.
[32] Allin. Ibid. 143.
[33] Allin. Ibid. 102.
[34] Allin. Ibid. 144-146.
[35] Allin. Ibid. 144-146.
[36] Jukes. Ibid. 184-185.
[37] Allin. Ibid. 146.
[38] Allin. Ibid. 146.

APPENDIX VIII

[1] Lehman, Fredrick M. "The Love of God." 1917. *"The Hymnal for Worship &Celebration."* Waco, TX: Word Music, 1986. #67.
[2] Chance, Kay. "Ah, Lord God." 1976.
[3] Mark Stevens. "All Of My Days." n.p. Hillsong Publishing, 2000.
[4] Charles Wesley. "Hark! the Herald Angels Sing." *The Hymnal for Worship &Celebration.* Waco, TX: Word Music, 1986. #133.
[5] Watts, Isaac. *The Hymnal for Worship &Celebration.* Waco, TX: Word Music, 1986. #125.

RECOMMENDED BOOKS

History of Opinions on the Scriptural Doctrine of Retribution by Dr. Edward Beecher, D.D., (1878). This is a book on Church History which also investigates the Greek word "aion." Beecher is unbiased and scholarly, without an agenda or denomination to defend. He writes as a sincere seeker of truth. It is comprehensive and yet readable for an older work. See www.HopeBeyondHell.net (Church History)

Restitution of All Things by Andrew Jukes, (1867). Pastor of St. John's Church and respected author, his works include: *The Law of the Offerings, Four Views of Christ, Types in Genesis,* and *The Names of God.* Some of his works have been re-printed by Kregel Publications, Grand Rapids, MI and are available on www.amazon.com. Jukes was a man of the Word with an exceptional depth of understanding in the Old Testament. This is not a light read, but an in depth and sound Biblical exposition. See www.HopeBeyondHell.net (Andrew Jukes) Concordant Publishing Concern 15570 Knochaven Road Santa Clarita, CA 91387.

Christ Triumphant by Thomas Allin D.D., (1890). Allin was a clergyman of the English Episcopal Church and ministered in North London in the late 19th and early 20th centuries. His works include *Race and Religion* and *The Augustinian Revolution in Theology* (1911). This is the most comprehensive book on this topic I have read. It has many times brought me to tears as I realized how loving and awesome God really is. Concordant Publishing Concern, 15570 Knochaven Rd., Canyon Country, CA 91351; 1878; Rpt. 9th ed

Absolute Assurance by Charles Slagle. Charles has also authored three devotional books, including the popular *"From The Father's Heart,"* which my daughter, Nicole, is enjoying. He is a prophetic psalmist, evangelist, and worship leader. He speaks candidly of his experiences and struggles with the inconsistencies in our tradition's beliefs. This book also brought me to tears as Charles expressed so clearly all that I had experienced. Here is a brother I can identify with. http://www.sigler.org/slagle/absolute.htm

The Savior of the World Series by J.Preston Eby. I thank Preston Eby for helping me understand God's unfailing plan for man revealed through his writings. Read them free online at www.hisremnant.org/eby/list.html

The One Purpose of God by Jan Bonda. Bonda shows clearly Israel's role in God's unfailing plan. Wm B. Eerdmans Publishing Co.; Cambridge U.K. ;1998; Originally published as *Het ene doel van God* ;1993; Baarn, Netherlands; ISBN 0-8028-4186-4. (See www.amazon.com).

The Inescapable Love of God by Thomas Talbott (2000). This book is scholarly, yet very readable for the lay person. He presents a sound Biblical and philosophical exposition for the Blessed Hope . His reasoning and arguments are compelling. This book has strengthened my conviction in this hope. <TTALBOTT@WILLAMETTE.EDU> www.amazon.com or $5 E Book: Visit: http://www.universal-publishers.com/book.php?method=ISBN&book=1581128312 ISBN 1-58112-831-2

The Word Study Concordance and *The Word Study New Testament* by George Wigram and Ralph Winter; This is a must if you want to do quick and easy word studies based on the actual Greek word usages. No background in Greek is necessary. Tyndale House Pub. Wheaton,IL 1978; ISBN 0-8423-8391-3 and ISBN 0-8423-8390-5.

THE AUTHOR

Gerry Beauchemin has been involved in fulltime missions since 1988. He has served as a missionary in Mexico, the Philippines, and Senegal, West Africa with Youth With A Mission (YWAM), The Luke Society, and Philippine Health Care Ministries. Since 2001, he has been directing Dental Training For Missions in Brownsville, Texas where he trains missionaries to provide simplified dental care with the love, gentleness, and compassion of Christ. He and his wife, Denise, (of 27 years), have three daughters.

What qualifies Gerry to write on this theme?

- He has extensively reflected upon, read the works of others, and for many years wrestled with and studied the Scriptures on this theme. He has found solid Biblical evidence for his conclusion of hope.
- He has agonized for most of his life over hell and understands the contradictions it brings upon the Christian faith and the Scriptures.
- Gerry asked himself and God, "Who am I to write such a book?" Then he recalled 1Co. 1:26-29, *"God hath chosen the foolish things of the world to confound the wise...that no flesh should glory in his presence."* KJV This along with Mt. 10:27 and 11:25 spurred him on.

Partner with Us!

Would you prayerfully consider partnering with us in helping to widely distribute this book? If we all pray and work together, we will have an impact! There are a number of tasks we all can do. We welcome whatever the Lord would have you do. Contact me. Let's talk, share ideas, and work together. I look forward to hearing from you. We need you!

Free Books!

To facilitate and encourage the sharing of books, we offer them free while supplies last. Just pay for shipping. Also, donations are welcome and appreciated! Please don't let books collect dust. Let's get them out there where they will bring joy, comfort, and peace. To order, see below.

Get Connected

May I introduce you to my friend Rick Spencer, of *Action Ministry* (A-C-T-I-O-N - *A Church That's In Our Neighborhood*). Rick has a vision to unite and connect believers across North America regarding the all-inclusive love of God. He is being used of the Lord organizing state conferences, round table leadership discussions, and home meetings. Rick wants to help you get connected, both in your region and nationally. His big event takes place every summer on Father's Day hosting a National Conference in various parts of the country. Visit www. restoration-nation.us Call Rick at (979) 540-9900 or email actionministry@hotmail.com.

ORDER BOOKS ONLINE
WWW.HOPEBEYONDHELL.NET

OR
Email Gerry@hopebeyondhell.net
Call (956) 831-9011 or (979) 540-9900
Write Action Ministry PO BOX 251 Lexington TX 78947
Make donations payable to: Acton Ministry (books)